Interpretation of Nietzsche's
Second Untimely Meditation

Studies in Continental Thought

EDITOR
JOHN SALLIS

CONSULTING EDITORS

Robert Bernasconi   James Risser
John D. Caputo   Dennis J. Schmidt
David Carr   Calvin O. Schrag
Edward S. Casey   Charles E. Scott
David Farrell Krell   Daniela Vallega-Neu
Lenore Langsdorf   David Wood

Martin Heidegger

Interpretation of Nietzsche's Second Untimely Meditation

Translated by
Ullrich Haase and Mark Sinclair

Indiana University Press
Bloomington and Indianapolis

This book is a publication of

Indiana University Press
Office of Scholarly Publishing
Herman B Wells Library 350
1320 East 10th Street
Bloomington, Indiana 47405 USA

iupress.indiana.edu

Published in German as Martin Heidegger *Gesamtausgabe 46, Zur Auslegung von Nietzsches II. Unzeitgemäßer Betrachtung*, edited by Hans-Joachim Friedrich
© 2003 by Vittorio Klostermann GmbH, Frankfurt am Main
English translation © 2016 by Indiana University Press

All rights reserved

No part of this book may be reproduced or utilized in any form or by any means, electronic or mechanical, including photocopying and recording, or by any information storage and retrieval system, without permission in writing from the publisher. The Association of American University Presses' Resolution on Permissions constitutes the only exception to this prohibition.

The paper used in this publication meets the minimum requirements of the American National Standard for Information Sciences—Permanence of Paper for Printed Library Materials, ANSI Z39.48-1992.

Manufactured in the United States of America

Library of Congress Cataloging-in-Publication Data

Names: Heidegger, Martin, 1889–1976, author.
Title: Interpretation of Nietzsche's Second untimely meditation / Martin Heidegger ; translated by Ullrich Haase and Mark Sinclair.
Other titles: Zur Auslegung von Nietzsches II. Unzeitgem?asser Betrachtung, "Vom Nutzen und Nachteil der Historie f?ur das Leben." English
Description: Bloomington : Indiana University Press, 2016. | Series: Studies in Continental thought | Includes bibliographical references.
Identifiers: LCCN 2016012767 (print) | LCCN 2016030783 (ebook) | ISBN 9780253022660 (cloth : alk. paper) | ISBN 9780253023155 (ebook)
Subjects: LCSH: History—Philosophy. | Metaphysics. | Nietzsche, Friedrich Wilhelm, 1844-1900. Vom Nutzen und Nachteil der Historie f?ur das Leben. | Philosophy, German—19th century. | Philosophy, German—20th century.
Classification: LCC B3279.H48 Z7513 2016 (print) | LCC B3279.H48 (ebook) | DDC 193—dc23
LC record available at https://lccn.loc.gov/2016012767

1 2 3 4 5 21 20 19 18 17 16

CONTENTS

Translators' Introduction   xi

A. PRELIMINARY REMARKS

- §1. Remarks Preliminary to the Exercises   3
- §2. Title   7
- §3. The Appearance of our Endeavors   9

B. SECTION I
Structure. Preparation and Preview of the Guiding Question. Historiology—Life

- §4. Historiology—The Historical On the Unhistorical/Suprahistorical and the Relation to Both   13
- §5. Section I. 1   15
- §6. Section I. 2   15
- §7. Section I   17
- §8. Comparing   17
- §9. The Determination of the Essence of the Human Being on the Basis of Animality and the Dividing Line between Animal and Human Being   18
- §10. Nietzsche's Procedure. On the Determination of the Historical from the Perspective of Forgetting and Remembering   22
- §11. "Forgetting"—"Remembering." The Question of "Historiology" as the Question of the "Human Being." The Course of Our Inquiry. One Path among Others.   26
- §12. Questions Relating to Section I   27
- §13. Forgetting   28
- §14. Nietzsche on Forgetting   30
- §15. "Forgetting" and "Remembering"   30
- §16. Historiology and "the" Human Being   42
- §17. "The Human Being." "Culture." The "People" and "Genius"   42
- §18. Culture—Nonculture, Barbarism   42
- §19. Human Being and Culture and the People   43
- §20. Nietzsche's Concept of "Culture"   44
- §21. The Formally General Notion of "Culture." "Culture" and "Art"   45
- §22. "The" Human Being and a Culture—A "People"   45
- §23. "Art" (and Culture)   46
- §24. Genius in Schopenhauer   49
- §25. The People and Great Individuals   50
- §26. Great Individuals as the Goal of "Culture," of the People, of Humanity   51
- §27. "Worldview" and Philosophy   51

C. SECTION II
The Three Modes of Historiology
1. Monumental Historiology

§28. The Question of the Essence of "the Historical," That Is, of the Essence of Historiology	55
§29. Section II. Structure (Seven Paragraphs)	56

D. SECTION III

§30. The Essence of Antiquarian Historiology	63
§31. Critical Historiology	64

E. NIETZSCHE'S THREE MODES OF HISTORIOLOGY AND THE QUESTION OF HISTORICAL TRUTH

§32. "Life"	69
§33. "Life." Advocates, Defamers of Life	69
§34. Historiology and Worldview	69
§35. How is the Historical Determined?	70
§36. The Belonging Together of the Three Modes of Historiology and Historical Truth	71
§37. The Three Modes of Historiology as Modes of the Remembering Relation to the Past	71
§38. Section II	71

F. THE HUMAN BEING
HISTORIOLOGY AND HISTORY. TEMPORALITY

§39. Historiology—The Human Being—History (Temporality)	75
§40. The Historical and the Unhistorical	78

G. "HISTORIOLOGY"
Historiology and History. Historiology and the Unhistorical

§41. "The Unhistorical"	81
§42. The Un-historical	81
§43. The Un-historical	81
§44. History and Historiology	81
§45. Nietzsche as "Historian"	82
§46. Historiology and History	82
§47. "Historiology"	83
§48. History and Historiology	83

H. SECTION IV

§49. On Section IV Onward, Hints	87
§50. Section IV	88
§51. Section IV (Paras. 1–6)	91

Contents

I. SECTION V

§52. Section V — 99
§53. Section V, Divided into Five Parts — 100
§54. Oversaturation with Historiology and with Knowledge Generally — 109

J. CONCERNING SECTIONS V AND VI
Truth. "Justice." "Objectivity." Horizon

§55. Life—"Horizon" — 113
§56. Objectivity and "Horizon" — 113
§57. Justice — 113
§58. Justice—Truth — 114
§59. Life—and Horizon — 115
§60. Beings as a Whole—The Human Being — 115
§61. "Truth" and the "True" — 116
§62. The True and Truth — 116
§63. Truth and the Human Being — 117
§64. Will (Drive) to "Truth" — 118
§65. Nietzsche on the "Will to Truth" — 118

K. ON SECTIONS V AND VI
Historiology and Science (Truth)
(cf. J. Truth "Justice" "Objectivity" Horizon)

§66. The Human Being—The Gods — 123
§67. Why the Primacy of "Science" in Historiology? — 123
§68. "Positivism" — 124
§69. Historiology — 124
§70. Historiology and Science — 125
§71. The Impact of Historiology on the Past — 125
§72. Truth — 126
§73. Historiology as Science — 127
§74. "Historiology" and "Perspective" and "Objectivity" — 127

L. SECTION VI
(Justice and Truth)

§75. Section VI — 131
§76. Section VI (Paras. 1–7) — 131
§77. "Objectivity" and "Justice" — 132
§78. On the Structure of Section VI as a Whole — 140
§79. Nietzsche's Question of a "Higher Justice" — 141
§80. Morality and Metaphysics — 145
§81. Justice—Truth—Objectivity—Life — 146

§82.	Justice as "Virtue"	147
§83.	Justice—Truth	148
§84.	Truth and Art (Cognition)	156
§85.	On Nietzsche's Treatise "On Truth and Lies in an Extramoral Sense"	156
§86.	Truth and "Intellect"—Justice	156
§87.	Truth and "Intellect"	157
§88.	Nietzsche's Conception of Truth (Determined from the Ground up by Western Metaphysics)	158
§89.	Justice and Truth	158
§90.	Truth and Science Conditioned by Worldview	160
§91.	Truth and Science	161
§92.	Historiology → Science → Truth—Justice	161

M. NIETZSCHE'S METAPHYSICS

§93.	Nietzsche's Metaphysics	167
§94.	"Life" in the Two Senses of World and Human Being	168

N. "LIFE"

§95.	Nietzsche's Projection of Beings as a Whole and of the Human Being as "Life"	175
§96.	Disposition	175
§97.	Recapitulation According to the Basic Questions	175
§98.	Concluding Remark	181
§99.	Nietzsche's Early Characterization of His Own Thinking as "Inversion of Platonism"	182
§100.	"Life" (*ego vivo*)	183
§101.	The Philosophical Concept	183
§102.	On the Critical Meditation	183
§103.	Decisive Questioning	184
§104.	"Life"	184

O. THE QUESTION OF THE HUMAN BEING:
"Language." "Happiness." Language
(cf. §15, "Forgetting" and "Remembering")

§105.	Language as Use and Using-Up of Words	187
§106.	Word and Meaning	187
§107.	"Happiness" and *Da-Sein*	187
§108.	"Happiness"	188

P. THE FUNDAMENTAL STANCE OF THE *SECOND UNTIMELY MEDITATION*

§109. The Guiding Demand of the Meditation	193
§110. Guiding Stance	193
§111. Concept Formation in Philosophy and the Sciences	193
§112. "Life"	195
§113. "Life"	194
§114. "Life"	195
§115. Nietzsche's Fundamental Experience of "Life" and Opposition to "Darwinism"	195
§116. Life	196
§117. "Life"	196
§118. "Life"	196
§119. "Life"	197
§120. "Life"	197
§121. "Life"	197
§122. Life and "Adaptation"	198
§123. Life—Health and Truth	198
§124. Life as "Dasein"	198
§125. "Life" and "Death"	199

Q. ANIMALITY AND LIFE.
Animal—ζῷον. (The "Living Body." cf. Lectures of Winter Semester 1929/30)

§126. Milieu and Environment (World)	203
§127. Soul—Living Body—Body	203
§128. Embodying	204
§129. The Animal Has Memory	204
§130. Animal (Questions)	204
§131. Delimitation of the Essence of "Life" (Animality)	205
§132. Animality	205

R. THE DIFFERENTIATION OF HUMAN BEING AND ANIMAL

§133. The Un-historical and the Historical	209
§134. The Unhistorical—(of the Human Being)	209
§135. Animal and Human Being	209

S. "PRIVATION"

§136. What Happens to us as "Privation"	213
§137. "Privation"—Inter-ruption	213

T. STRUCTURE AND COMPOSITION OF THE *SECOND UNTIMELY MEDITATION*

§138. On the Advantages and Disadvantages of History for Life ... 217

ADDENDA

I. Seminar Reports ... 221
II. Summary by Hermann Heidegger ... 287

Editorial Postscript ... 309

Translators' Introduction

This volume is a translation of Martin Heidegger's notes for a weekly seminar on Nietzsche's second *Untimely Meditation*, *On the Advantages and Disadvantages of History for Life* (1874), held in the winter semester 1938–1939 in Freiburg. These notes were first published in German in 2003 as volume 46 of the *Gesamtausgabe* ("GA"—"Complete Edition") of Heidegger's work. Although the notes were originally supposed to form the basis of seminar exercises, the number of students actually present meant they were delivered in the form of lectures, and this seems to be one reason why Heidegger chose to have the notes appear in the second division of the *Gesamtausgabe*, which contains his lecture courses, rather than in the fourth division containing notes and recordings.

In this lecture course, Heidegger returns to Nietzsche's early essay *On the Advantages and Disadvantages of History for Life*, an essay that was of great importance for the development of his thought in the 1920s. *Being and Time* (1927) indicates clearly enough the positive influence that Nietzsche's essay had for Heidegger's project of "fundamental ontology." In contrast, in his more critical readings of Nietzsche in the first set of his lectures on Nietzsche's philosophy beginning in 1936 (GA 6.1),[1] Heidegger does not refer to this early essay, and claims that the essence of Nietzsche's philosophy is to be found in his later works, especially in the posthumous *Notebooks*. Nevertheless, in the present lecture course of 1938–1939, Heidegger returns to Nietzsche's essay of the 1870s in order to argue that his fully developed philosophy is already marked out in the essay's reflections on history, life, truth, and justice. This will allow him to argue in later lectures on Nietzsche

---

1. Martin Heidegger, *Gesamtausgabe*, vol. 6 bk.1, *Nietzsche* I ed. Brigitte Schillbach (Frankfurt am Main: Klostermann, 1996).

(GA 6.2)[2] that Nietzsche's early concern for truth as justice is, in fact, the core of his metaphysics. The present lecture course, then, is pivotal in Heidegger's interpretation of Nietzsche, and in the development of that interpretation from the project of fundamental ontology to the *Seinsgeschichtliche Auseinandersetzung*—"the confrontation in terms of the history of being"—advanced in the 1930s and 1940s. The lectures focus in particular on the underdetermined notion of life that appears in the title of Nietzsche's essay to argue that this notion lies at the root of the later philosophy of the Will to Power. This is one of the key ways in which the present lecture course casts new light on Heidegger's confrontation with Nietzsche's philosophy.

Lecture course though it was, Heidegger's notes are for the most part schematic and fragmentary. They contain incomplete sentences, diagrams and aides-mémoire, rather than a full transcript of what Heidegger actually said. This of course presents special difficulties for the translator. We have endeavored to reproduce the notes with as little textual intervention or embellishment as possible, but occasionally it has been necessary to add missing verbs or articles, for example, in order to avoid producing nonsensical and unduly impenetrable passages in English. Yet we have done so only in cases where the meaning presented by the German text was unambiguous.

We have followed the general principle, in line with other Heidegger translations in this series, of attempting to reproduce in English the effect that the notes would have on Heidegger's German listeners and readers. This entails that ordinary German words that become terms of art with extraordinary senses are, as much as possible, translated by ordinary English words. Heidegger's idea of being as *Ereignis*, for example, means something other than what we think of ordinarily as an "event," and the German word contains rich etymological significance absent in the English, but it is nevertheless best translated by that English word. Similarly, the sense of Heidegger's *Auseinandersetzung*—literally, a setting apart—with Nietzsche and other key thinkers in European philosophy might not be captured fully by the cognate English term *confrontation*. Yet Heidegger's attempts to draw original significance from the etymology of common words takes nothing away from the fact that they are common words; and it is for the reader, not the translator, to decide exactly how he uses words in ways that go beyond their everyday meanings.

---

2. Martin Heidegger, *Gesamtausgabe*, vol. 6 bk .2, *Nietzsche* II ed. Brigitte Schillbach (Frankfurt am Main: Klostermann, 1997).

The most intractable translation problem posed by this lecture course concerns its central theme, namely history. Heidegger attempts to establish a clear distinction between *Historie*, understood as the knowledge and the study of the past, and *Geschichte*, meaning the past as such, the past as foundation of our reality, whether it is known or not. Heidegger's critique of the second *Untimely Meditation* turns on the claim that Nietzsche fails to see this distinction and thus that his concern for *Historie* is both philosophically limited and ambiguous. Now, we have translated *Historie*—signifying in Nietzsche's text, on Heidegger's reading, if not simply the study of the past, then at least our approach to it, even when living without an explicit intellectual concern for it—by "historiology," which we prefer to "historiography," since the latter can name a metareflection on the writing of history. The three modes of *Historie* that Nietzsche analyzes in his text are thus monumental historiology, antiquarian historiology, and critical historiology. While this translation is occasionally unduly precise and sometimes makes for odd reading, one ought not to forget that for the contemporary German reader the word *Historie* is slightly odd too. Today, the German teenager has *Geschichtsunterricht* and might decide to study *Geschichtswissenschaften* at university, while *Historie* suggests grand events in the past or the painting of grand tableaux more than a sober science of historical fact. Of course, the second *Untimely Meditation* has never been known in English as *The Advantages and Disadvantages of Historiology for Life*, and thus the title of Nietzsche's text has to stand as an exception to our rule of translating *Historie* by "historiology" while reserving "history" as a translation of *Geschichte*.

The adjectival and adverbial forms present extra but not insuperable difficulties. We render *historisch* not as "historiological" but with the more natural *historical*, and this in accordance with Heidegger's argument that it is precisely when Nietzsche discusses the human being as a *historical* animal—and conversely, as one that needs to live *unhistorically* to a certain degree—that the ambiguity in his approach is at its most flagrant. However inchoately, this approach at least points to the recognition that the human being is *geschichtlich*, which we have consequently translated as "historial," in its essence.

Another key translation problem relates to Heidegger's distinctions between various forms of memory. A German reader might find that with some of his terminological distinctions Heidegger attempts to introduce more clarity than the German language allows. This compounds the problem of rendering these distinctions in English, but we decided to translate *Erinnerung* as "remembering," *Gedächtnis* as "memory," *Andenken* as "remembrance," *Behalten* as "retaining," and

Vergegenwärtigung as "making present." Wherever some ambiguity remained, we have reproduced the German word in brackets.

A set of problematic terms appears in Heidegger's renewed attempt—following the winter semester lecture course of 1929–1930, *Die Grundprobleme der Metaphysik: Welt, Endlichkeit, Einsamkeit* (GA 29–30)[3]—to reflect on the notion of life via the distinction between human and animal life. We have, in the main, followed established translations of the key terms, translating *Benehmen* as "behavior," *Verhalten* as "comportment," *Benommenheit* as "captivation," *Beraubung* as "deprivation," *Umfeld* as "milieu," *Dunstkreis* as "opaque milieu," *Umwelt* as "environment," and the more or less untranslatable *Entrückungseinheit* as "unity of rapture." Wherever there are other terms giving rise to difficulties we have reproduced the original German in brackets.

---

3. Martin Heidegger, *Gesamtausgabe*, vols. 29–30, ed. *Die Grundprobleme der Metaphysik: Welt, Endlichkeit, Einsamkeit*, ed. Friedrich-Wilhelm von Herrmann (Frankfurt am Main: Klostermann, 2004); *The Fundamental Concepts of Metaphysics: World, Finitude, Solitude*, trans. William McNeill and Nicholas Walker (Indiana University Press: 1995).

Interpretation of Nietzsche's Second Untimely Meditation

A. PRELIMINARY REMARKS

§1. Remarks Preliminary to the Exercises

In its broad outlines, the work that we are planning has three aims:

1. *An introduction to philosophical concept formation*. But this as
2. *A reading and interpretation of a specific treatise* (*On the Advantages and Disadvantages of History for Life*[1]), and therefore
3. *An engagement with Nietzsche's philosophy*.

* * *

With regard to (1): Instead of "introduction to philosophical concept formation" we could just as well have said: instruction in learning *to think*. That sounds clearer and apparently simpler, but it also gives rise to a doubt regarding our project: thinking—for example, "historical" thinking—we learn best and most securely when we concern ourselves with the "science of history" [*Geschichtswissenschaft*]. The same holds for medical, economic, juridical, technical, and also for political thinking: we learn "to think" in each case when we participate in the elaboration of a specific subject matter, in the mastery and formation of a specific field of activity, and thus *practice* the kind of thinking that is demanded in each particular field.

In contrast, *learning to think* as a general task seems, if not impossible, then at least useless.

Yet in speaking of learning *to think*, we do not mean thinking in general, a thinking that, without object or foundation, is only an indeterminate, undifferentiated thinking. Instead, we mean thinking in an accentuated and more specific sense: the thinking of those who are called "thinkers," [4] as in our talk of "poets and thinkers [*Dichter und Denker*]." To learn to think in the manner of *thinkers* is what matters to us. Of course, whoever learns to think in such a way is not yet a thinker, a "philosopher." And we do not *want* to become "philosophers" for the simple reason that one cannot "want" such a thing. Someone either is or is not a thinker; and if one is a thinker, then that means that one *must* be the thinker that one is.

What we want to learn here is something preparatory, something that is contained in the thinking of thinkers as their *invisible craft*: "philosophical concept formation." An introduction to this is what

---

1. Friedrich Nietzsche, *Nietzsches Werke* (Großoktavausgabe), ed. Fritz Koegel, vol. 1, *Unzeitgemässe Betrachtungen: Zweites Stück: Vom Nutzen und Nachtheil der Historie für das Leben* (Leipzig: Kröne, 1917), 277–384, trans. and ed. Daniel Breazeale, "On the Advantages and Disadvantages of History for Life," in *Untimely Meditations* (Cambridge: Cambridge University Press, 1997), 57–124.

concerns us here. We would rather not provide a long justification of why we are attempting this. It may be that if we really are willing to learn the thinking practiced by thinkers in a genuine way, there comes a point when seeking the answer to the *Why?* and the *What for?* of such endeavor suddenly becomes superfluous. Such a moment can arise if we notice how the possibility of thinking in the manner of thinkers grants a peculiar determinateness to more habitual "thinking," that is, to practical and calculative, technical and scientific thinking, bestowing on it a hitherto unknown luminosity. The possibility remains that we suddenly see and evaluate "philosophical thinking" differently. Otherwise, from an ordinary, everyday perspective, philosophers are considered as people who lose sight of the ground under their feet (the ancient Greeks already told such stories about their thinkers); people who "think things up," things that no one can verify and that are useful to no one, and which are at worst harmful, since they confuse and twist minds. It would be childish to attempt to refute this general conception of "philosophers," for it accompanies and follows every genuine thinker, belonging to him like smoke belongs to fire.

All the same, the possibility remains that one day we will see all this in a different light: perhaps the thinking practiced by thinkers does not groundlessly float above so-called reality and above the [5] oft-invoked "life," with its tangible and productive mode of thinking, appreciated always from the perspective of its practical advantages. Perhaps this "realistic" thinking, in whose element alone everydayness justifiably moves, is only a final offshoot and the outermost branch of that sort of thinking of which ordinary thinking has no idea, and about which it does not need to have any idea, as long as it is satisfied with its habits and values its usefulness above all else. Whether or not the human being wishes to content itself with its everyday thinking [*Alltagsdenken*] is a matter and question of the rank that it assigns to human being [*dem Menschentum*]; it is decided according to what the human being demands of *itself* and of *its essence*—as an individual, a group, a community, a people, or an age—for such demands are the wellsprings of wealth. Hence we shall refrain from calculating the *uses* that learning to think in the manner of thinkers could possibly have. For once, we are daring to undertake a useless task, and to consider what is first of all required for it.

With regard to (2): *A reading and interpretation of a specific treatise.* We want to learn the thinking proper to thinkers by thinking-*along-with* [*mitdenken*] a particular thinker, and by thoughtfully following him [*nachdenken*] on his path; that is, not by studying a "logic" in the traditional way, and not by constructing an empty "theory" from an equally empty thinking with empty forms, thereby taking up a position that from the beginning is external to the enactment of genuine thought.

§1. Remarks Preliminary to the Exercises

With our aim, on the contrary, to think-along-with a thinking that has already been carried out, it is also already decided that we will not blindly repeat and reconstruct the philosophical thinking in the treatise under discussion. We are rather to take it immediately and continually as an occasion for what characterizes philosophical thinking, that is, as an occasion for *questioning*. The inner condition, however, for a *questioning* dialogue with an essential thinker is veneration, which must be maintained even when a confrontation [*Auseinandersetzung*] with that thinker is required, and even when it becomes necessary to overcome his fundamental position. In truth, there is no other form of a genuine encounter with the thinking [6] of a thinker than that of a struggle which puts this very thinking in question. And that brings us to the third point.

With regard to (3): By reading and interpreting this particular text, so as to learn thoughtful thinking, we are, at the same time, attempting to gain an initial insight into *Nietzsche's* philosophy.

Nietzsche is not just any thinker among the great German thinkers; and we are certainly not turning to him because today he is "fashionable" here and there or because now and again his name is mentioned. Nietzsche rather has his distinction in being the last thinker in the history of Western philosophy up to now; and he is the last, not merely in the sense of being the *last* to have appeared, but rather in the sense that he constitutes *the end* of previous philosophy, which means that he completes it and in a particular manner returns to its beginning. Hence to think through and alongside a few steps of *his* thinking means at the same time to grasp Western philosophy in its essential structure and to raise it up into a primary knowing. The essential structure of the history of Western philosophy is characterized by the fact that it is "metaphysics." We will experience what that means when learning to think according to the guiding thread of Nietzsche's text.

The "greater" a thinker is—that is, the more what is thought and questioned by him is essential—, the more indifferent the thinker remains for the public and for those who come after him as a particular human being with a particular life story. Anaximander, Parmenides, Heraclitus: we know almost nothing about the so-called personalities of the greatest thinkers of Greece. And it is better that way. Their thinking, often handed down to us only through a small number of aphorisms, thus stands in history in a purer and more solitary manner as an inexhaustible impulse and as a continual challenge.

Admittedly, modern and contemporary human beings live according to a constant and unrestrained craving for analyses of the life and soul of creative people. Contemporary interests are to an unusual extent "psychological" and biographical, so much so that it is held that a work can be understood only from the material conditions of the life of its author. [7] But neither in the domain of art nor in that of thinking will psychological, biological, and biographical explanations of the emergence of a work ever reach into the vicinity of its inner origin.

In this way, the question that forces itself upon us—*Who is Nietzsche?*—remains ambiguous. It can and must mean, what is most essential to his thinking? But it could also mean merely, what is his life story? If it is not to remain as an object of mere biographical curiosity, then this life story can be understood only on the basis of the work, and not vice versa. Now, admittedly, it is precisely Nietzsche's thinking, or at least the widely held view of it, that is *partly* to blame for the extreme escalation of the contemporary psycho-*biographical*, and in the widest sense "biological," way of thinking. Hence we always find ourselves in an ambiguous situation with regard to Nietzsche: it is essential for us, on the one hand and in all decisiveness, to comprehend his thinking, while on the other hand, we have to consider his life story, even if *not* from a biographical-psychological perspective.

To summarize, our task is "provisionally" learning to think, read, and question, or in short, a first instruction in *mindfulness* [*Besinnung*].

Given that demands for the fulfillment of immediate needs and for the realization of instrumental goals are forced upon us everywhere, and that this distress is everywhere maintained in an extreme way so that nothing "urgent" is overlooked or neglected, we should allow ourselves from time to time the "luxury" of the useless undertaking of an aimless mindfulness. Our work can be successful only as long as we keep this in mind and refrain from immediately looking for some sort of benefit in it, which would mean to leap out of mindfulness and out of its proper path.

At the beginning we will proceed, in appearance at least, biographically and will acquaint ourselves briefly with Nietzsche's life story up to the point when our particular text appeared.

From the very beginning of his thinking onward, Nietzsche repeatedly looked backward and forward at his own "life."[8] See, for example, the recently discovered account of his life, written when he was 19 years old.[2]

Important dates: 1844–1873/1874. . .

Reference to Jacob Burckhardt's "Force and Freedom: Reflections on History."[3] Nietzsche's letter to Gersdorff of November 7, 1870.

From Nietzsche's account:

---

2. Friedrich Nietzsche, "Mein Leben. Autobiographische Skizze des jungen Nietzsche" (Frankfurt am Main: Diesterweg Verlag, 1936).

3. Jacob Burckhardt, *Weltgeschichtliche Betrachtungen* (Wiesbaden, DE: Marixverlag, 2009), trans. James Hastings Nichols, *Force and Freedom: Reflections on History* (Pantheon: New York, 1943).

§2. Title   7

Beginning: "I was born, as a plant, near God's Acre, and, as a human being, in a presbytery."
Plant: *life*, to which "death" belongs, unfolding itself.
Human Being: conception—constitution—formation [*Bildung*]—History—*Historiology* (culture) of life.
Conclusion: Question of the "circle," which holds the human being together and encircles it, of where it belongs, and of the relation in which life and its embodiment must be brought together.

Ten years later (autumn 1873) Nietzsche wrote his *Second Untimely Meditation*.

---

§2. Title

Elucidation of the title as an indication of the domain of our reflections:

1. "Historiology" as a theme?
2. "Life"
3. "Advantages and Disadvantages"

Domain
Calculative measure   > "Life"
Enactment
Demand

[9] With regard to (3), this is the real topic: the *calculative account* [*Verrechnung*] of the relation between historiology and life.

   a) *The domain*, within which they relate to each other (only when both historiology and life have been defined).
   b) Advantages and disadvantages can be evaluated in each case according to a *particular purpose* and *aim*. "Life" as purpose (of life?) and life as a domain.
   c) The form of the calculative account; *which truth it* demands, *how it accounts for itself, where* and *by which means it has been enacted*. (*Describing* "sentiments"! "descriptions of nature," portrayal. Meditation—*life!*)

With regard to (2): "life"—human "life"? or which form of life?

"life" < as beings as a whole
       < as being

With regard to (1): "historiology"—*the science of history*, historiology and history, in Nietzsche and elsewhere these are not properly distinguished.

With regard to (3): *the calculative account*—"life": the domain—the criterion and *enactment* and *origin* (*demand—need*)

* * *

Life itself *can* pose the question, and life, as human life, continuously poses the question. And it does *not* only ask what might be advantageous and disadvantageous at any given moment—advantageous or disadvantageous *"for what"*—but rather it asks whether it itself is *worthwhile* (Schopenhauer): a "business," something to do, to see through to the end, to run, to pass a test. The *"justification"* of *life* itself—but *on what basis* if life is "beings as a whole"? (The question of "happiness.") Consequently in relation to (3), (2), and (1) the question of life "itself" is the most decisive question (compare (3)(b)).

What "life" might be is not to be determined through "biology," because "biology" necessarily involves essential concepts that, as "biology," it cannot justify.

What *history* might be is, for the same reason, not to be decided by means of the "science of history."

[10] Not even what the *science* of history is can be determined on the basis of historiology, for no science can ever be in possession of the means to account for its own essence. And furthermore, historiology as the science of history can be determined only on the basis of *history*.

Thus *another manner of thinking and questioning* is necessary. Affirming this is not to disparage science. On the contrary—it is an indication that science brings with it something that wholly surpasses it, and thus that it is more than what it knows of itself, more than what it can know of itself.

The preliminary reflection on the title provides a still more essential indication with respect to our confrontation with Nietzsche. The theme in the narrow sense is "history" (compare the title that Nietzsche gave to the text in 1887: "We Historians: On the History of the Illness of the Modern Soul"). But it has emerged that the inquiry occurs essentially within the region of *life* itself, in view of life (happiness), and as a *questioning* on the part of *life* itself; and this not merely as posing just any question, but rather as a question that it—"life"—has to pose to itself ("happiness"). Hence what is decisive in the first instance is not which concept of "history" Nietzsche bases his reflection upon, and whether he exhausts all possible modes of historiology, nor whether there are historical methods that do not appear in his classification, but rather: what is at *stake* with this situating of *"life,"* what the significance of such situating is, and what it includes (cf. "fundamental experience").

"Philosophy of life"—the comfortable and quite fatal impropriety [*Unwesen*] of such a name as a haven for thoughtlessness.

The greatest "danger" for the thinking of thinkers is not posed by those who oppose them, for these can only ever be other thinkers, but rather by the supposed "followers": Leibniz and the Leibnizians, Kant and the Kantians, Hegel and the Hegelians; but the worst case is given with Nietzsche and the Nietzscheans. What is important in this is only: no texts "on" the thinkers, the so-called literature, but rather the thinkers themselves. It is still more valuable, following a real and genuine effort, [11] to have grasped little or nothing about a thinker, than to have "understood" one or more of the texts about him. Hence it amounts to a misguided effort when someone now feels the need to inform themselves about the literature on Nietzsche.

§3. The Appearance of our Endeavors

A concern with the "meaning of words"—with the univocity of words:

1. focusing on the matter at hand and the right relation [of the word] to it.
2. univocity of the word—not a semantic pedantry concerning the use of language.
   a) no *standardization*, no "apparatus of signs"
   b) only where there is univocity can the original play of the mysterious plurivocity of language come into its own.
3. *The essence of language* (in the context of our considerations). [13]

B. Section I

Structure. Preparation and Preview of the Guiding Question. Historiology—Life

§4. Historiology—The Historical
On the Unhistorical/Suprahistorical and the Relation to Both

1. The animal (and human being): caught up in the moment, constantly forgetting, without past, lives *unhistorically*.
2. Human being (and the animal): cannot forget, braces itself against the past, constantly related to the latter, lives *historically*.
3. To all human action and happiness the unhistorical (being able to forget) *also* belongs; the historical sense. *Both* in the human being, that is, in *relation* to each other.
4. *What kind of relation* between the unhistorical and the historical in the human being? *Belonging-together*—not merely existing next to each other. And what is the ground of the unity that unifies in each case? "The *plastic power*" of the human being, of life. The *"horizon."* The historical characterizes the human being: *animal rationale*.
5. But the *limitation* of historical sense emerges here, and even a *primacy* of the unhistorical (not only "also"; cf. (3)), that is, for the sake of *enactment*, the *deed*, calculation (therefore for "life" as power; but then is there a primacy at all?). The unhistorical as primary, the historical as the distinction!
6.–8. The suprahistorical is ambiguous (cf. sec. X, p. 379); that is, what kind of responses are possible? Those human beings who are only historical and those who are suprahistorical, those who *deny such belonging together* (cf. 4.):
    a) through one-sidedness,
    b) by leaping beyond it.
9.–12. *Cognition and life*, hierarchy, *"theses," fundamental meditation*
    a) Historiology, for itself, absolute.
    b) Historical education in the wake of life.
    c) Historiology in the service of an ahistorical power: *life*.
    Transition to the second and following sections.

* * *

[16] All these key questions are distributed throughout the various paragraphs of the section as a whole, and that in turn holds for the particular sections with respect to the whole meditation.

Thinking—not progress along a straight line, but circling around a middle, emerging from the latter, and in an always more originary way (*maelstrom*).

Added to this is the peculiar character of the *Untimely* Meditation as aiming to unsettle and arouse; not a learned treatise. Furthermore, the *rigorous* style has *not yet been attained*, not even as a demand. Equivocation [*Vielspältigkeit*].

The way of saying proper to each great thinker is determined from the fundamental trait of questioning, and therefore from a fundamental position. Leibniz—Kant—Hegel—Nietzsche—and then again the Greek thinkers. *No common sense schemata* [*Allerweltsschema*].

The prevalent opinion: Nietzsche is *easier to understand* than Kant, for example, Zarathustra: reveling and rooting around, individual "aphorisms"; yes and no.

* * *

Beginning with a comparative consideration of the *animal. What is singled out?* That it *feeds*, jumps about? No! That it constantly *forgets*, and this as: "being absorbed in the present." "Presence"—time? *Not what is initially essential*. First of all: *forgetting*, what it is. [17]

Approach:

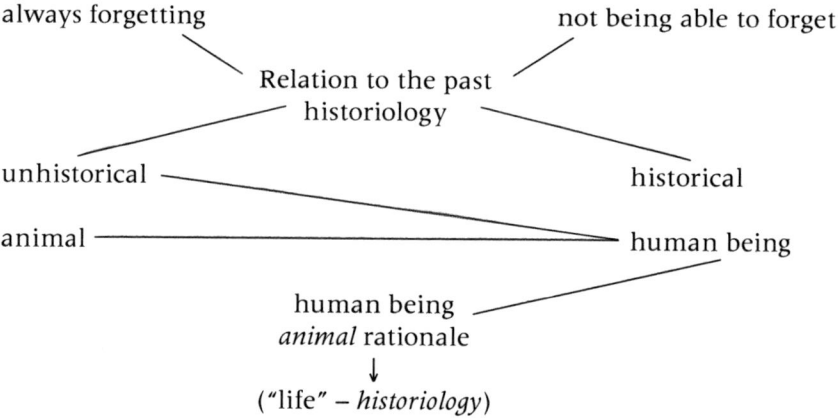

A series of questions concerning the microcosmos and the macroanthropos, cf. *Überlegungen* X, 70.[1]

This means now: *if* "life" *is the domain, measure, and demand of a calculative account* of historiology, and *if* "life" *is being as such and in general, then* we have to ask: how and from what perspective it can be

---

1. Martin Heidegger, *Gesamtausgabe*, vol. 95, *Überlegungen* VII–XI (*Schwarze Hefte* 1938–1939), ed. Peter Trawny (Frankfurt am Main: Klostermann, 2014).

determined! From "ourselves," from human beings? Then everything is *anthropomorphization?*

---

§5. Section I. 1

A. What "is seen":
  1. Being bound to the moment. Cf. section I, para. 2: being absorbed in the present.
  2. Not knowing what is *today*, what is *yesterday*, i.e., *not knowing* suchlike. ("We" do not "know" that *either!*).
  3. this absorption *as* "happiness." [18]
B. *How "the human being" copes with this experience.*
  "The" human being—who? Human "happiness"—*the same*, but different in its "how."
  The human being's "envy" (that he is not an animal! no, rather that he cannot make himself happy by his own efforts).
C. *Attempted dialogue between human being and animal.*
  How the animal's "forgetting" is brought to light.
  Only an "image"—an imaginary situation?
  The animal's wanting to say something and its silence.

* * *

The animal—untroubled by the past as such (unhistorical, cf. para. 2). And yet in every animal—something "prior," that which always and already reigns (e.g., instinct).

---

§6. Section I. 2

A. The human being is assailed, harried by the past ("I remember"). In contrast, the animal . . . unhistorical.
B. *The human being, conversely*: bracing itself against the past, somehow getting to grips with the past, being delivered over to it.
C. The *most extreme antithesis. Imperfectum* signifies: *"unfinished."* In what sense? With reference to the "was" as imperfect? The relation to the "was" is furthermore—*imperfectibile.* In contrast, the animal: *Praesens semper perfectum.*

* * *

The relation to the past is drawn out in a completely one-sided way, from the perspective of the "animal."

"The perfect and the imperfect drank champagne." (Morgenstern)

* * *

"*Bound to the moment,*" being absorbed by what is at each time present, being *captivated* by *it*, without knowing it *as* "present." [19] Neither *melancholic* because everything passes by, because nothing lasts—*weighed down by* the past and by *everything*—, nor weary of *the continuous monotony*, which is to say, of what is still to come. This only where there is *"was," rift, and overview* [*Riß und Überblick*], and in relation to what is given as such, to "beings" and that means to what comes and goes.

The "thin line of the present" (vol. X, p. 268). Does the animal "forget," if it is captivated by . . . and never takes or retains? If it "saw" *every moment fall away*, it would have to be capable of pursuing it into the *no-longer*—(too much), "because it vanishes in the present" (sec. I, p. 284).

Relation to *the present* (and yet it does not know what today is); and yet again: sees dying. Presence—is also "time" (even the genuine and the *only real time*).

How to consider the animal—the herd? (*An almost fleeting view*) and what is immediately expressed: *"it does not know what yesterday, what today is,"* is ignorant of any differences in time, past—present. *Migratory birds* and the days when it is time! Storks in St. Gallen. "To be mistaken" [*sich versehen*].

What is seen: *being absorbed in the moment* as *a happy living along with things*. "Happiness"—always constituting itself—leaps, feeds, digests. Investigation of "movement" (muscles, ligaments, nerves), of mouth and teeth, stomach, chemistry of the metabolism, circulation. Microscope and experiment, nothing of all this, but rather only from the "outside," *how it behaves*. Is that "externally" or *the most internally*? And if the stomach and the lungs are *"external,"* what does outside and inside mean here? The living being as "organism." The living body [*Leib*] and the body [*Körper*]—*cf.* animality.

It, "the animal," where is the boundary of the animal—*the surface* of the "body"? *The inside is outside,* captivated-by-its-milieu.

"Feeding" as the combination of chains of muscle contractions and excretions of salivary glands, caused [20] by the effects of other things. *Or? From the relation to food* and within this relation.

The "somatic" (the animate) as only an entangled and not yet disentangled corporeal materiality. "*Living mass*" [*Lebendige Masse*]—the turning of the plant toward the sun and the searching for a "truth" in reflective thought, as 'forms' on the same level of maturity (Pavlov).

§7. Section I (pp. 283–294)

This section anticipates the whole of the treatise in its fundamental traits. The treatise itself returns in section X, pp. 379ff. to its beginning.

The structure of the first section (twelve paragraphs) *opens* with a *comparative consideration* of animal and human being. (cf. no. 9)

Comparing: e.g., motorcycle and primrose.
             "machine"   "growth" (plant)
                    Automotive
                    A way of being

or the number three and Kleist's "Prince of Homburg"— incomparable? Yes and no!

1. With respect to . . . taking the same into view in advance
2. Differentiating: singling out what unites them and the *differences*; why, and with what intention?
"Contrasting," what is intended by it:
a) merely comparing,
b) balancing out,
c) deciding
Which difference
is accentuated: The animal lives unhistorically
                    The human being lives historically
[21] *What remains in view:*   Life "how"—historiology
                               "life"   —"happiness"
How life stands in and in relation to itself. ———▶ Life
Life — Beyond itself, and back into itself.
    Remaining within it and advancing toward it.

§8. Comparing

To look at something aiming at what is common to them and thereby at what is different. The common and the different, and both exist as they are with respect to *the same thing*. What is decisive in a comparison: the *whereupon* of a taking into view. *How this unfolds and is justified, whether it is questioned for itself* or *only made use of.*

Different types of comparison; everything is in some way comparable to anything, *which is why* the choice of perspective is crucial, how something is taken up and come by, from a *preview*:
- *mere comparing—arbitrary, limitless choice,*
- *avoiding taking a position,*
- *balancing out,*
- *decision.*

§9. The Determination of the Essence of the Human Being on the Basis of Animality and the Dividing Line between Animal and Human Being

In our discussion so far we have drawn out and clarified in advance the perspective within which the reading, and this means at the same time the interpretation, of Nietzsche's *Second Untimely Meditation* has to be developed. This reading and learning to read becomes an introduction to Nietzsche's thought, in such a way that we can practice thoughtful thinking and thinking-along-with [*das denkerische Mit- und Nachdenken*].

It is not a matter of expanding our stock of knowledge, but rather of *seeing with different eyes*, so that we can take into view what ordinary views and [22] opinions are *not* able to see and do not need to see for their most immediate aims and purposes.

The fundamental word "life," which governs all of Nietzsche's reflections, signifies both beings as such and in general, and the *kind and the mode* of this being. But from the above we have learned that "life" also, and often in an accentuated sense, means "*human* life" and even simply the human being in its being human. From here it follows:

Granted that "life" is all at once the domain, the measure, and the ground of the need to calculate the advantages and disadvantages of history, the question of *human life* plays a prominent role within the reflection on life as such and in general.

From the overview of the structure of section I we learn that:

The human being is in its very essence characterized and distinguished by the historical. At the same time, the unhistorical has a primacy within human life. Within the human being this characterization by means of the historical and the primacy of the unhistorical belong together; in such a belonging together reigns the antagonism of what is different within itself. The *unity* of this belonging together—of the historical and the unhistorical—in the human being can therefore not be described as an external concatenation of the two after the fact,

§9. The Determination of the Essence of the Human Being 19

but rather must have the character of a foundation that lets both—the historical and the unhistorical—arise from themselves *in* their belonging together, so as to reign pervasively over their antagonism. We have thus not understood anything as long as we restrict ourselves to merely stating the existence of the historical *and* the unhistorical in the human being; only in considering their unity and the ground of the latter are we able to bring light into the essence of the human being so conceived.

The belonging together and its unity will come to light all the more clearly *the more decisively* the *distinction* between them has been established beforehand.

[23] This distinction of the historical and the unhistorical is gained according to the guiding thread of the difference between "forgetting" (more precisely: constant forgetting) and "remembering" (more precisely: always having to remember again). The characterization of this difference begins with a consideration of the *animal*.

This approach forces the following question on us: in a text concerned with the calculative account of *historiology*, that is, of *human* being for life, and thus first of all with *human* life—in a text where the *human being* is thus put into question, was it necessary or merely accidental, merely, say, an artifice of artistic composition to begin with a reflection on the *animal*? Starting with a consideration of the animal is, as we will see, not accidental. With the question of the human being, we move *necessarily* within the realm of the distinction between animal and human being. Here the question becomes inescapable: where does the dividing line between animal and human being lie? And does such a dividing line exist at all? And if it does, how can we determine it? These questions extend far beyond the limits of Nietzsche's treatise; they are also prior to the questions of any "biology" or "anthropology." The question of the dividing line between animal and human being is in fact not at all a question of an academic nature, and neither is it a "question" of a "worldview" or one of Christian faith. Within the realms of these—science, worldview, religious faith—such a question either *cannot be raised* or is always and already decided by some doctrinal statement, and thereby dismissed as unworthy of questioning. And yet the destiny of the historial Occident, of its sciences and its worldviews and the faith of its churches, is decided by either posing the question of the dividing line between animal and human being or by avoiding it. We will not be able to solve this question here, not even to pose it adequately. But we have to recognize, following these initial interpretative reflections, that this question reigns over our exercises of thinking, even when we do not explicitly talk about it, and even though we are not yet capable of fully assessing its import. Yet referring [24] to this profound question is necessary; otherwise we might come to labor under the misapprehension that the discussion concerning, for example, the essence of forgetting is nothing but an empty quarrel about empty words.

At the end of the last session one participant in these exercises said to me: where he comes from, namely America—and thus in American thought—"there is not such a big difference between animal and human being." This might be true not only for America. But here and now we are not really interested in taking stock of currently prevailing views concerning the distinction between animal and human being. Instead, we want to think about something *more essential*, and that is the fact and the reality that the European human being has, for the last two millennia, determined itself as an animal, which is to say: has posited the realm of animality as the fundamental measure for any essential delimitation of being human.

ἄνθρωπος: ζῷον λόγον ἔχον
homo: animal rationale
Human being: the rational "animal"

We would do well to remark that in this essential determination of the human being, it is not simply equated with the animal. Rather, and much more significantly, animality is posited as the generic realm within which the essence of the human being is specified. Western thinking, however, has right up to the present day failed to think through this positing of the essence of being human on the basis of animality. The reason for this uncanny thoughtlessness is quite obvious: the interpretation of the human being as a psychosomatic being, a being that imposes itself with the help of "instinct" and "logic," has long been taken *for granted*. It is for this reason that we are incapable of grasping the consequences of this characterization of the human being as an animal, while we often think that when attributing an "immortal soul" and a "spirit" to the human being, or when we understand it as a "personality," we have already overcome its determination as animal, [25] whereas the truth is that we have now presupposed it all the more radically; for "soul" exists only where there is body [*Leib*], and body only where there is animal, and the person as a "center of acts" with "experiences" exists only where there is "life"—"living being"—*animal*—animal.

Nietzsche says at one point that the human being is the "not yet determined animal" (*Beyond Good and Evil*, p. 88 frag. 62, vol. VII), that is, the animal whose essence has not yet been fixed. With this statement Nietzsche at any rate bears witness to the fact that *he* too, and he especially, thinks wholly in the sense of the Western tradition: the human being as ζῷον—animal.

§9. The Determination of the Essence of the Human Being 21

In the further course of our inquiry, however, we will have to ask whether, as Nietzsche says, this animal, the human being, *has not yet* been fixed, or whether, conversely, it has been far too conclusively determined in its essence.

Although Nietzsche regrets the absence of fixation of this particular animal, it has to be said that this fixation has already been effective for several centuries—since the philosophy of Descartes. This fixation of the human being consists in the following determination: the human being is that being which immediately *finds itself existing* as spirit and soul, and consequently knows itself as a living body. Thus when Nietzsche says, in apparent contradiction to Descartes that it is not spirit and the soul—consciousness—that are first given to the human being as what is properly human, but rather the living body and its bodily states, he nevertheless thinks, at bottom, in accordance with the modern conception of the human being as the self-conscious "animal" that can conceive of itself as such—the human being as the being that can come upon itself and which by means of its power [five words are illegible here]—overanimal, but still an *animal*. The fixation of the human animal, which, though long established, Nietzsche thought to be still outstanding, consists precisely in this interpretation of the human being as the animal with access to itself. The modern human being is now determined in such a way that on account of this delimitation [26] of his own essence, he is not able or willing to determine himself other than as an animal, to understand himself in any other way than as so determined.

With the modern determination of the human being as "subject"—that is, as the being that grounds the encounterability and mastery of beings as such and in general as their governing center and goal [*maßgebende Mitte und Ziel*]—the old interpretation of the essence of the human being as a reasonable animal is not done away with but realized for the first time in the full breadth of its meaning.

And this brings us to the next question standing in the background of our investigations: is the familiar delineation of the essence of the human being as ζῷον, as *animal*, really as self-evident as we have taken it to be? Such a question touches on the possibility, perhaps even the necessity, of determining the essence of the human being in a more originary way, that is, not first and foremost as belonging to the genus animal, and thus not primarily as a "living body" and, consequently, neither as "soul" nor as "spirit," and therefore definitely not as the admixture of living body, soul, spirit. To be sure, this cannot be taken to mean that the human being exists *without* what one calls a "living body" [*Leib*] or even a "body" [*Körper*]; the question rather concerns whether what we call the "living body" is merely something allowing for a spirit or a personality to be grafted onto or built into it.

But first of all we have to observe that the essence of the human being is thought on the basis of animality, that such an approach is not at all accidental or arbitrary, and that it can even rely on the tribunal of everyday experience and its immediate intuitions.

Therefore if Nietzsche, in his *Untimely Meditation*, begins the essential delimitation of historiology, that is to say of the human being, with a consideration of animal life, then the *real* reason for this is that the human being, according to an ancient tradition of Western thought, has already been fixed—in terms of its genus—as "animal." It is because the human being has already been grasped as a *special* animal that it has now to be interpreted as distinct from the animal. And the question of the dividing line between animal and human being now acquires a particular [27] significance, and this question can now be posed in the following form: Does the dividing line between animal and human being run its course and does it exist in such a way that it distinguishes the animal in the usual sense from the human being as a "superior" and "special" animal, or is it such that the human being *cannot* in any sense be predetermined as animal and *animal* [*als Tier und* animal]? In the second case the dividing line between animal and human being would present itself as a *chasm* between what is—*despite an apparent proximity*—abysally distinct, a chasm that cannot be bridged; a chasm, moreover, that is covered over precisely when one claims to have elevated the human being above animality by means of its determination as a *rational creature* and as a person.

Supposing that a chasm separates animal and human being, the question whether a universal biology or "anthropology" determines the essence of the human being "correctly" or "incorrectly" becomes meaningless, because they are unable to determine it at all. Only *one* necessary question remains here, namely that of how biology can claim to establish anything at all about the *essence* of the human being.

But we are *still* standing within the horizon of the traditional determination of the human being on the basis of animality. And therefore to begin with we will follow Nietzsche in his consideration of the animal: "Consider the herd. . ."

§10. Nietzsche's Procedure.
On the Determination of the Historical from the Perspective of Forgetting and Remembering

a) "Animal"
"Organism" and "Wholeness" [*Ganzheit*]

Wholeness is a unity that unifies in an originary way and that gives rise to the manifold and retains the latter within it. *When* something

§10. Nietzsche's Procedure

is [28] taken to be whole—supposing this to *occur* rightfully and *adequately*(!)—the decisive question has here merely been *initiated*, and not yet even posed, let alone answered (the people as "a whole").

Wholeness—ὅλον—καθόλου / Aristotle—Heraclitus
Leibniz—Herder—Goethe. ——————→ Nietzsche
Leibniz—*Schelling*—German Idealism.
    "System"—σύστασις;
    apparent antonym: "composition" [*Zusammenstellung*]

Animal: contour of the living body ——→ space
    milieu-boundary   *being-captivated-in-space!*

The animal (and the plant?) takes up "more" space than the contours of its body [*Leibkörper*].
Different relations to space:
1. *Filling up space*—a body
The living body does not only fill up space, not even as a living body [*Leibkörper*], but is characterized by the *captivated* taking up of space.
2. *Taking up* space—*reaching out*—sizing up while moving through [*verfügendes Durchmessen*]; in the animal in terms of captivation— "the eagle"—the swooping hawk.
    a) Space—is not given as such
    b) is *as such* mastered—not mastered.

- The next question: the essence of historiology;
- on the basis of the *differentiation between the unhistorical and historical*;
- the most extreme limit cases posited: animal—human being;
- what the difference is grounded on: forgetting—remembering. The dividing line: *"relation to time"*—different (*imperfect* and *praesens perfectum*);
- where does the explanation and the justification begin—*"animal!"* animal—although it is an absolutely original and particular being [*Ureigenes*]—still only from the perspective of the *"human being."*

[29] *Human Being?* ← Microcosm—Human Being
                ↖ Cosmos—Macrocosm

The significance of the question of the human being.
- Therefore unhistorical-historical—forgetting-remembering in the human being.
- The points of discrepancy
    a) In the notion of the unhistorical (cf. (b) Procedure 4),
    b) With respect to the characterization of forgetting (cf. (b) Procedure 8).

b) Procedure (the Center of the Circle!)

1. First of all the account of the essence of historiology is clarified—in relation to the *historical-unhistorical* distinction; but this at the same time as the distinction between human being and animal.
2. Yet Nietzsche's definitions are not to be considered simply in their content, rather we have to be mindful of *how he comes by them*—namely
    a) *Starting from the animal* (thus the short, preliminary reflection on animality) and
    b) By means of stipulating two extreme and opposed limit cases: the animal lives unhistorically, the human being lives historically.
3. This leads to a focus on different relations to *time determinations*, in which relations animal and human being can move:

    Human being—*Im per fectum—semper imperfectibile.*
    Animal   —*Praesens perfectum.*

The dividing line between human being and animal runs *within* the different possible and hetero*geneous* "time relations"; distinct relations to "the past" and "the present." [30]

4. In the end, we will have to ask whether this distinction between the historical-unhistorical (and at the same time the determination of historiology) is sufficiently grounded and whether it can be maintained at all in this form. On the basis of our preceding reflections we can already bring to bear a fundamental reservation: only that which is historical can be *un*historical. Therefore the animal, in order to be able to be *unhistorical*, would need to be a *human being*; but the unhistorical was supposed to be precisely what characterizes the animal as an animal.

    The animal is not unhistorical, but much rather *without history* [*historielos*]—and these are not the same. ("Privation"! "Negation"—"thinking"). Consequently, when Nietzsche characterizes both animal and human being as *unhistorical*, then the word unhistorical means something essentially different in each case, without Nietzsche ever having clarified this distinction sufficiently. Nevertheless this distinction emerges—without his knowing it.

    Cf. the account of the unhistorical (sec. I, para. 2, p. 284) in the animal: the constant, immediate (by itself) forgetting.

    Cf. the account of the unhistorical in the human being (sec. X, para. 9, p. 379): "the art and the strength of being able to *forget.*" This is what the animal ultimately "lacks"—and on what? is this grounded!

    In the account of historiology there are essential obscurities, the illumination of which casts some light on the treatise as a whole.

    But: this illumination cannot be brought about by merely formal considerations, but only in following the path of mindfulness

[*Besinnung*] and confrontation [*Auseinandersetzung*]; and that means working one's way into that within which this account of the historical and the unhistorical unfolds, into what it is grounded on.
5. This can only happen by means of the distinction and characterization of *"forgetting"* and *"remembering."*

To be absorbed in the present—to drag the past behind oneself.

What is this a matter of, *how* is it emphasized and delimited? (Again we have to remark: not a reckoning up of "errors," not a schoolmasterly [31] pedantry, and if there is here anything unclarified, then this is an aberrance [*Verirrung*] of an essential kind, which reaches far back into and is rooted in Western thought; and for this reason it cannot simply be overcome by a more adequate determination of concepts.)
6. The characterization of *forgetting* and "remembering"' by means of a comparative *consideration* of *animal and human being*. ("Life"), in which the guiding perspectives with respect to animal and human being are:
   a) Relation to what is encountered and its temporal determination (present—past).
   b) Animal-being and human-being not just in general, but always grasped with respect to "happiness" or "health."
   c) *"Human being"* ("the" human being) not only as an individual, but as a *"people,"* with respect to "culture."
   Always: humankind—"humanity [*Menschheit*]" (Kant)—just as "animality [*Tierheit*]."
7. Nietzsche's approach begins with the *animal*! And *how* exactly—from "outside," that is, from "inside." The animal as such is related to food, prey, enemies. Related to its milieu, but this not in such a way that there is first the animal—the so-called organism, and then also this relation, but the relation is essentially *animalistic* and also "immediately" *"visible" from our perspective*: the hawk swooping down on its prey and suchlike.

This interpretation is nevertheless *quite difficult*: "to put oneself in the place" of the animal; who? "oneself," the *human being*, therefore *the animal from the perspective of the human being*—certainly. The legitimate and illegitimate mistrust within zoology of such a perspective; (cf. *Kantianism*!; 'world'!; von Uexküll: *Environment and Inner World of the Animal*;[2] von Frisch: *On the Bee*[3]).

The more essentially and the more definitely the human being has determined itself, the more securely is it able to *distinguish* "it-

---

2. Jacob von Uexküll, *Umwelt und Innenwelt der Tiere* (Berlin: Springer 1901).
3. Karl von Frisch, "Über den Geruchsinn der Biene und seine blütenbiologische Bedeutung," in *Zoologische Jahrbücher (Physiologie)* 37, 1–238 (1919).

self" from the animal, and *therefore* with respect to *forgetting and remembering* first of all: *Consider* [32] *the human being*:

Human Being:	"the world" writ small, microcosm
and	or macroanthropos or?
World	"the human being writ large"

but?! "everyone is farthest from himself"! Nietzsche.
8. Beginning with a difficulty in Nietzsche's characterization of *forgetting*.

I. 1)   The animal does not know what is yesterday and what is today—it is bound to the moment. The *moment* is *a "stake,"* with which the animal cannot part—the animal is in each case only what it is captivated by. It is absorbed *in what is in each case present*, but cannot see or understand it as such. No looking back onto the past and the bygone. No outlook on to that which is to come. "Migratory birds! Winter is coming, come on, we soon have to set off!" Against this

II. 2)   it is absorbed in the present, *forgets immediately* and sees the moment sink *"back"* and *"expire,"* and thus its *passing away* (into the past), its *being no longer* and its *gone just now*, as a no longer present, therefore as presence and thus *after all* related to the moment, to present things as such?
Seeing disappear — as *forgetting?*
Being absorbed in the "present" — as *forgetting?*
Neither. *Everything indeterminate.*
What are present things *as such?*
Presence—itself?
First of all: *looking away from the animal*, to look at the human being, at ourselves (cf. §15, "'Forgetting' and 'Remembering'").

---

§11. "Forgetting"—"Remembering"
The Question of "Historiology" as the Question of the "Human Being." The Course of Our Inquiry. One Path among Others.

1. Forgetting
2. Forgetting and retaining [*Behalten*] [33]
3. Forgetting and remembering [*Erinnern*]
4. Forgetting and "memory" [*Gedächtnis*]
    a) Faculty of making present [*Vergegenwärtigung*] and of retaining
    b) *Remembrance* [*Andenken*]
5. The context in which Nietzsche looks at "forgetting and remembering" (as kinds of relations toward the past): in view of the differen-

tiation of the unhistorical and the historical, and this with the aim of a comparison of animal and human being; *in view—of* historiology and its relation to "life."
6. Forgetting and that of which it is an *abruption. The domain*—but this in its "essence" is retaining, comportment toward something, *remembering, thinking ahead*, expecting, *hoping, fearing*.
7. The essentially different direction of questioning: captivation (in being captivated by the milieu [*Umfeldbenommenheit*]), comportment (from being-in-the-world).
8. The decisive difference:
   Relation to beings —human being
   Lack of relation —animal
9. How to conceive from this perspective the differentiation of the *unhistorical and the historical*.
10. This differentiation and "the" domain "life"; and with a view to "happiness."

---

§12. Questions Relating to Section I

1. What has been placed *first of all* (thematically) into the comparison (sec. I and II), that is, what is the immediate topic? *Of forgetting and remembering*. First of all the forgetting of the *animal*:
   a) How to establish this (cf. end of sec. I)?
   b) How do we know about it at all?—human being;
      Where does this belong? What is it? Relation to the past?
      But *forgetting*—a relation that is not a relation; which is given up. Or? *What is forgetting* (cf. §13)?
   c) General inability to retain. To sink into oblivion—[34] *even the forgetting* (the forgetting is constantly forgotten!), (does the stone forget?).
   d) Inability to bring to mind [*Vergegenwärtigen*]. *Not being able to recall*. "Having"—forgotten
   e) Not being able to remember.
2. Why is "happiness" spoken of here?
   Life and happiness of life.
   What significance does this direction of questioning have with respect to the essential determination of forgetting and remembering?
3. If the historical and the unhistorical are determined on the basis of the account of forgetting and remembering, from where, then, can historiology derive its essential boundaries?
4. Do we gain in this way an adequate starting point for the differentiation between animal and human being?

5. To what extent is the orientation by means of animality at all necessary? (Human being—*animal* rationale)? "Life."

§13. Forgetting

Gezzen	—*to get*, to encounter, to attain, to hold
For-getting	—not to encounter, not to hold, not to retain
oblivisci	—*oblino*? To *besmear*, to smudge,
(medial)	to *cross out*, to erase (wax tablet)
ἐπιλανθάνεσθαι	—to conceal something (from oneself), to let disappear into concealedness.

1. *forgetting*:
   a) something *slips* one's mind—"it"—a name
   b) *not* retaining—*we*—let something escape us,
      α) because we do not want to retain it
      β) because we have moved on to something else.
        The aspect of something (to lose from "sight," being out of "mind")
   c) *not* thinking of it—(bringing the book).
      Giving up—no longer holding on to something.
   d) No *longer coming* back to it (the [35] wrong inflicted shall be forgotten), no longer thinking *about it*! In what sense?
   e) For-getting oneself (losing one's composure).

everywhere a movement-away — to leave; *de*-port; a *"not"*
                    to veil   — into concealedness
                  privation — *of something*—cf. *blindness*; cf. death
                  of what?   possessions—belongings; to "break off"
                                retaining, having before-oneself.

2. Retaining—to have present to oneself—to be able to make something present to oneself, so that it *always comes to mind, without one's calling it to mind.*
   a) Things that exist, but are not immediately present— "the Feldherrnhalle in Munich."
   b) The course and the appearance of a past event or thing. What the area looked like where now the university stands.

3. *Forgetting and remembering*—to remind "oneself"!
   Remembering: 1) as an "*act*"'—a particular thinking-back-to,
                    2) as a "state"—re-membrance (attitude).

Remembering is a making present of something past, and the latter *as* something that *I* have encountered, something I was there with, to which I have belonged. In what is remembered the *one who remembers* is, as the one he was then, *brought to mind too*—therefore remembering [*Sicherinnern*].

To *remember* [*Er-innern*]—to throw into the inside, that is, to relate to one's own self, making it present *as what it was—in its having been.*

Remembering—making present of something past as such (not merely retaining what has passed). In contrast: coming to mind again is not a genuine act of remembering.

From this perspective, then, *forgetting* also as a *not remembering* [*Sich nicht erinnern*], different from mere *not retaining*, insofar as the former is a flight from that which has been, an evasion, a cutting oneself off, a *forcing out of mind*, a having done with. Here we find the site for "not being able to forget" = the always having to think of it:

1) against one's will, not being able to shrug off, to be haunted (binding); [36]
2) as attitude, *re*-membrance [*An-denken*] (doing), turning toward.

4. Forgetting and *"memory"* (*"mneme"*)

Now the essential ambiguity comes to light:
a) Memory as the faculty of retaining and *constant making present. The ability to imprint on one's memory* so as to keep *hold of something.* "*Learning*"—practicing so that one can always come back to it immediately—remembering a "name."
b) Memory as *re-membrance*—to think toward something *that has been.*
c) *The relation of both*:
   i) Without retaining there is no remembering,
   ii) The remembering *changes* the ability to retain with respect to b) re-membrance.
   i) As a preserving, being inclined toward;
   ii) As the unfolding safekeeping of a bequest, that is, of an essential imposition beckoning toward the origin.

What kind of "thinking" is required here?

5. The context in which Nietzsche considers "forgetting" and "remembering"—the limits of his analysis.
   a) forgetting and remembering—as different kinds of a relation toward the past,
   b) with regard to the differentiation between unhistorical and historical—"historiology" as being fixed (as a representation of things past),
   c) with the intention of comparing animal and human being,
   d) with the aim of a calculative account of historiology and its relation to life (*human* life); ("we historians").

§14. Nietzsche on Forgetting

Dawn (1881), no. 126: "*Forgetting.*—It has not yet been proven that there is any such thing as forgetting; all we know is that the act of recollection [37] does not lie within our power. We have provisionally set into this gap in our power that word 'forgetting,' as if it were one more addition to our faculties. But, after all, what lies within our power?"[4]

From the time of *Zarathustra* (vol. XII, p. 303): "That there is such a thing as forgetting has not yet been proven: only that there is much we cannot remember when we want to."[5]

Forgetting—*inability to retain and* bring *back,* to bring to *mind.* Forgetting as a complete slipping away.

§15. "Forgetting" and "Remembering"

1. "Forgetting"—the word; (although we cannot simply reveal the essence of the thing in question from the meaning of the word, the *word*—if authentic—is never simply accidental, and therefore we can gain essential instruction from it, *supposing* that we have already turned our gaze toward the thing in question, and even if this is still only as a function of questioning).
   a) *For-getting—gezzen,* disappeared early in German; (English "to get"), to encounter, to attain, to hold
   For-getting—not to attain, not to hold, *not to retain*; the forgotten is what has not been held on to, what has been dropped, has "*gone.*"
   b) Oblivisci—(*oblino*—to besmear, to smudge the wax tablet, having written on it, crossing out, erase); medially: *to wipe itself away, no longer to take for real,* the forgotten is erased, "*gone.*"
   c) ἐπι λανθάνεσθαι—*toward something, to let* this "something" *pass* into the concealed (λανθάνω, λαθ-, ἀ-λήθεια!), because and insofar as one is closed against it!, that something (for us) *sinks*

---

4. Friedrich Nietzsche, *Nietzsches Werke* (Großoktavausgabe), vol. 4, ed. Fritz Koegel, *Morgenröthe* (Leipzig: Kröner, 1923), 126; *Daybreak: Thoughts on the Prejudices of Morality,* ed. Maudmarie Clark and Brian Leiter, trans. Reginald John Hollingdale (Cambridge: Cambridge University Press, 1997), 78.

5. Friedrich Nietzsche, *Nietzsches Werke* (Großoktavausgabe), vol. 12, 5th ed. Fritz Koegel, *Unveröffentlichtes aus der Zeit der Fröhlichen Wissenschaft und des Zarathustra* 1881–1886 (Leipzig: Kröner, 1919).

§15. "Forgetting" and "Remembering" 31

away into [38] concealedness.[6] "Away"—to bring oneself into a non-relation, but in the Greek sense: to be covered over by it-self—*in relation* to...

2. what can we take from this elucidation of the word?
   a) The forgotten: that which has slipped one's mind   *the inaccessible*
              that which has been erased   no longer
              that which is concealed   "present"

the ab-sent [*Ab-wesende*]—and *what for?*—*for* this: having-before-(oneself)—re-presenting it, *immediately* disposing of it.

The professor "forgets" his umbrella, we say, *he leaves it behind*. The umbrella is *therefore present*, it thus has not really disappeared; but the professor says: my umbrella has "gone," that is, from the vicinity of what is immediately available to him, of what he *holds onto* and retains; *gone* from *the sheltered-recollected* [*die Behältnis*].

For-getting: *not-retaining*—(gone), and therefore like something we have already encountered a few times: *"death," loss of life, lack, breaking off*:

"blind"—"not-seeing"; "poor"—not "possessing."

"negation," but of a *peculiar* type!, whereby what is negated (vision—"life"—possessing) is precisely the *presupposition* (root) of the possibility of the *negation*.
not red, *but* 1) quadrangular, proud, heavy, etc.
not *red, but* 2) blue (i.e., *within* the realm of color).

From here we gain an important pointer with respect to the characterization of the essence of "forgetting":

i) For-getting—as *not-retaining* has to be understood from the perspective of *retaining* and what belongs to it, from the perspective of that in which forgetting is grounded, that is to say, as a specific "kind" of retaining (perhaps occasionally as a perverted kind). [39]

ii) And if there were different kinds of forgetting, then these could only be understood together *with* and on the basis *of* the various kinds of "retaining."

iii) Only where the possibility of re-taining (that is, of holding-before-oneself and re-presenting) exists in the first place can forgetting itself be possible.

---

6. On ἀλήθεια cf. the Freiburg lectures of the winter semester 1942–1943 published as Martin Heidegger, *Gesamtausgabe* vol. 54, *Parmenides*, ed. M. S. Frings (Frankfurt am Main: Klostermann, 1982); *Parmenides*, trans. André Schuwer and Richard Rojcewicz (Bloomington: Indiana University Press, 1998).

The stone does not forget, this does not mean that it always retains everything; rather it cannot forget at all, because it cannot retain anything. And why can it not retain anything?

b) The elucidation of the word offers us a second hint, particularly if we pay attention to the Greek and Latin words; they are *medial* (between *activum* and *passivum*), that is, what is named contains within itself the relation to an agent and that which effects it, and yet it is not completely subject to the "power" of the latter.

The *self-relation*! Oneself—as something given (to lapse, letting slip into concealedness—*for* itself). *The relation* of that which slips away to the one *from whom it slips away. For-getting*: relating— "oneself" to. . . . directing oneself to oneself, genuinely standing out *as what one is; not-retaining*, "losing" expresses the same point—without a "medium." The forgotten is "related" (unrelated) to a having-*before-oneself; a mode of the latter*.

Thus we arrive at the necessity of reflecting first on "retaining" ("impressions" and traces in "the brain").

3. "Retaining" in the mode of having-before-oneself. The ability to re-present something as something "present" and that means being capable of making something present. Present: in the vicinity of what is currently represented,

  a) *although not present* in its *own actuality*, but still a being: Strasbourg Cathedral (I have retained what it looks like),
  b) something that is *no longer*
   • for example, how things *used to "look" in* the district of *Herdern*. I can still *re-present* this quite vividly, as if it were *today*. . . . [40]
   • report: the ground plan of a Greek temple, neither *present* nor existent in any sense, for the foundations have been destroyed. Being able to make it present [*ver-gegenwärtigen-können*] and only this. To bring and place it-before-oneself as re-presented.
  c) something that "is" not yet
   • how the house *is going to "look,"* making something "futural" present to "oneself"
   • "look at the herd"; for example, *when we cannot* immediately *perceive it*! "Oneself": to bring into *the vicinity of what is currently represented*. Retaining as not-forgetting, remembering.

4. *Remembering* [*Das Sicherinnern*]—(not a simple making present of something, if a making present at all. "I remember Strasbourg Cathedral." Cf. above! The same as above (3)(a))? No; I can never remember Strasbourg Cathedral, but "only" that and how and when I *have seen it*, that I stood in front of it, that *it towered above me*, that somebody showed *me* an image depicting it. *So what is the difference between this and mere making present?*

§15. "Forgetting" and "Remembering"

To remember that which has been, in its having-been: a "teacher," him, that is to say, the relation I had with this teacher in the past, the context of these relations. Remembering *as also remembering oneself having been* in that which has been, as a *placing oneself back and into* that which is remembered, which is precisely *not* a taking "inside" as in the case of making present, but a *taking over* of the belonging to that which has been as a *reciprocal* "retaining" and holding "oneself" within what is retained (and thus *within* remembering there is a *making present*).

5. Mere making present and remembering are fundamentally different.
    a) Remembering with respect to that which has been *as* such. Making present—is, however, not remembering, for though possibly related to something past, this not as something past, or perhaps even as this too! And yet still not, because not. . .
    b) Remembering into *that which has been* as such, where *I too* [41] was present and in some way affected by it.
    c) Remembering as *attitude and action ("self")*.
    Making present—"enactment," therefore:
    • retaining as the ability to make present, cf. (6)(a),
    • as the ability to remember;
    to make present: to take up into the present.
    Remembering: placing oneself *into* that which has been and as belonging to it.
    Fundamentally different, and this becomes clearer with respect to the ambiguity of what we call "memory."
6. "Memory"
    a) To have a good memory, for example to retain without effort "historical dates," "facts," "book titles." *No relation to* "remembering" [*Erinnerung*]. A mathematical formula, which I had forgotten, comes back to me. There is no remembering, except when I think back to the moment that it was explained to me in the lecture theater by the lecturer.
    The ability to commit something to memory and to retain it, *so that it remains*, so that one can refer *to it* immediately and at any moment (*not* as coming "back" to it), but simply grasping a name, for example, or a formula "again"; "learning," "practicing"; "*mneme.*"
    b) "In" "memory" of the soldier fallen in battle, that is, *remembrance* [*Andenken*] as a "sign" of *re-membrance, turning in thought toward them*—as—those who have been *sacrificed* for us, as those who *have been*. But how to think "remembering" here? indeed! (what is bequeathed to us is an imposition essentially pointing toward an origin).

B. Section I

Relation between Making Present and Remembering

Does making present presuppose remembering and is it always only within the latter, that is, only possible by means of an exclusion of remembering proper? [42]

Or is making present possible freely in itself, insofar as it can also aim at something "present" or futural?

Is remembering in need of making present or is it independent?

For-getting and Forgottenness

1. *forgetting* as a relation in the sense of *comportment*. This comportment on the ground of *forgottenness. Being-gone; non-comportment.*
2. forgetting as non-comportment and forgottenness. *mathematical formula*—lack of relation and non-relation, cf. (7)(b) *Apparently the same!* ("At night all cows are black," as long as we are only looking toward the "not"!)
3) *vortex character* [*Sogcharakter*] and *forgottenness*, cf. 7.
4) the (most abysmal) and the most questionable forgottenness, cf. (8)(a).

* * *

7. Memory [*Gedächtnis*] and forgetting; forgetting is *correspondingly ambiguous*, cf. above, (2)(a)
   a) *As not retaining*—to let it slip away from the ability to make it present to oneself, from the sheltered-recollected [*der Behältnis*]— "we" forget = *it* slips "someone's" mind, *"we" are exposed to such slipping away.*
   b) *As not remembering*
      α) No longer being able to place oneself into that which has been as such: (1) *how* it was and how one was alongside it, (2) *that* it was at all.
      But here it is not simply that the thing retained falls out of the sheltered-recollected, but the determinate relation, the relationship to that which has been is interrupted and thereby one's own having-been is changed. *To shut oneself away from what has been.* This transformation does not take place merely by way of an accumulation of "remembered things," but by means of the way in which *having-been* is in each case formed [*gestalthaft*] respectively and prospectively—out of? *This having-been* as such determines the particular enactment of individual memories and their possibility. [43]
      β) Distancing oneself from that which has been; against it. Putting it behind oneself. Driving it out of one's mind. No longer thinking of it. Throwing the past behind oneself. Turn-

ing away from that which has been. (The question of success? Whether the past does not come back all the more insistently? But how?) Here we are not asking whether it does not in fact "come back to mind," *but* how what has been *forgotten*—in our sense of the term—is still determinative or not.

8. *Modes of "forgetting" in the broadest sense of the word*:
   a) The slipping away on account of *indifference* with respect to retaining; something comes, is encountered and slips away again.
   b) Not being able to recollect ("I" always again forget that name), "just about forgetting to do something" [*verschwitzen*].
   c) "Not thinking about it" (*I* forgot to bring the book), "not paying attention," "idling" (absentminded—forgetful); *one way of forgetting "oneself."*
   d) Not wanting to come back to it (that the affair "be" forgotten, "settled"), "to let it be dead and buried."
   e) *Forgetting oneself*—
      α) Losing one's composure, *not retaining oneself*, the "genuine" self is "gone."
      β) As pure devotion, from the *greatest* composure, "oneself"—the "self"—the *improper*—"gone."
9. Modes of not being able to forget. *Coercion*.
   a) To be haunted by a throng of "representations," Something, the very same thing, constantly "comes to mind" (for the *animal* also?! Or not; the so-called conditioned reflexes, the "world" of the lunatic, paranoia; schizophrenia; Pavlov! wrong!).
   b) Always *having to* remember—from *resoluteness* toward what is remembered. Re-membrance, turning toward, freedom, self-legislation.
10. *Forgetting*:
    We are now able to take from the previous discussion an *essential* determination of forgetting (cf. p. 36f.), on condition that we adequately understand "retaining" [*das Behalten*] in the aforesaid modes of [44] *making present* and *remembering*, that is to say, according to that in which it is wholly grounded; and this is something quite simple: that retaining in the mode of its relation to what is recollected in each case maintains a being as such in the open.

    Such a relation to . . . within which what is intended by the relation shows itself *as* a being, is what we called a *comportment* [*Verhalten*]. *Comportment*—a relation to, within, and by virtue of a disclosedness of beings as such. Non-comportment—a closing down of beings, which itself moves toward concealedness. (This is always a comporting oneself toward, on the ground of a *conducting oneself* (attitude), which in turn is based on steadfastness [*Inständigkeit*]).

If therefore forgetting is a variant and perverted form of retaining, then we find in forgetting a non-relation to beings as such, a non-comportment, and therefore a not-comporting-oneself to beings, which non-comportment is not nothing, but quite the opposite.

If we wish to grasp the essence of forgetting (its inner possibility and where it belongs), then indispensable preparatory work is necessary in that we first need to be able to survey the plurality of its forms in their essential traits. It is even more essential *to grasp forgetting in its unity with retaining.* "Unity" here means the *ground* on which retaining and forgetting stand: through which they can be *what they are,* each for itself and in their "interrelation." And what is this "ground"? *It can be indicated* through *what carries and determines retaining and forgetting from the ground up.*

Forgetting and Forgottenness,
The relation to beings as such and in general

Making Present:	Presence	*what-being*
	Absence	past, becoming being [45]
Remembering		*Having-been-ness*
		Not-having-been-ness as *even* deeper having-been-ness

"*Comportment*" (cf. p. 35), even if something is "only" slipping away *without one's having done anything*!

Forgetting—"loss"? "Detachment" from *beings in general,* Shutting oneself away from, turning away from: beings.

Forgetting—a *fundamental mode* in which beings in general are gone *for* the human being; in which the human being itself has—while right in the middle of beings—gone from beings (being-gone).

"*Forgetting*"—only in the being that "is" in that and insofar as it stands within the disclosedness of beings, by directing itself in relation to beings and comporting itself in their midst (cf. above 8.a) and b)).

But of what does *the essence* of such a being consist? In what is such *steadfastness* in the midst of beings grounded? (In its being assigned to the truth (and that is, equally, to the untruth) of beyng [*Seyn*].)

(Wherein and as what does this being assigned to beyng prevail—in *language*—*the word.* Therefore the human being is a deployment of steadfastness in the truth of beyng. But the word is not something *that* the human being "has" and only uses up, but that *within* which he can in each case be the one who he *is.* Cf. below p. 187 (language—word).

* * *

§15. "Forgetting" and "Remembering"

11. *Forgetting*—*not* being able to make present something which is represent-able, present-at-hand, represented.
    —*un*willingness to remember *what has been*.
    a) *In each case a relation leading to (bringing about) an abruption:* Losing—slipping away. Shutting oneself away and turning away. It is not at all the case that we have no relation to the thing forgotten; rather we precisely have a remarkable *non-relation* to it. But this non-relation is not necessarily a relation [46] to *something past* or even being apt for the latter. *Non*-relation and lack of relation (as in the case of the stone) are different.

    The non-relation, that is, a relation that has been perturbed or disturbed, somehow tampered with, or a relation that has been *refused* and thus never yet been *granted; a forgotten formula is something essentially different from* a formula that has never been represented or that could never be represented in such a way *that it can come back to me*!; such *non-relation* can only be the consequence of an existent relation as a non-relation.

    With the help of the "brain"! Yes, but only when there is something like a relation *to* beings as such and, therefore, being-gone. Non-relation says: that there is a relation, but (*as non-comportment*). *It is disturbed* (*first of all and in truth* by virtue of an understanding of being).

    Lack of relation (in the sense of comportment, but in captivation within the region of the milieu—taking in and letting go)—there is here no possibility of representing, of being able to be alongside with, *the mouse* and *Pythagoras's theorem*.

    Non-relation and nonrelation are thus not the same; even the not (not yet) knowing of the knowable is a *non-relation*, whereby *relation always* means relation to beings as such and in general.

    For-getting is a *non*-relation of the retaining (*non-comporting*) and commemorating relation; a particular kind of non-relation, the *"no longer"* and *not-yet-again*.

    b) *But* we have still not seen something decisive: the *vortex character* of forgetting (vortex—the suction when a ship sinks, with a dam or hydroelectric power plant): what gets drawn into forgetting, what is forgotten, sucks even this being forgotten into forgetting. The *non-relation itself is no longer* re-presented, moves out of the *being related* of the representing-oneself-with and takes on the appearance of a *lack of relation* and generally of the *nothing*—and yet! It is now that it is a *non*-relation in the most essential sense and never a *lack of relation*. [47] The *non-relation* is drawn into itself, and nevertheless it is only what it is from the root of the relation, of the *retaining and remembering* that makes present.

    Forgetting—

Ordinarily "forgetting," something *slipping someone's mind*, is what happens without our help and often against our will. But as the Greek and Latin names already indicate, *forgetting* is more than a "passive" letting something happen to one, although it is not a *merely* "active" willing and achieving:

(1) As the complete slipping away of something, in such a way that one has also forgotten that one has forgotten the forgetting;

(2) As not being able to or not wanting to remember, also *to shut oneself away from* the shutting oneself off [*von der Abschnürung abgeschnürt sein*], *to turn away even from the turning away*.

But what is this vortex character of forgetting?!

Forgottenness of Being

The deepest forgottenness occurs with the *highest and most constant retaining* (and holding [*Haltende*]), and where this, as what *generally* grants a hold [*das überhaupt Haltgebende*], is precisely *not made present (the belongingness to the truth of being)*. Comportment—as relation to beings *as such and in general; what is this to say?*

This forgetting is not a slipping away, not a letting-go; *for being is always understood*. The *forgottenness* as an essencing of *Da-sein*! Therefore forgetting is not a shutting oneself off, not a turning away. Forgottenness is not a consequence of forgetting, but the latter is possible only by virtue of the former. *What then? A mere* oversight and *not thinking of it??* A necessary forgottenness and *yet at the same time* a need! *Not considering something* and *thus still an understanding* and availing oneself of it. The more forgotten, *the more retained*! the more exclusive the holding fast to it—*being*!

What sort of forgetting sinks here into *what sort of* forgottenness, and in such a way that this sinking back is precisely what keeps the abyss [*Ab-grund*] open! [48]

Forgetting generally

Where there is no retaining or commemorating relation to the represented, no relation: as lack of relation, as modification of the *relation* into a *nonrelation. Misleading use* of the name (where no representing, and therefore retaining, is at all possible). All ordinary forgetting is first of all possible on the ground of an originary *forgottenness*.

* * *

12. To return from the reflection on the human being back to the consideration of the animal. Question: does the animal forget? *If yes*, in what sense, since we now have a double mode of forgetting? Cf. (a) and (b); *if no*, in what sense can one still speak of "forgetting" with respect to the animal? Cf. (c).

§15. "Forgetting" and "Remembering" 39

Does the animal forget in the sense of
a) *Forgetting*—as the *not* being able to remember ["oneself"]? No, because the animal cannot remember ("is almost without memory"!! says Nietzsche), that is, cannot place itself into that which has been *as such* and as belonging to it, for to do so it would have to be able to "know" the past (relation to time); Nietzsche himself says right away: "the animal does not know what yesterday is." This not-knowing = not being acquainted; not just not having an explicit *concept*.
b) Forgetting—as not retaining = not being able to make present? No, because the animal is not *capable* of placing something *as* "something present" in front of *itself and possessing it*; Nietzsche himself says: "it does not know what *today* (now, *presence*) is."

With the first sentence Nietzsche *negates* the possibility of what he later affirms, and which he posits as an essential starting point of his reflections: namely that the animal does not only generally *forget*, but that it does so *constantly*. (This constant forgetting = not-retaining = generally and essentially *being unable to retain*— because? no relation to beings as such and in general.) [49]
c) "Forgetting"—but the animal certainly has "memory": the *tit* always finds its way back to its nest, and therefore must be able "to retain" its place and aspect. The *robin* waits every morning for the mealworm that has been put out for it. *Migratory birds* always return to the same region. The dog comes back to the buried bone. Habituation—"learning"—training.

What kind of "retaining"? Something "remains" for the animal: how? It is not that the animal retains something for itself in the mode of a constantly possible making present; rather the animal is held within its milieu as captivated by it, in such a way that, depending on the sort of animal it is, now this now that emerges in a withholding manner and then *sinks back,* again within the indeterminate contours of its milieu. This emerging and taking away and taking in happens in each case within a circle of relations that is not present *as such*.

Therefore: in the midst of the field of captivation there is—according to this field and governed by it—a constant change of that which, in the milieu, emerges and sinks back; within the field of captivation there is a being-taken-along-with and a *falling back*. But this exchange, in the sense of the sinking and stepping back, cannot be understood as a *forgetting*, as that is grounded on a *retaining* that has an essentially different character.

The animal does not forget, because it cannot retain, and it cannot retain in the sense of a making present, because (it) does not ever need to forget something as present in the way of re-presentation; it never encounters such an exigency. The mode of "life"—does this automatically mean being sustained in and by milieu-captivation? The "devotion" of the animal; the "loyalty" of the human being. How does the following sentence relate to the above: *the stone does not forget*, not even the *sinking back*.

The animal does not *comport itself*—no comportment; the animal [50] behaves "itself" [*benimmt "sich"*], is sustained by captivation [*Benommenheit*], and determined in its *capabilities*; its "possibilities" are those of a captivated capability. Captivated "by": the "by what" is in a specific sense given: surrounding field, "milieu."

The stone "lies" about somewhere, has weight, it neither behaves nor comports itself. *Course of events—relations—the atomic image* of "matter"—"field."

Everything leveled—*in advance*—toward "comportment" as a free relation—mutual relation; "behaviorism."

Not to be equated with *Leibniz*: "Monadology." *Gradation*! but! "*ratio*," though only metaphysically, not in terms of the history of beyng.

Behaviorism—that, for example, even the "stone" has "heart" and "loves." This conception appears to be very "deep," but is in truth quite *superficial, leveling everything—explaining everything—the "uniformity" of the correct*! Against this: *the abyssal nature of that which is fundamentally different!*

13. On the *Critique*
   a) The characterization of forgetting remains in Nietzsche underdetermined and contradictory, because he fails to clarify the essence of remembering and of making present and, more generally, that of retaining as a being able to represent "beings";
      i) Cf. above: the various characterizations of forgetting, cf. p. 286: the animal is "almost without memory,"
      ii) That he claims there is forgetting here at all. He has nevertheless an essential phenomenon in mind: the sinking back of that which in each case captivates within milieu-captivation; the sinking back, not a slipping away (but is it essential to consider it here at all?).
   b) Taking a position in relation to one of Nietzsche's maxims: "without forgetting it is quite impossible to *live* at all" (sec. I, para. 3, p. 286), that is, forgetting and the ability to forget necessarily belong to "life."
      i) *With respect to the animal*: it is precisely the animal that is not in need of [51] forgetting. "Life" (the animal) is characterized by the fact that it is *not* in need of forgetting, because it is in itself a being sustained in milieu-captivation—captivation al-

ready says: impossibility of re-presenting, making present and retaining;

ii) *With respect to the human being*: cf. later on.

c) The animal, because it stands outside of the possibility of forgetting and being able to forget, is *also not unhistorical*. "Life" (the animal) is without history [*historielos*]. But Nietzsche speaks of life as "the unhistorical power." On this point the fundamental observation; only what is historical—*can* be unhistorical.

14. The question of historiology—historical and unhistorical—is *not* a question of the distinction of human being and animal, but is solely one posed within the essence of the human being; "human life" (cf. p. 42).

Yet Nietzsche also determines historiology (secs. 2 and 3) with regard to human life. But—the "unhistorical"—is at the same time proper to the animal, although an essential ambiguity has certainly come to light here: *"life"*? and *"life"*?

Paying attention to how Nietzsche proceeds is essential: Nietzsche does not determine forgetting as a variant of retaining (making present to oneself and remembering), but vice versa: *"remembering" is a variant of forgetting as not being able to forget*. Historiology —understood from the vantage point of such a "remembering," that is, as a *bracing oneself against*, somehow never coming to terms with the past. The importance of this approach! and the guiding concept of "life." *Before we* enter into *his understanding* of the un-historical (its primacy and relation to "horizon" and "plastic power"), we will first anticipate the characterization of historiology in sections 2 and 3 (on secs 2 & 3, cf. part E), and also of human life and "culture"; "the essence" of "culture." The question of the unhistorical and the historical, and therefore of [52] *historiology*, needs *to be posed* within the realm of the *human being. It needs to be torn out of the comparative consideration of the animal.*

But *then* we will be forced to consider what it is, *in* the essence of the human being, that historiology is to be *determined* from; whether the essence of historiology *from* the essence of the human being and how? or whether we need to go through *historiology* in order to reach the essence of the human being—*whereto*? But in this case how to determine historiology?

The question of the *essence of the human being now* becomes in a sense more pressing insofar as its elucidation must ensure that it is not misled by reflection on *animality*. This means more than just avoiding the comparative consideration, especially if we bear in mind: human being = *animal rationale*. A completely different question concerning the human being announces itself, and perhaps with it an overcoming of the traditional understanding of the human being as *animal rationale*.

In this way the question of *historiology* stands at the very center of the question of *the human being* (and therefore the question of "life" (*domain, measure, enactment*)). And even Nietzsche, despite his peculiar and important comparative approach with animal life, asserting the primacy of "life" as such, cannot escape the defining importance of a reflection on the human being.

§16. Historiology and "the" Human Being

"The human being" does not here mean first and foremost a particular human being; but "the human being" is here taken as a generic concept: "humanity" (Kant), "*humankind*" [*Menschentum*], and within this the individual human being, groups, unions, collectives, societies, communities, "nation," "people," "cultures."

We need to begin by clarifying the concept of "culture," as this is essential for *Nietzsche*! Cf. "*culture*." [53]

Being oneself ≠ "egoity"; and egoity ≠ "*individualism.*"
   ↑
"authenticity"

§17. "The Human Being." "Culture." The "People" and "Genius"

The individuals!? Not just anybody who has written a book or painted a picture. Six *or seven in a few centuries*. "*Individualism*"? "*Nietzsche*"—just as little denied that there is no personality? "Limitations" are never immediate, *and if they are taken to be*, they are *not understood*.

The "people" does not need to know about these purposes and objectives. *On the contrary*. It is essential that it takes itself to be the "purpose."

§18. Culture—Nonculture, Barbarism

"Civilized people"; the cultured human being; primitive people [*Naturvölker*].

Culture as "*surplus*," "*possession*" of culture, "*humanity.*"

"Culture" *as such*, only where there is humanity as "*subjectum*"; from the modern age, but used retrospectively in historical interpretation—"Greek culture."

"Culture" as a mode and form of knowing and forming oneself. Barbarism; βάρβαρος:
1) the one who does *not* speak Greek.
2) the stranger, the foreigner without denigration; thus the Romans called themselves "barbarians," until the language and writings of the Greeks found their way into Rome.
3) Since the Persian wars: the brute, the serf—the one despised.

---

§19. Human Being and Culture and the People

We are in the habit of thinking of the *higher* human as a cultured human being and to demand that it be such. (Humanism, *humanitas*, the higher [54] human, human being as human being; why higher?) Only from this demand and with it is the difference between higher and lower given at all.

This habit—that is, this notion of the human being is familiar to us—without our knowing and properly thinking about its ground: that, in the modern understanding of the human being as subject,[7] the human being produces itself and asserts itself as the center of beings and in such assertion develops its possible perfection and sets itself up as the purpose. Presupposition: the human being as *"sub-jectum."*

"Culture" is the taking into account and regulation of all the developments of all faculties in their interrelatedness within *humankind* as the "life" of the *animal rationale* ("historiology" and "technology" as metaphysically identical).

Culture as "unity," unification, is already a concept derived from *culture* as art, that is, τέχνη *as historiology.*

The more the organization of life is all-encompassing, and the more masslike become those living—human beings and peoples—and the more manifold the needs, the more indispensible culture becomes (with the fundamental presupposition of the human being as *subjectum*). The more indispensable it becomes, the more it enters into calculation and therefore itself becomes an "end," *either in itself* or not "in itself"; in the latter case it is conflated with what is supposed to be "unified": "the people." The more powerful culture becomes in its bustling activity, the more unquestionable *"life"* is confirmed in *its demands*. The more questionless "life" is, the more final is the alienation from beyng.

---

7. But compare Hellenes and barbarians! *We* interpret this difference with a view to *culture and nonculture*.

§20. Nietzsche's Concept of "Culture"

1. The essential mark of culture—*the unity of artistic style* in all expressions of the life of a people. [55]
   Culture—people. What is culture with respect to a people? Means or end? If only a means, then what is the *end* of culture? *Culture* as *means*, path, *therefore* necessarily the question of the *"end."*—opposite: "barbarism" = "the lack of style or the chaotic confusion of all styles."
2. *The goal of culture*. From where can the originary unification be determined? From where *the imposition of goals*—essence of *"goal"*?
3. The essence of culture—*as "art" in the broadest sense of formation* [*des Bildens*]? *"Culture: the reign of art over life."* (vol. X, p. 245)
4. *Therefore* the emphatic role of "art" in the more narrow sense. Culture as "expression" of *an age*, testimonial, *memorial, "monumentum"*; "the centralizing significance of an art form or an *art work*" (vol. X, p. 188; cf. ibid., p. 124). Forming a center! *Agreement* on *style*; the latter is what genuinely unifies.

"Culture is, first and foremost, the *unity* of artistic style in all expressions of the life of a people" (vol. I, p. 183; cf. ibid., p. 314). The opposite: "*Barbarism*, that means: lack of style or chaotic confusion of all styles" (vol. I, p. 183); "true culture" presupposes "at any rate a unity of style" (ibid., p.186). Cf. vol. X, p. 278: "the German as a proper artistic style is still *to be found*, just as with the Greeks, Greek style was found only very late: there was no earlier unity, but rather a dreadful κρίσις."

"Unity of national sentiment [*Volksempfindung*]" (vol. I, p. 317; cf. ibid., p. 314).

"The concept of culture as a new and improved *physis*, without inside and outside, without dissimulation and convention, of culture as the *accord* of life, thought, appearing and willing"[8] (vol. I, p. 384).

"The generation of genius—that is the aim of all culture" (vol. I, p. 411); "in its highest *specimens*" (vol. I, p. 364). "the generation of great works" (vol. X, p. 124); "*the generation of the genius as* the only one able to *evaluate* and *negate* life truthfully" (vol. X, p. 420); (Schopenhauer). [56]

---

8. Cf. vol. I, p. 411: "corrector" of the "foolery and gaucheness" of physis.

§21. The Formally General Notion of "Culture." "Culture" and "Art"

Colere—to look after, to nourish, to build, to cultivate, to work on, to form something, to meliorate something, *"to improve,"* to admire, to celebrate (*unifying* in unison and unanimity).

Forming—τέχνη—"art"—inventing—illusion.

The decisive nature of *"art in the broadest sense"* for culture. "Culture is, first and foremost, the *unity* of artistic style in all expressions of life of a people." (*First Untimely Meditation*, vol. I, p. 183; cf. ibid., p. 314). *The same conception!* On *"the unity of a people"* and "education" [*Bildung*] (cult) (cf. vol. X, §7, p. 245).

"culture and style":	"culture has always to start out
"culture" and "historiology"	from the centralizing significance
"unity"—"unison"	of an art form or an art work"
"the plastic power"	(vol. X, p. 245)
of life and "art"	Centralizing—to collect toward
	the center into the *unity of a style.*

Cf. vol. X, p. 124: "the correct proportions of the development of all the talents of a people," "unitary taming of the drives" of a people. Recognition of works of art.

"Culture: the reign of *art* over *life"* (vol. X, p. 245).

§22. "The" Human Being and a Culture—a "People"

Indication of the *essence* of culture (following vol. I, p. 314].

Already a reference to the "people" here. Correlation of culture and people. Culture is always the culture of "a" people (equivocal), from the people, "for" the people. Is a people always the people as the people of a culture?

The question of the "role" of culture—whether means or end? And if end—what does that mean? Realization of cultural values! "Science"! [57] Realized by the value of truth!! If *means*, what then is its end? (The people as the goal?)

The more precise determination of the "concept of culture": *"Culture*: the mastery of *art* over *life"* (vol. X, p. 245). Culture as *art*. *The degree* of this mastery; *the value* of art. Art as "formation" [*Bildung*]—the essence of "formation."

§23. "Art" (and Culture)

A) Culture as Art, that is, as Formation [Bildung]

a) To what extent and in what sense is culture thus a *unity*?
b) In what sense is the word "style" meant here and in general?
c) *What* is to be unified, that is, to surge forth from this unity (inside and outside)? "*Expressions of the life* of a people" (cf. vol. X, p. 245) (living—thinking—appearing—willing): language, customs, convention, technology, science, art, faith? The two main determinations of the essence of culture.
d) Culture as "improved physis," (because already a form of art) (see above, §20).
e) Culture and "art" in the *more narrow* sense (their "centralizing" significance).
f) Culture and *the people*.
g) *The "goal"* of "culture"—of the people.

B) Art in the Broader Sense of "Formation" [Bildung]

(Our contemporary "concept of education" [Bildung]—its misuse—being educated:

a) "Knowledge"—knowing.
b) "Education" in terms of its value for rank and class; given to the whole of the people as expansion of education to all without regard to any differences of rank and class. In opposition to this, "education" in German Idealism.) [58]

Forming:

1. As shaping, bringing into a shape (*Gestalt*), to bring forth a *figure*. ("to form" from "inside" out, contents, the what and the how are the *consequences*—not "matter").
2. To give, to provide an "image," to reduce to an image—imagination, "'illusion." "Images" ("ideas," "ideals"—something unreal but *as* that which is to be realized).
3. This twofold forming is interrelated (where? within the living?)—in itself as unifying:
   a) simplifying with a view to that which is essential (leaving out, passing over),
   b) drawing attention to *one thing* and fixing this as what gives the measure.
4. Art as "education"—and "nature"; the "organic"; "with the organic" begins "also the *artistic*" (vol. X, p.1 28), (Goethe—Kant); within us reigns "an *artistic force*" (vol. X, p. 127), (here the passage concerning the "plastic power"). Thus: *Even nature herself is imitation of art.* (vol. X, p. 320)

§23. "Art" (and Culture)

5. Art—as a possible improvement of nature. Forming:
   a) Overcoming of the formless and of the empty and reduced "form" (of the confused and "raw" nature of mere "drives" and needs).
   b) To lift out from the dull and from degeneration into mere intelligibility. (Incitation—elevation—transfiguration), "stimulant"! (cf. *Will to Power*.)
6. Art in the broader sense and art in a *more narrow* sense. "The centralizing significance of the *work* of art" (the total work of art).

C) "Art"

a) *Culture* as "unity"—not a bringing together after the fact, but standing in one light, univocity, consonancy, all that forms itself and all forming *in itself and from out of itself* is intrinsically related, because it is harmonized toward a unity and this, because it is *determined by means of a unity*—the originary *unification* that reigns over everything. [59]
b) Unity "of" artistic style in the sense of (ii), below; when opposed to *"lack of style."*
   i) that the style is everywhere consistently the same? (*genitivus objectivus*) or
   ii) that the *artistic style* determines this unity? (*genitivus subjectivus*). Unity derives from and exists on account of style, *that a style shall be!* That is, *self-legislation of the forming*—(art) *style*—that which first of all properly "*forms*" the formation [*das Bilden "bildet"*], that which creates the law and the rule. Law, "rule"—*condition of the unity of possible order, necessary order.*
c) *What is to be unified*, that is, what is first of all to emerge in its essence from *such* unification: *the people*. The people become a people by means of *"culture."* But culture is now run by *"politics"* as the fundamental form of the securing of the continued existence of the "people" and of its shaping [*Gestaltung*]. "Inside" and "outside" of "*life.*"
d) Culture—as "*improved physis*" (see above, §20, art and "nature"). "Physis"—itself already artistic (*therefore* to be improved only by "art"), but primarily and often blind, urging and lashing out, confused, untamed drives and talents.

D) "Style"
Writing Implement, the Manner of Writing or Speech

Manner and mode, "form," "rule" of formation, but not as an *empty* one. Style is not the law ("rule") *according to which* formation and art are executed and accomplished, but that which is the truly "forming"; the law of such formation needs to be fashioned and exposed within the work, not as a formula, contained within it alone. The originarily unifying [*das ursprünglich Einigende*], that which pre-fashions and thoroughly forms unity. The mode of legislation *determines* the playspace of the *"what"* and the *"that."*

The law as condition of the representing and production of the unity of a *necessary* order, *the rule* of a *"possible"* order, [60] and when there is *style* the ordering is at once predetermined and *co*determined, and the inappropriate is eliminated.

Style—consequently also determines its own range and limitations and the time *when it is to cease;* it does not fizzle out, but posits its own end!

Style—is not *uniformity*, but *its contrary*. The ground of *the most extreme contradictions and their* unity.

Style—releases these contradictions into the freedom of their altercation and struggle.

Style—in the essential style—the law *as law* is never isolated according to rules, but rather *brings itself to disappear in the work.*

E) *"The People"*

"Create for yourselves the concept of a 'people': that concept you can never think nobly nor highly enough" (sec. VII, p. 346). Therefore in creation as the work of *thought* (the "metaphysics" of a "people"); therefore not by means of *"social anthropology,"* not by means of "prehistory," nor through *politics* nor through "worldview" and especially not through a "national [*völkisch*] worldview"; for the latter precisely takes the "concept" of the people for granted and can never let it be what is most worthy of question. The people is its own purpose.

In a planned preface to the *Birth of Tragedy* (1870–1871): "Preface to Richard Wagner." (vol. IX, p. 140).[9]

"People" (language—customs, tradition—state). [61]

F) *"Essence and Goal of 'Culture'"*

"Culture"—as "unity."

Why "unity" ἕν—ὄν? *Permanence and continuance in the collection.*

Culture—the securing of the continued existence (of the essence?) of a people. The essence of a people is not determined by culture, but is carried and developed by it. From where is the determination of the essence of a people to be derived? From the *goal* of culture?

---

9. Friedrich Nietzsche, *Nietzsches Werke* (Großoktavausgabe), vol. 9, 3rd ed. Fritz Koegel, *Nachgelassene Werke: Aus den Jahren 1869–1872.* (Stuttgart: Kröner, 1921).

§23. "Art" (and Culture)

What is the goal? Posited by what? ("Unity of national sentiment." The *genuine* needs! *Genuine*: befitting its essence and secure in its essence.)

G) The Goal of Culture

Vol. I, p. 411; vol. X, p. 124; vol. X, p. 420; vol. I, p. 364)

The production of "genius" (Schopenhauer). *"The goal of humanity"* lies *"in its highest specimens"* (vol. I, sec. IX, p. 364).

Great individuals are the aim of *"a people,"* "not the product of the masses" (vol. X, p. 109) (in what sense is this meant?). Nietzsche's early and his late interpretation develops according to the *"concept of life."* Thinkers—artists—saints.

"The engendering of genius as the only one able to *evaluate* and *negate* life truthfully" (vol. X, p. 420; Schopenhauer).

"Legislator"—the one setting goals, that is, the *highest yes* to "life."

Is *the Genius an end in itself* or also merely a "means"? No! When do we have the highest form of life? "The goal and the last intention of nature" (vol. IX, p. 147); not here for the sake of humanity, but for its highpoint and *final goal*! But later a revision concerning genius in the context of the inversion of Platonism; nonetheless the fundamental idea remains: "the over-man." [62]

H) The Goal of "Culture" ("of the People")

"A people is nature's roundabout way of getting six or seven great men.—Yes, and then of getting round them" (*Beyond Good and Evil*, part 4, §126, p. 1886; vol. VII, p. 102).[10]

How does this goal determine the *essence* of culture as "unity"? *Why does "culture" on account of this goal* have to exist as such "unity"? To afford the *realm* within which and with respect to which the creators as the evaluators can posit "values"! (In the early work "the concept of life" and "value" are not clearly *thought through*—and later?)

---

§24. Genius in Schopenhauer

Negation of "life" by means of the affirmation and intuition of the "ideas" of the "eternal," the "suprahistorical" (cf. sec. X, para. 9, p. 379).

---

10. Friedrich Nietzsche, *Nietzsches Werke* (Großoktavausgabe), vol. 7, *Jenseits von Gut und Böse*, Fritz Koegel (Stuttgart: Kröner, 1921), 3–279; *Beyond Good and Evil*, trans. Rolf-Peter Horstmann and Judith Norman (Cambridge: Cambridge University Press, 2002), 66.

For Nietzsche, the possibility of *this* interpretation of genius falls away with the inversion of Platonism. The overhuman—"the one who *transfigures* existence" (vol. XII, p. 413), the "type that has the highest constitutional excellence" (vol. XV, p. 51).[11]

"Not 'mankind,', but the *overhuman* is the goal!" (vol. XVI, p. 360).[12]

The yes to *this* life (not another life beyond), therefore vol. XII, p. 397: "to teach the return *from the perspective of the Overhuman*"; (in contrast, the second *Untimely Meditation rejects* the eternal return). [63]

Nietzsche's distinction is not political or anthropological (not a matter of worldviews), but rather metaphysical. It intends beings as such and as a whole and determines its highest and most proper pinnacle, that is, it in its most proper beingness, and it wills "only" *that* determination, rendering impossible any positing of utility as a standard. The individuals—neither *for* nor *against* the people.

"Goal"—(does not signify the intention of the people), but *that* self-presentation of beings, which in *its* way even the *people* are, without being the highest. This positing of goals also lies outside of the Christian way of thinking.

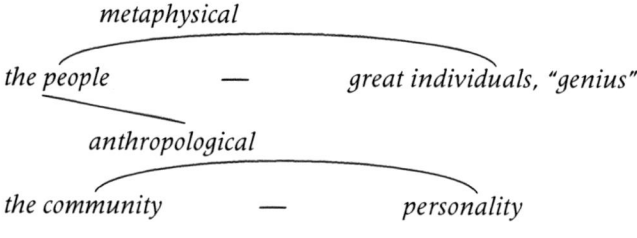

---

§25. The People and Great Individuals

The decision for the people and its eternity is not only *different* in terms of its content than the one about the positing of great individuals, but is *different in kind*.

Therefore both are to be brought neither into opposition, nor into unison.

---

11. Friedrich Nietzsche, *Nietzsches Werke* (Großoktavausgabe), vol. 14, 2nd ed., *Ecce Homo*, Fritz Koegel (Leipzig: Kröner, 1911), 1–127; *Ecce Homo*, in *The Anti-Christ, Ecce Homo, Twilight of the Idols and Other Writings*, ed. Aaron Ridley and Judith Norman (Cambridge: Cambridge University Press, 2005), 101.

12. Friedrich Nietzsche, *Nietzsches Werke* (Großoktavausgabe), Vol. 16, 2nd ed., Fritz Koegel, *Der Wille zur Macht: Drittes und Viertes Buch*, (Leipzig: Kröner, 1911); *The Will to Power*, trans. Walter. Kaufmann and Reginald John Hollingdale (New York: Vintage, 1968), §1001, 519.

This remark on Nietzsche was supposed to make the following clear; that is, to say at the same time: judged from a politico-worldview perspective, the *rejection* of Nietzsche bears witness to a higher insight and a clearer consistency than any mere half measure. Taking a stance. [63]

§26. Great Individuals as the Goal of "Culture," of the People, of Humanity

and that means the "goal" of *"life"* for Nietzsche; but life is understood as an "unhistorical" power, and thus "history" is only an "experiment" of life to see whether the great specimens are possible; metaphysics—the interpretation of beings in general as life—is essential to this laying out of goals.

Apparently the highest goal is posited, but only in such a way that the abandonment by being of beings becomes final. This setting of goals is only the inner consequence of the human being's position as *subjectum*, but this does not signify "subjectivism"; on the contrary, it signifies the opposite, that life within humanity is at once center and *summit*, and in this way accomplishes its subjective character.

The overcoming of metaphysics as such by means of the history of beyng encompasses the overcoming of this goal setting. Not that we would then elevate "the people" and the "community" to the position of ends, but over and against all these anthropologico-subjective interpretations of the human being, there is a necessity for the projection of *Da-sein* from the perspective of the grounding of the truth *of beyng*, within which the human being will for the first time come to a stand within beyng as the event of a possible play-space of decisions [*Entscheidungsspielraum*].

§27. "Worldview" and Philosophy

Meaningless—attempting to contradict a "worldview" by means of an external appeal to a metaphysics (e.g., that of Nietzsche). Realms that cannot be related.

In fact, the political worldview (in which *politics* determines the worldview, care for the people as the foundation and the goal of itself, and that means of its eternity) *can* interpret *metaphysics* "politically" as an "expression" of "life" and therefore as dependent on the latter, and it *will* indeed interpret it in this way if [65] it wants to remain coherent. But *this* never touches metaphysics itself and neither the ground opened up in it: beings as such and in general. *On the contrary*: the "worldview" is not only an "expression" of metaphysics, but is also grounded on it. But if we finally make the step toward the other beginning of thinking in terms of the history of beyng, then the *un*relatability of worldview and philosophy really becomes abyssal.

Philosophy, however, does not need to make use of the dependency of "worldviews" and various forms of faith on it; it has no need to refer to these in order to be what it is. [67]

C. Section II

The Three Modes of Historiology
1. Monumental Historiology

§28. The Question of the Essence of "the Historical," That Is, of the Essence of Historiology

Because the historical, according to Nietzsche, goes hand in hand with "remembering," that is, in some way with representing *that which is past as such* (that which has been as such), because knowledge of having-been and the past belongs to this representing, and because this knowledge is proper only to the human being, the question of the essence of historiology has to be raised in the horizon of the essence of the human being. (*"Relation between life and history"* (p. 310)).
1. What does historiology mean as such (indication of its essence)?
2. On what is the inner possibility of this essence grounded?
    To 1. For the characterization of history [Historie] the following two points are to be noted:
    a) Nietzsche discusses various modes of history. Both the manifoldness of the essence of history and its thoroughgoing unity ought to become visible here; and we should also gain an indication as to what its inner possibility is grounded on (Way).
    b) Nietzsche accounts for history—according to advantages and disadvantages—in a calculative fashion. History is something that can be calculated and that has to be calculated in such a way. With this we gain an indication as to what it is that demands such a calculative account, what is it that exists as calculating and which is therefore directed toward settling accounts [Abrechnung] (result) and toward goals and the setting of goals (Manner).
        Accounting for oneself and including oneself in the calculation—(ratio)
        "Value—nonvalue" as condition of the intensification and diminishment of life. "Life," "happiness" (what stabilizes and drives on), "victory" of life (relation of the "historical" in the sense of the past to the "present"). (The historical: (1) the past, (2) the relation to it.)
        "The present"—not merely currently present "life," anything that occurs and is brought about, but rather the explicit or implicit settling of accounts on the part of "life" with itself that has in each case come to be and that sets the standard—but reckoned up with what aim? Where does the [70] right to take history into account in one way or another derive from? What enables this right to avouch temporarily for history? Power!
    c) Nietzsche treats (a) and (b) together, and first of all in the structuring of sections II and III. According to the three modes of the

"historical" relation (constituting history) to the past, the latter (what has been) is related to:

1. choosing an exemplar	Here what is past (has been) is in each case related to:	1. striving-power
2. conserving		2. venerating
3. judging		3. suffering (being bound)

(Remembering)
This relation to the past is in each case such that what relates itself to it is affected by it (by what has been), therefore a "remembering" [Erinnern] (and yet it is not a having been alongside with, but rather a being concerned by it, a belonging to it, a being motivated by it, descending from it, and being bound to it.) Remembering is a relation that transposes into what has been as such, in the mode of a confrontation.

(The Present)
The relation to the past from the position of a present, in direction to that present. The concept of "the present" (cf. 2.), not what is in each case present-at-hand, but what is "present day"; life, and this with regard to how it has fixed itself and to the direction in which it settles its accounts—essentially, the in each case (present-day) dominant settling of accounts of life with itself and the directions of this calculation, the remit of this calculation (cf. above (1)–(3)), how "life" takes and enacts itself, and what it projects itself onto—"future."

(Past—present—future). "Temporality."

---

§29. Section II: Structure (Seven Paragraphs)

1. Threefold *characterization of life*—(with a view to what?) according to which three modes of history *belong to it*, and [71] from this it follows *that* life is in need of history in these respects. What is "life" such that it is in need of history? An unhistorical power? Or history? (monumental, antiquarian, and critical historiology). Here "historiology" not as "science," but? Representing and producing of the past *for* the "present."
2.–6. Monumental historiology.
7. Back to (1)—on all three modes as *growths* (of life), which each need their *own particular soil and climate* ("life"!). (Not every "truth" is for everyone.) *If transplanted then weeds are produced.* The advantages and disadvantages are principally clari-

§29. Section II, Structure

fied by an anticipatory projection (cf. sec. II, para. 2 and para. 7; also sec. IV, para. 1).

2. What monumental historiology is (see below, the concept of the *monumental*). The *thinking back* into what was once present (looking behind oneself), which here searches for and divines the summits of human life, and which originates from the understanding of life as harboring greatness and as what ought to harbor greatness again and again. *Faith in humanity*: faith in the persistent heights of humanity. *Enlarging the concept of the "human being,"* and thus an interpretation of *human life, but what sort of interpretation? Activity—struggle—striving on the part of the powerful,* "those who become," "those who will," who want "to create great things"! Monogram of their essence (that is, those who "genuinely" "live," *"those asserting themselves"* by means of formative action and creation—but how, what for, and why?).

The Monumental

(Moneo) that which remembers—monu-ment—a sign of commemoration. That which makes us remember, the past in the sense of something exhorting us, motivating us, urging us on to "great" and essential things; what concerns the present and brings it to a decision.

The monumental—for that reason always something already past, that is, [72] belonging to the past and standing in it like a statue, lifted out of "becoming."

The "not yet monumental" = that which is present (p. 301).
The "monumental" = that which is "already there" (p. 302).

The *"monumental"* in the sense of the gigantic, *the colossal*, therefore also *"in the present,"* and this precisely when the present already *wants* to secure itself as a future past *and calculates accordingly* (propaganda for what, one day, will have taken place).

And therefore:

1. One strives for what is the most impressive and overwhelming, and consequently for something that, in the eyes of the present, has never existed in these dimensions before, and that will later allow the past to ground itself as something "great."
2. And this in such a way that there is constant reference to it, while everything else is suppressed and eliminated.

The "monumental" aspect of an architectural work is, then, a monumentality [*Denkmalhaftigkeit*] that is calculated beforehand and willed in advance by focusing on the exceptional and thus also on what has not yet been attained in such dimensions.

The mode of history—from the kind of *position toward life* ("happiness").

History • a making something present? of that which is merely past?
- Or a re-membering? of that which was present *as such*? Remembering—but of *humankind* concerning *human* possibilities—related to "oneself" as the one *remembering*, as what *already stands, is statuelike, exemplary, and thus binding.*

* * *

3. The "advantage" of this (monumental) historiology for *human life*. The *advantage* of the "classical," of the "rare" in former times for the *present human being*. There is *encouragement* and *confidence* in the possibility of greatness; it addresses itself to the present as present-day human being, and is thus *remembrance* of a past humanity, which addresses itself to him. [73]

   Remembrance as *exhortation, provocation, motivation!* "strengthening effect" (p. 16). *Remembering* [*Sich-er-innern*] as *placing oneself* into the greatness that has been and that is still present.
4. *The truthfulness and truth of this mode of history.*

   This history is *possible* only as long as its *previously mentioned effect is secured*; its "truth" conforms to the *advantage* demanded. It is *supposed to* motivate. But it can do this only by a corresponding retouching, leaving out, making up, rewriting, that is, it is aimed at "effects" as such and presents these accordingly.

   Historiology cannot make any use of the portraying presentation that simply records the sum total of all relations of causes and effects. *Non facta—sed ficta* (truth as "correctness").

   "Not the true historial nexus of causes and effects" "completely understood" (p. 299); "how it was" for an *absolute perspective* (does Nietzsche still work therefore with the guiding understanding of an objectivity in itself, that is, for an absolute *subject*?).

   Monumental historiology as the collection and conservation of "effects in themselves" that cause great effects ("effects without sufficient causes," causes which are passed over, ignored). Thus monumental historiology is not "true," but *advantageous* (to learn from it = transforming what is remembered into a "heightened praxis" (p. 301)).
5. The *disadvantage* of this history consists in its:
   a) *exclusive domination*, when it presumes to present things as they were, that is, when *its impetus* (to will greatness) counts as the only valid one. The past is only ever accessible in an *inadequate* manner (and *yet*! a completeness!).

§29. Section II, Structure

b) in that it might possibly—in the hands of great villains—lead to new gruesome effects in themselves (which by themselves could even effect the elimination and obliteration of causes and circumstances).

c) in the hands of the powerless and the idle.

6. With the example of "art" (reference to Richard Wagner), [74] weak and inartistic characters *take refuge* in a great, historical exemplar in order to negate in its name everything *that becomes and wills. Making greatness impossible!* by appealing to the fact that it is *already there.* Here the meaning of monumental historiology is turned into its opposite: instead of bringing forth greatness, it hinders its emergence.

7. Cf. above, p. 57. [75]

D. Section III

Paragraphs 1–4   antiquarian historiology
Paragraph 5   *critical* historiology

One has to *know* what is most perilous and most essential, but one will want to speak little of it, and will much rather hold one's own while remaining silent. (As when a "danger" or a "need" became a subject of gossip, a concern for everyone and thus something harmless?)

(This kind of historiology is quite rare, and if it turns toward the *essence* of the human being—the history of its essence [*Wesensgeschichte*] and thus its relation to being—, it becomes the rarest.)

Critical historiology is not really the mere vilification of a past age, and it certainly does not exist in order to glorify the present against this backdrop. *Critical historiology* is addressed equally to the present, and *brings it into question.*

---

§30. The Essence of Antiquarian Historiology (Paras. 1–4)

1. The essence of antiquarian historiology and its advantages.
   a) Looking back into the *origin of provenance* (in order to preserve the past conditions of emergence for coming generations), finding oneself in the tradition, that is, giving oneself over to it and taking refuge in it. To be on the scent of nearly expired traces. Goethe, the cathedral of Münster, "a German work," the Italian Renaissance (wrong).

   Rediscovering oneself in the past, that is, as already given and completed within it, and this with the aim of holding fast to oneself; the "historical sense" as a mode of being oneself.

   b) *Becoming reattached to one's origins, settling down, justifying* even simple and meagre circumstances. Faithfulness to earlier ages; preventing *the surrender* to rootless novelty and the ever-new.
2. The truth of this form of history—not a pure knowing. Here too history suffers. [78]
   a) *This history has a limited horizon*—enclosed in what is properly its own and only in this (folkloric regionalism).
   b) These *past events*—always grasped *intimately* and *individually*—as equally important, insofar as they are all one's own and from far back in the past. *Truth—the past is covered over* by the desire to rediscover what is one's own. No freedom, no license is granted to the tremorous [*Erschütterung*], and *therefore* one is at the same time delivered over to the past.
3. *The disadvantage (degeneration).* The past here comes to predominate in a particular sense. The past as such *justifies* (not greatness taken

for an example, but the mere *having been*), therefore the past as *rigidified*, immutable (the old), has a primacy in relation to everything that *becomes*, anything new; the former is the venerable, the latter the worthless. Historiology is here no longer spurred on and enthused by the fresh life of the "present."

4. *The disadvantage* arising from the singling out of this history as the only one, even if one ignores the degeneration: it only retains and preserves *bygones*, and does *not create*. For this reason, it essentially underestimates what becomes, and lacks an instinct able to divine creative forces.

§31. Critical Historiology (Para. 5)

("Critical": not *historically critical* with respect to sources, (scientifically) verifying them!, but in relation to the *past*, and this in judging and negating it!). Rather than conserving and even indiscriminately holding on to the past—just because it is the past—the human being has to *break the past into pieces and dissolve it*, so that life remains life (ahead of itself, beyond itself) without solidifying. Dragging the past before the court, interrogating and convicting it. Every past merits condemnation, *in any of its strengths or weaknesses*. Life *itself* judges the past. "Life" as what? As an *"unhistorical power,"* the *un*-historical! [79]

"Annihilation of forgottenness" in order to make clear that these things deserved to perish. What is dangerous in a form of historiology possessing such advantages is not at all its disadvantage. Such human beings:

1. are dangerous, because *they uproot*! apparently (bringing danger) and being irreverent.
2. endangered (they are themselves pulled into the ground-less, (standing in danger) being pushed to the brink).

The *disadvantage*—derived from its exclusive domination—the *perilousness*? (This does not need to be a disadvantage, nor necessarily an advantage). The condemnation of the past *is not, in the end, able to efface it*. From this a "conflict" arises between the tradition and that which is *newly desired*, between a *first* and a *second* nature. The creation a posteriori of a past that one desires (cf. the first mode).

The aggregation of the third mode with the first (its advantage) *liberation for* . . . the third in the service of the first: the knowledge,

    a) that first nature was once a second nature (i.e., strife with a first nature),

    b) *that every victorious nature is the second to a first*.

Conspicuous: the *third* mode is dealt with relatively briefly and the first the most elaborately. The reason for this:

1. because it has an intimate connection above all with the first,
2. because it is (*within* such a connection) the one in which Nietzsche predominantly leads his fight, and the one in which he later on has to fight more and more tenaciously ("nihilism"),
3. because it is *the most dangerous* mode of history and *the most essential*—when? *at that moment that* Nietzsche himself makes out as the end of Western metaphysics.

E. Nietzsche's Three Modes of Historiology and the Question of Historical Truth
(On Sections II and III)

§32. "Life"

Domain—measure—enactment;
Beings as such and in general and *human being*.

§33. "Life"
Advocates, Defamers of Life

The ambiguity of "life":
1. Life as the name for *beings as a whole*,
2. Life as the name for *"human* life."
   A relation between beings as a whole and the human being is hidden in this ambiguity.
   What is the significance of this relation?
1. *Beings as a whole as such* (as beings and as a whole) are understood in their beingness by the human being;
2. The human being is itself the one who understands, and whose essence is grounded in this understanding.

Thus human life *is* in an emphatic sense "life itself" (beings as a whole); the one can stand in for the other.

Conversely, insofar as this ambiguity has not been recognized in its necessity and its origin, while one nevertheless makes use of it as if compelled to do so, a fundamental happening remains hidden in it: the forgottenness of being in the sense of no longer being able to place oneself into a relation to being and into the truth of being as the essential ground of the human being. This forgottenness of being is in turn the consequence of the abandonment by being itself, and this arises from being itself as refusal (cf. N "Life"). [84]

§34. Historiology and Worldview

When historiology is determined *from* a worldview and *for* the latter, this is itself a historial moment of a specific kind. The more resolutely and the more clearly it is carried out, the more unequivocal is the event.

In order to see this determination clearly, we need to understand that
1. Historiology comes to be necessarily and *completely dependent* on worldview. It becomes meaningless here to speak of "freedom," quite apart from the fact that the defense of the "freedom" of sci-

ence, itself bound up with worldviews, is but a belated squinting in the direction of the ideal of "liberalism" that has supposedly already been overcome. Why, then, "freedom"? Why not muster one's "courage" and declare that the sciences are essentially dependent, and to affirm them as bound in this way?

A "slave" condemned to work as a forced laborer in a mine is certainly still "free," insofar as he has to be able to move his arms, his legs, and his head to and fro, so as to be able to do the work forced upon him; that is, if one still insists on calling this "freedom," so as to grant some "freedom" in this sense to "research," one can certainly do so, but it should be borne in mind that this remains a mere play with words.

One only damages the coherence of the worldview when one persists in making such concessions to past ideals.

2. When historiology is put into the service of a worldview, it is necessary to know that the truth of this "historiology"—like that of the others—remains a *semblance* and that its validity remains dependent on the force by which that worldview imposes itself.

But this worldview, to the extent that it is a product of modern metaphysics, is bound to *those* presuppositions that it can never have access to, and which it therefore cannot bring into a decisive questioning. [85]

The power to impose itself, indispensable to worldview, is the essential consequence of the abandonment of beings by being. It therefore has to determine "history" ["*Geschichte*"] completely from the nature of historiology, and it will never be able to understand or admit its origin in the essence of beyng.

---

§35. How is the Historical Determined?

From the *unhistorical*, from mere life? No. *But from where, then? From taking a position toward* life? (Life itself takes a position toward itself as human life), and what is it within which felicity and happiness are sought? And this "searching" itself (from where can that be determined?)? Which decisions? Therefore "happiness" again, again the *human being itself*, that *it* succeed!

To take oneself and to bring the genuine needs into the open and to fix one's aims accordingly (cf. *on* sec. II, no. 34)	("historiality," "temporality")	*to be* historial to have "history" (an essence), To be in need of *historiology*

§36. The Belonging Together of the Three Modes of History and Historical Truth

The predominance of the one over the others, their *simultaneous* reign, the different ways they attain equilibrium under the domination of one.

What is the significance of this belonging together for the *reification* of History?

What does "objectivity" mean ("correctness"—how is this possible?), if historiology *as such* is a putting-into-order [*Zurecht-stellung*], but *of* "life" and *for* "life"! [86]

Is there, next to the three modes of history, also an *objective history*? (How does this determine the *object*—by means of projection?)

Cf. Nietzsche's treatise on the "philosopher's book" from the same time: summer 1873: "On Truth and Lie in an Extramoral Sense" (vol. X, p. 189ff.).

§37. The Three Modes of Historiology as Modes of the Remembering Relation to the Past (in Their Respective Belonging to "Life")

To what extent life is—in itself—"historical," *related to the past*. What *is* "life," such that it is "in need of" history? (p. 294, sec. I–II), such that it "possesses" history (as *belonging* to it)?

The *first* mode of belonging to—of the relation to the past, to life—is determined by a character of life, which is not already, like conserving and suffering and wanting to liberate oneself, bound to the past, but is a relation in the *opposite direction*: "striving," planning, power, wanting to rise beyond oneself (the "against" here on the *basis* of "temporality"). The "life" of the human being needs historiology insofar as it is essentially *"historial."*

"The *demand* for monumental historiology" derives from the "belief in humanity." This demand appears as *its fundamental thought*. Monumental historiology is supposed to exhibit the "classical"; the "rare"; that which is *great* (as archetype, teaching, consolation).

§38. Section II

The three modes of "history," that is, the way the past as such is represented by and for a present.

The mode of the objectification of the past in its relation to "history" ["*Geschichte*"]. [87]

There is an "understanding" all pervasively at work here, one which explains—by means of its presentation—the domain that is in each case posed and projected in one way or another.

Is there, next to this, another special kind of history, an "understanding history," and if so, what sort of guiding projection of the past does it enact? One often talks of "contexts of meaning." (What does meaning mean here and how are these contexts conceived? And are they then to be corroborated and guaranteed in relation to "facts"; but what are "facts", how are they to guarantee the contexts of meaning, if they exist only *by means of these as* "facts"!) The *"circle,"* the question of "objectivity," history as research. [89]

F. THE HUMAN BEING. HISTORIOLOGY AND HISTORY. TEMPORALITY

§39. Historiology—the Human Being—History (Temporality)

The *three* modes of historiology correspond to *three* comportments of human life: life-intensification, life-preservation, life-liberation. What is the origin of this double triplicity? Why these three modes and only these three? Why does this triple historiology *belong* to human life? Why and *when* does this life need historiology?

Nietzsche does not pose these questions; but neither does it appear that he has come across this triplicity of life's comportments and historiology by chance (*Schopenhauer, Goethe*)

We are questioning historiology in order to gather from it and from its relation to the human being (the human being is historical, the animal is unhistorical) something concerning the essence of the human being (yet this—human *life*—is now "life" in the sense of beings as a whole) .

What is historiology? The knowledge of the past in the service of the future and the present, desired and needed by (human) life.

Historiology exists only where there is a relation of the past *as such* to the futural and to the present *as such* (the relation is opening-open). The original unity of *this* relation between future, past, and present is what we call "time." (This relation does not derive from some representation after the fact, but is *in itself* and out of itself (temporalization).) And we call this, that is, that and how the past *as such* and the future as such and the present as such are related to each other, *temporality and its temporalization. It* is the reason for the possibility of creation (into the future), of preservation (of that which has been) and of liberation (of the present). The triplicity of the essential comportments of human life is therefore grounded, in itself *and* according to its unity and possible belonging together, in the *temporality* of the human being.

Temporality establishes and makes possible not only historiology as such, but also the triplicity of its modes. Here [92] the question remains open as to whether, conversely, the triplicity of life's comportments and the triple modality of historiology, as posited by Nietzsche, necessarily arise from temporality (cf., e.g., Hegel's threefold differentiation of historiography [*Geschichtsschreibung*]: original (immediate, belonging to it), reflective, and philosophical).

The Essence of Temporality:

a) Contrasted with *intratemporality* (something is "within time").
b) Temporality—transience (and that even in the Christian sense). Temporality precisely the ground of the "constancy" of the human being as a historial entity.

F. The Human Being

c) Temporality—as the ground of historiality.
Temporality and *the unity of rapture* (the possibility of return, authenticity, selfhood).
d) Temporality and the truth of beyng,
(the essence of the human being and the understanding of being), beyng projected from "time."
e) Temporality and the *more originary* determination of the essence of the human being: it is decisive for the grounding of the essence of the human being that we do not and do not only ask about the place of the human being within the whole of beings, but rather, in a different and original way, about the relation of the human being to beyng: *meditation on the steadfastness [Inständigkeit] in the truth of beyng.*

The question of historiology and its "relation" to the human being can—when asked in a more originary way—lead us to a meditation in which any interpretation of the human being on the basis of "life" and "animality" will be shaken to its core. [93]

Historiology and History

The clarification of the essence of historiology and the pointing to temporality as the ground of its possibility has now brought us into a position where we are able to carry out from the matter at hand the *differentiation*, set out at the beginning, between historiology and history, and to determine their relation.

First of all differentiated only according to the sense of the words [*Wortbegriff*]:

Historiology: it provides, within representation, something that has been present or something formerly present-at-hand—"knowledge."
History: what is happening and has happened. What has happened as a possible object of historiology.
But: History" is not only the "object" of historiology, but also the ground of its possibility. Only that which is properly historial can also be historical; the human being is historical, because it is historial, and it is historial, because it is "temporal" (the "because" here thought in the sense of thinking, and not in an explanatory sense).

History

1. Happening [*Geschehen*]—this means, to begin with, any change and transformation, becoming and passing away (events of "nature").
2. Occurrence—an incident, something "happens," takes place, passes by and through.

3. *Happening*—that kind of being, which in itself enacts something present in such a way that, being ahead of itself, it preserves that which has been (not only "in" time, but in itself "temporal" and therefore intratemporally). [94]

Historial

The human being "is" this, not because it "has" a "history" that is, not because it can calculate historical events and settle their accounts, but instead it "has" a history and a tradition because it *is* historial in itself, and it is this because and insofar as *temporality* constitutes its essence. Human being is grounded in this (temporality as the truth of being), which is at the same time the ground of the possibility of history. The more originarily this happens, the more historial the human being is, the less it needs historiology.

History is

the steadfast insistence [*inständige Beständnis*] in the truth of beyng within *Da-sein*, insofar as beyng has been projected as e-vent and has issued into its essencing as refusal.

Consequently, the essence of history can be determined neither from the position of "life" in general, nor from that of *human* life. Rather historiality first of all informs the essence of the human being on the ground of its assignation to beyng.

And from here: the essence of temporality is determined from out of beyng as the *clearing* of eventuation [*Ereignung*], which unfolds with beyng and is eventuated by it.

The question of "temporality" is not an *anthropological* question, nor is it one belonging to a so-called existential philosophy, but it is rather the "fundamental ontological" question, whereby "ontology" is *no* longer to be understood in its conventional sense, but as a questioning of the truth of beyng.

If in such elucidations the title and concept of "existence" emerges as the character of *Da-sein*, then this does not justify in any way the claim that it is a matter here of an "existential philosophy," or a philosophy of "death" or the nothing. All of these are comfortable [95] titles for mere cowardice in thought, which does not dare (or is completely unable) to follow in its questioning the simple guiding question and thereby to put to the test its flaunted superiority and condescension.

The "improvements" in "existential philosophy" that one apparently desires, and its timely accommodation to a political worldview, are but the unequivocal proof that the simple question of *Being and Time* has not yet been understood and, above all, is not to be understood.

Our age is more distant from such understanding than ever before.

§40. The Historical and the Unhistorical

The unhistorical in Nietzsche is ambiguous:
1. = lacking historiology—no possibility of historiology—the animal.
2. = not chained to the past, and this by virtue of forgetting on the basis of creativity [*das Schaffen*]. Moreover, we need to
3. posit (which Nietzsche did not):
the *not-yet*-historical, but as what first of all makes historiology possible.

The unhistorical is (in this sense) *history*. The "un-" does not speak of a deprivation, but of the *priority* that Nietzsche himself *assigns to life*.

Furthermore, for Nietzsche, "history"—when he does not simply equate it with historiology—is what first of all comes into being by means of objectification on the part of historiology (history from historiology); but, viewed properly, history as a temporal happening (not merely as intratemporal) is, conversely, the ground of historiology (historiology from history).

G. "Historiology"

Historiology and History.
Historiology and the Un-Historical

§41. "The Unhistorical"

says: 1. *that* which is unhistorical (life) (cf. p. 294, 308).
    2. what being un-historical consists in (cf. the ambiguity!):
       a) not being *overloaded* by historiology,
       b) *not being at all* capable of historiology (the animal).

§42. The Un-historical

Its characterization depends on two points:
1. on the delineation of the historical and of historiology
2. on the *mode* of negation and privation.

For Nietzsche, the un-historical is the more primary, that which grounds, *life* itself; the un-historical is surging life not yet limited by historiology (p. 308); life with its restricted orbit (the animal *and* the ordinary human being), its *formative power*, that it would be better to name the *prehistorical*.

The historical first appears with *ratio, thought, calculation* (sec. I, p. 288). With this the unhistorical finds itself "limited," which means that beforehand it was life itself, expanded and expanding itself.

§43. The Un-historical

determined from the historical, and from the ground and root of the latter, that is, from the *historial*. The various forms of the unhistorical, the ways in which the historical is limited by the unhistorical. The concept of *"life"*! [100]

§44. History and Historiology

Nietzsche's *identification* of the two (p. 294).
    The historical and the past (p. 382).
    The unhistorical? The "present," but how?
    The *historical* and that which *"has become,"* that which "becomes" (p. 379) (thus that which lives?).
    "History conceived as pure science" (p. 294).
    Making "history" from what *has happened* by means of "the power to use the *past* for life" (p. 288). Therefore "history" arises first from historiology and means *the remembered past*.

But remembering then means: *incorporating into life* in *several ways.* "Only strong personalities can endure history [that is to say, historiology]; *the weak are completely extinguished by it"* (p. 324).

§45. Nietzsche as "Historian"

Daybreak (vol. IV, p. 251, no. 307 [1881]: *"Facta! Yes, Facta ficta!*—A historiographer has to do, not with what actually happened, but only with events supposed to have happened: for only the latter have produced an effect. Likewise only with supposed heroes."[1]

§46. Historiology and History

History— as a kind and form "of life," i.e. of "nature." "Laboratory of life," in which the highest specimens succeed and much miscarries.

A struggle for the augmentation of power and more power, and yet self-preservation and affirmation not as something present-at-hand, but as [101] self-intensifying and determining "rank." All "aims" and "purposes" are added after the fact and according to rank.

"*Values*"—conditions of the *intensification of life.* But why this at all? Because "life" is the *fundamental reality. What kind of experience of what truth?*

ἱστορεῖν— ϝιδι—to see—to inspect—to witness—to *hear* (a witness, *eyewitness*), that is, to look over something again.

ἴστως— that it has to do with such things in particular (referee).

Cf. Heraclitus, fragment 35: χρὴ εὖ μάλα πολλῶν ἵστορας φιλοσόφους ἄνδρας εἶναι. It is absolutely necessary that those who have the love of wisdom are those who *perceive much* (qualitatively) in witnessing beings as such.

ἱστορεῖν— also *the futural.* Referees—in the essential sense—being able to hear, to distinguish, to value, whose "critique" is *extensive,* and this not in the sense of knowing it all; cf. fragment 40: πολυμαθίη.

---

1. Friedrich Nietzsche, *Daybreak: Thoughts on the Prejudices of Morality,* ed. Maudemarie Clark and Brian Leiter (Cambridge: Cambridge University Press, 1997), 78.

§47. "Historiology"

ἱστορεῖν versus μῦθος—an investigating, explanatory clarification of what is *given* and already there (and also of what once was)

as a *mode of representing things present-at-hand as such*—ἴστως and (calculative account),
as *representing* of what is already present-at-hand as the past as such,
as "science," as *research*,
as scientifically *formed* representing of the past ("Education" [*Bildung*]) and calculative account of the present in the direction of the future,
as *a form of thought*. [102]

§48. History and Historiology

What if historiology is not grounded in history, but in beingness as — *cogitatum*—objectness?

The origin of history—history and the human being.

H. Section IV

Transition to Section IV and Following

What character the meditation takes on now (advantage and disadvantage)!

"*Untimely*," (i.e., critical historiology) in comparison to sec. I–III? Sec. I–III *only a prelude*, but of an *essential* value?!

§49. Section IV Onward, Hints

1. *The confrontation* [*Auseinandersetzung*]:
   It is necessary to repeat the hint given at the beginning of our exercises: our confrontation with Nietzsche is only a careful feeling our way toward the realm of an essential reflection [*Besinnung*], which has to remain foreign to most people.

   Feeling our way not only because these are "beginners' exercises," but *necessarily* and *essentially*, because since Nietzsche we have not yet been able to develop and master a more originary "principle" in order to question Western metaphysics and to take a position in relation to it. ("life")
2. Every philosophy is *untimely* (untimeliness), that is, every essential philosophy thinks "against" its age, not in the sense of the discontentedness and surliness of the know-it-all, but as the unconcealing of the essence of the age and as a decision concerning its future: thinking-ahead to the essential necessities. Not an antagonism in the sense of a merely "historical" confrontation; that remains wholly incidental.

   It is for this reason that we should not get stuck in what stands in the foreground of Nietzsche's text. Instead we have to take the realm of the essential decisions into view: "life."

   Here we first need to ask to what extent Nietzsche's philosophy is as a whole *un*timely in this essential sense, and to what extent it is all too timely. The timely "acts" and "is" in [106] the mode of what is effective. The untimely does not "act" and is not in need of "effects" in order to corroborate being.

* * *

The critical-historical reflection, the judging, the untimely meditation begins with section IV.

The judging of present historiology and its relation to present *life*, that is, *the truth* of historiology: how life itself is taken up and posited, what one takes to be genuine being, and where truth is to be found. *Critical historiology* is *philosophical reflection*.

We will clarify this and what belongs to it within the following sections by means of a few fundamental questions, in order then to bring it into an inner connection with the guiding question ("life"):

Historiology—science—knowledge—truth → life: beings as a whole—the human being; position.

But these questions not in abstraction from Nietzsche's work; therefore we begin by addressing the following sections in their structure and their correlation, in order then to mark out those passages (6) which are particularly significant for the fundamental questions.

§50. Section IV

With this section we see the beginning of a historical meditation in the sense of a *critical historiology* (whereby *critique* is understood philosophically; judging, liberating), and indeed the judging and condemning concern historiology itself, historiology in a particular form, the form that it had for Nietzsche and his contemporaries, and this according to the aim of liberating life (the present future) from this *burden*; to what extent can one speak of a burden and excess?

The *burden* consists in the *oversaturation* with historical knowledge, the oversaturation originates from the primacy of "science" within historiology. Where does this primacy arise from? The inner consequence [107] of the oversaturation is the rift between the *"inside and outside" of life*: destruction of the unity of life, of the possibility of culture.

The meditation *judges* the past and the present that is determined by it, *it liberates itself from the present, from the timely*, turns against these, becomes *untimely*.

Critical → *monumental* → *antiquarian historiology*.

* * *

According to the orientation of the meditation toward the mode of history predominant at the time, the question of *science* acquires a *particular* significance. But the question has at the same time—although Nietzsche is unaware of it—a fundamental significance in that it concerns the nature of the "knowing" and "cognizing" proper to historiology as such. Nietzsche says nothing about this but he still has to deal with it. *Truth—justice* (cf. sec. VI).

It is only because historiology (remembering) is here always "knowledge," "cognition," that science as a special mode of knowing can possibly and perhaps necessarily be *called into service*.

On the other hand, and for the same reason, there arises the danger and temptation of understanding the essential character of knowing pertaining to historiology immediately and solely as *science*, particularly when this "science" has had a primacy in the realm of thinking for a long time, and has even been conceptualized as absolute knowing (Hegel—German idealism). Here "science" is not to be understood from the positive concept of "particular" sciences, but as the essential development of the first knowing of the first *certainty* (*ego cogito*).

"*Certainty*" is the modern form of "truth." (Knowing, cognition and not only this, but any relation to beings as such and certainly any relation to beyng is grounded in *truth*.)

The *question of truth*—fundamental question—("life"). [108]

The "question of science"—today partly overestimated and partly underestimated. That *science* has misrecognized its essential object domains, or, respectively, has lost itself in them.

The reason for this does not lie in "liberalism" or in a lack of a national worldview and political aims, but much rather in that it has been incapable (and still is incapable) of *concerning itself with its essence* and of mustering from an understanding of what it is the force to gain access to the essential, that is, to the knowledge of its own limitations and of its low rank (truth and the question of beyng).

Conversely, the addition of new object-domains and perspectives in no way guarantees a *change in the essence* of the sciences, but on the contrary it will by necessity tend toward and lead to a rigidification of science in its traditional form. (Cf. the "type" of the contemporary "professor," the archetype of a lack of character: seizing any opportunity to court prestige, with a complete lack of sincerity regarding the question of truth, dancing around the cut-price golden calf of "results" and "research records," and all this with puffed-up "cleverness.")

From the beginning onward the essential ambiguity of the guiding word *life* has brought us to the question *of the connection of historiology and "life."* A question for the human being, but *not* from an anthropological perspective. "Life," the guiding word of Nietzsche's meditation, of his philosophy as a whole, and of the explicit and implicit metaphysics of the age; even when, whether in a schoolmasterly fashion or not, one fights against "life-philosophy."

This question has now been more closely determined:

1. through the clarification of historiology (triplicity of historiology derived from the triplicity of "life"),

2. through the transition to the genuinely untimely meditation: historiology "and" life.[109]

Historiology → science → knowledge → truth

Life ⟨ Beings / Human Being ⟩ —Being

The question of the essence of truth is the same as (that is, belongs together with) the question of "life"—in the ambiguity previously identified, and *with regard to the relation* between the two "meanings" and to what is thought in them.

From the following sections we only want to single out those points relating to the question about the scientific character of historiology. Here two points that belong together come into view:

1. Scientificity: science as a *form* of knowing, to be more precise: appropriation and conservation and protection of knowledge. But knowledge is: standing within *truth*.
2. Historiology itself—before all scientificity—a knowing relation to the past, to history itself.

    Re-membering, making present, understanding, projection! As knowing, already *standing within truth*.
3. The question of the *essence of truth* and of the stance within it. *Truthfulness*:
   a) in relation to "history,"
   b) in relation to beings as such and in general,
   c) in relation to beyng.
4. Truth and *justice*.
5. Insofar as "truth" is understood as semblance and, indeed, as a necessary semblance, a semblance posited in each case from the perspective of justice, "art" as the positing of *semblance as semblance* gains a quite singular *primacy* in relation to "cognition"—the latter remaining within semblance; but if semblance is taken *as* semblance and is not, once again, falsified as the seemingly true (i.e., here that means: as truth), then "art" is the highest "truth" (and then truth is again *adaequatio?*).
6. When art, as *the true illusion of the true*, is the foundation of *culture*, then all culture rests on the *dissimulation* of [110] life (cf. vol. X, p. 206). Truth and culture and human being.

With this question of "truth" we encounter at the same time what in section I was preliminarily called the *horizon*-character of "life," without this having been specifically brought into connection with the question of truth.

The question of life and truth, of the "will to truth" and "life," fulfils itself here and does so in a double sense:

1. The truth about life = beings as a whole.
2. Truth as determination of human life, which stands within it.

How from the position of the *question of truth*—in relation to historiality and temporality—the *animality* of the human being and the interpretation of beings as such as "life" are both shaken to the core, and how from here a more originary questioning arises as a need and necessity.

Nietzsche's metaphysical fundamental position (chap. M).

"Privation" and beyng (chap. S).

---

§51. Section IV (Paras. 1–6)

1. *Summary*: once more the consideration of the three modes of history, before and as the transition to the genuinely untimely meditation.

The three modes of history:

"Growing plants" • each *on their own soil* and in *their own climate.*
                   sec. II, paras. 1 and 7 (monumental historiology).

                • Each according to aims, strength, and needs
                   sec. IV, para. 1 (transition).

Each mode is not right for every age (what remains decisive is the way in which the human being is *historial*).

The "natural relation" between "historiology" and "life" (the "constellation"): [111]

a) occasioned by "hunger"	i.e. by
b) regulated by the degree of "needs,"	"life"
of, that is, the *already* present past	"nature,"
c) held in check by "plastic powers"	the
(what is currently becoming, the present).	"animalistic"!

What can be drawn out concerning the "natural constellation" of history and life; the "natural" constellation accords with "nature."

Nature is ambiguous here:	1) the "nature" of the thing, essence, that is to say, temporality.
	2) "nature" according to "life," as per animality (*hunger* . . .).
"Natural"—"nature"	• how is what sets the standard each time to be determined ("growing plants")?
"Constellation"—Historiology	• life like two "stars," each existing for itself!

(Historiology is the knowledge of the past in the service of the future and the present, which is desired by life, because needed by life.)

2. *The leap over* into the untimely mediation, that is, *into the timely* (the present, and indeed the German present). "And now a quick glance at our time!" (p. 310) "A quick glance"—indeed, while all that follows concerns itself with nothing but that (!) Nevertheless, "a quick glance" in order to turn away from it at the same time and immediately. *What is it that is asserted in advance by means of this glance?* The disruption of the "natural constellation"; another *"celestial body"* has emerged between historiology and life, a "powerful and hostile" one (because it is "against" "life"), a "radiant and glorious" one (Western history, knowledge, "science" in the broader sense, *the passion for original science, research, and learned expertise*): science; and more precisely the *demand that historiology be a science.*

   a) *Where does this demand come from?* Manifestly from an *accentuated evaluation of "science"* for *knowledge* and truth and life. *Certainty* as truth. [112]

   b) *The sense of this demand*: not only that historiology is to work with scientific means, but that science as such is to furnish the ground and the essence of historiology as a form of *knowledge*, that is, that it first and foremost determine the *relation* to the past, and in turn its relationship to the present and future. "Science" produces the true and determines "truth."

   c) *The determinateness of this demand*: in what sense are we to understand "science" here? Science: factual research, *scientia*; ἐπιστήμη; νοῦς; λόγος—*fundamentally different.*

   What is Said in this Paragraph about Science?

   i) Everything past, that which once *was*, lays claim as something knowable to *knowledge and knowing*. Knowing and wanting to know are limitless, they set their own limits, *knowability* as such becomes that which determines the contours of what is *to be known*.

   In relation to what we earlier discovered about forgetting, remembering, and making present we can say: representing—bringing before oneself—derives from a mere making present (free and unrestrained), which is not carried and governed by remembering (the *being concerned* by what has been, being affected by it). Now this being concerned is never more than not yet knowing the past that affects us; that nothing has yet been written about it, that it has not been dealt with—*a gap!*

   ii) *The past itself.* Each and every thing in the context of its becoming and its consequences, concatenation of cause and effect. Historiology: the science of "universal becoming," the entirety of factual connections in their sequence (the inversion of the Hegelian metaphysics of history [*Geschichtsmetaphysik*] into positivism). [113]

* * *

3. The hegemony of science in and over historiology comes to inundate the "knower" and the human being capable of knowing with *knowable things*. (Not merely with "material," no mere accumulation, as this would soon become unbearable; the danger lies in this: that now, on account of this knowing, a limitless *comparability* of everything with everything and anything with anything is established and promoted. This is what drives everything. This *comparing* gives rise to the illusion of *mastery*, of vanquishing, of being able to go further; delectation in explanation and understanding. Hölderlin *and* the retreat from the incomprehensible and from the necessity of enduring it, cf. conventional art historiology).

Nietzsche understands the effect of this oversaturation as the "rift" between inside and outside; that is, the difference and the opposition are of a special kind. The *opposition* between inside and outside is such that *no outside corresponds* to the inside and no inside to the outside; "the most distinctive property of this modern man" is "an opposition unknown to ancient peoples" (p. 311).

This opposition as a difference will remain and is essentially modern ("conscious-ness"—Schopenhauer's idealism!). But the question still stands: *what form it takes* in each case and how it is mastered.

On the Differentiation of "Inside" and "Outside"

On (3), the differentiation of inside and outside. Wherever a "rift" is possible, there is a togetherness and unity [*ge-eintes*], and this not as an indifferent mishmash, but precisely as differentiated. How does the differentiation occur? It is first meant "spatially" ("living body—body") but:

Inside: the *mere re-presenting* of things alongside oneself, *opining* [meinen], "considering" things only within this relation—the observer ("*theoretical*" things made present, *from oneself and for oneself* in the "I" or "we"), "oneself" [*sich*] and "one's self" [*Selbst*].

Outside: the effectuating of what is not only meant, [114] but present from itself as something effected and existing ("*practical*"). To convert this into *performance* and success ("the *palpable*," effective and effected).

But: 1) even the theoretical aims at *"exterior things,"* as knowledge of deeds and works and aims.
2) even the *external*, "the practical," "the effected" is in each case, as something effected (e.g., the transformation and education and formation of human beings—the people), something *interior*.

What is named here?: the "subjective" and the "objective": subject-object relation.

The differentiation in its accentuated form presupposes the interpretation of the human being as the *self-related subjectum—thinking and being aware of itself*—as ground and *fundamentum—res cogitans*; differentiated from *res extensa*. The certainty of the I (the certainty of experience) as the fundamental form and foundation of anything "true."

What occasions the excess of *historiology* with respect to this differentiation? The inner, *what has been learned, instruction*, "knowledge"—which does not become "life." Is it simply the case that the practical and its realization are lacking, or are cognition and knowing in themselves groundless, and therefore and at the same time, our idea of praxis—of effect and the outside? And *it is for this reason that* the unity and correspondence are disturbed!

The Opposition between Inside and Outside

is not first of all created by historiology as science, but the differentiation is only developed in a particular way. The primacy of *science* is a later but prefigured *consequence* of the same ground, which beforehand grounded not only the *possibility* of the contradistinction of inside and outside, *but also their "unity"*! and that is: *modern subjectivity*. The sheer fact that the human being and "life" are differentiated according to "inside" and [115] "outside"; which they also are precisely where one seeks and wants *unity* and presumes to possess it (cf. sec. IV, para. 6, p. 317). Nietzsche's belief in "unscathed interiority." This is consummated in the interpretation of beings as a whole as life, whose *center* is human life in its animality; only on its soil and within the range of its representations is there "culture" as such (*anima* and *animus* as *cogitatio*; from here also Pascal's *cœur*!).

When the "rift" is made to disappear, then "culture" is salvaged, but at the same time animality is consolidated and the human being has been brought into the highest danger and removed from any questioning.

Nietzsche says (p. 312): the ancient peoples do not know *this* opposition of inside and outside. This phrase is ambiguous; it can mean: for them the differentiation does not come to form a "rift," so that the unity and harmony of inside and outside remains, which means that the inside has its outside and the outside its inside (and *this* is what

§51. Section IV

Nietzsche means to say). But the phrase can also mean: this differentiation and the unity that carries it—the relation of an inside and an outside—is here completely impossible because the presupposition of an "inside" and of *its primacy* is lacking (self-certainty as essence and ground of all truth and of beingness as objectivity).

This primacy begins, though clearly in a different mode than the modern *subjectum*, in sophistry. It is only in terms of a *vague* correspondence that we can see the same thing here; *Protagoras's theorem*; here ἄνθρωπος is not yet the *subjectum*.

A simple return—in abstraction from the question as to whether or not this sort of thing is possible in general—to the classical ideal is as impossible as the reinterpretation of early Greek thought by means of a metaphysics of universal life.

* * *

(The "unity" of the subject-object relation is what originarily unifies and legislates, but how! In such a way that this relation disappears completely!) [116]

The rift is not first of all created by historiology as science, but it is *developed* here in a particular way. It already *exists*—since modern *science has* come to determine and set the standard for "knowledge" per se, and since *conscious-ness* sustains being-human—even when and where consciousness, having had the un-*conscious* added to it, appears to be replaced by "life."

Nietzsche's hatred for someone as insignificant as Eduard von Hartmann is grounded on the fact that the latter "represents" precisely what Nietzsche is chained to, and which he wants to overcome without being able to—"life."

* * *

Life		Structure
Truth	*Nietzsche's*	IV. 1. Exercise
Knowledge	*conception and its*	2. Celestial Body-Disruption
Science	*"grounding"*[1] *of truth*	3. Rift:
History		Inside—Outside

Destruction of true education [*Bildung*] (culture) by means of educational refinement. *The concept of culture*, cf. §§20ff.

---

1. The later interpretation is already in preparation at the time of the *Untimely Meditation*; without understanding Nietzsche's conception of truth his thought cannot be understood at all.

"Unity"—originarily unifying, forming—an in-formed life. Not a "style," no legislation as forming; at the most a "rule" and formation of parties and "views."

* * *

4. *The contemporary Germans*
Lack of form and disregard for form, "convention" with reference to the possession of "content" (interiority). (Hölderlin!—but how different!) and yet! [117]

5. *The danger of interiority*
That it suddenly evaporates, is falsified. That it *is* precisely what is constantly appealed to *that disappears*. That it remains "weak" despite its riches! *But: its depth* demands a strength that essentially overwhelms the strengths of what is foreign. It becomes easy for the superficial to be "strong"!

6. *The belief in "unscathed interiority"*!! in opposition to *historicism*!

"The true, immediate unity of national sentiment" as the ground and the origin of "culture," *as a historical form of the existence of a people*; "the great productive spirit" has to become the judge and the people has to help *it*! "German unification."

The *essence of the Germans*! *The struggle concerning the determination of this essence!* Against everything "roman" (politically and ecclesiastically) and prior to the "political," that is, the mere "governmental" "unity of the German spirit and its life." Not a simple *interconnection* (!), but first of all the German people must find its essence. Culture as the way, the mode and the "form," not as a goal. And the latter? Merely formal also? [119]

I. Section V

§52. Section V

With section V begins, following section IV which had immediately prepared for it, the properly critical, judging deposition against the age and what belongs to it. The untimely meditation really begins here, and *precisely for this reason what follows is marked by the all too contemporary* and by a *degraded* attitude—in part a victim of its enemy!

Despite this there are important clues in the following sections V–IX, which have to be taken into account by ignoring what is all too contemporary and this in view of our guiding question: *"life"—human being* (cf. chap. N, "Life").

Insofar as the untimely meditation judges, it brings out the contemporary perniciousness of historiology, that is, the contemporary, immediately palpable disadvantage of history for life.

This disadvantage is rooted in an oversaturation with historiology; this oversaturation in historiology having become overpowering; this having become overpowering in history's exclusive domination; but the latter is rooted in a purported independence of historiology as knowledge, as *science*.

But this is not to say (and we need to insist on this repeatedly) that the *disadvantage* and the harm of historiology lies in its scientific character as such, lest one draw the consequence that in order to avoid this harm one ought to give precedence to an unscientific historiology and to change "science" accordingly (cf. vol. X, p. 255).

The ground and the nature of this essential harm lie in the fact that life—as it appears in each case as that to which historiology has to be related—is judged miserable and desolate, lacking standards and purpose (later thought as nihilism). Precisely because the relation to them is essential, it is decisive how the present and future *understand themselves*.

With respect to the critical reflection on historiology as *scientific* historiology that follows, and with regard to historiology's relation to life, we always have to bear in mind: the disadvantage and the harmfulness that arise from history do *not* lie in its scientific character as such, [122] but rather in that one particular mode of scientific knowing lays claim to bring into being, and this a priori, the only *authoritative* relation of the past to the present and vice versa; in short, the pretension of science to take the place of the fundamental prescientific relation (*prescientific relation*: choosing a guide, veneration, liberation). In other words, the decisive question always remains: *how and by means of what* is the relation of the "living" present to the past *determined* and sustained, *which* involves the question, *how and according to what does life in each case value itself?*

The following possibility thus arises: the present can be judged as so low and superficial—and concomitantly the *pre*scientific relation to the past, which proceeds from the present and turns back on it—that the primacy of the scientific relation and its "objectivity" has to be valued even higher than the *pre*scientific relation, notwithstanding the harm it is doing to "life."

This possibility of the *primacy* in terms of the value of a purely scientific historiology in relation to—what one calls—an immediate apprehension of the present [*Gegenwartsnahme*] is what Nietzsche has in mind in this passage, which we have already quoted a few times (cf. vol. X, p. 255).

§53. Section V, Divided into Five Parts

1. The first part presents an overview of *five* noxious effects of the oversaturation by historiology in a *particular* historical epoch; thus it now *appears* as if, following section IV, the text would here after all—"now . . . quickly"—fully enter into a fundamental meditation. And yet this fundamental mediation is not timeless, but futural in an *un*timely fashion, and this is the reason why what follows is dependent on its time.

   These effects—the five consequences of oversaturation—are treated in this (section V) and the following sections VI–IX; here we find the idea of the rift and the destruction of the possibility [123] of culture and, therefore, of the true creativity of genius.
   1) The production of the rift between inside and outside, *consequently* the weakening of *personality* (sec. V, pp. 319–326). (The enduring of "historiology" on the part of strong personalities.) The essence of "personality"?
   2) As the origin of the presumption that one possesses a higher *justice* (sec. VI, pp. 327–338). (Justice—objectivity and truth of historiology.)
   3) Through the destruction of "instincts" and the *atmosphere* necessary for the maturation of a people and of the individual (horizon) (cf. sec. VII, pp. 338–347).
   4) As the emergence of an awareness of being latecomers and living in the end times (of having grown too old) (sec. VIII, pp. 347–357).
   5) As the spread of a mood of "irony" and cynicism. Casual indifference (sec. IX, pp. 357–372).

   According to these five aspects, the meditation becomes increasingly contemporary and more "polemical," shallow, a rant, and therefore for Nietzsche himself more discomforting. See volume X, notebooks. What Nietzsche knows and brings into question in these years. Nietzsche divines, if unclearly, that he is not keeping to the prescribed path on the mountain tops. (The as-yet-unacknowledged seduction by Wagner. All the same, it was precisely this meditation that first perplexed Bayreuth).

2. Concerning (1), the modern human being suffers from a *weakened personality*. What is the meaning of *"personality"*? Only when we know this can we understand the weakening. The word is the translation of *personalitas*, which points us toward the fact that what is named here—the concept of "personality"—has a long history reaching far back in time.

Nevertheless, for us the word "personality" stands for *the modern understanding of the true humanity of the human being*. Somebody is a "personality"—we also say he is a *"character."* How this name and concept relates intimately to [124] the modern concept of personality will have to be shown.

If "personality" characterizes the real essence of the human being, indeed, the human being as an individual [*Einzelne*]—though not as an isolated individual [*Vereinzelte*]—we have to take as the foundation of the concept of personality the Western interpretation of the human being as *animal rationale*; the concept has to be determined from the latter and particularly from its modern form (the human being as subject).

We will begin with the clarification of the concept *personalitas—persona*.

a) *Persona* is the Latin, Roman word for πρόσωπον: that which is in front of the face (ὤψ): the mask [*die Larve, die Maske*].

The mask: that in which and as which a human being can portray "something"—another human being—and how it is in such portrayal.

Consequently:

b) *The role* that somebody plays; here "role" also has two senses:

i) In the generally indifferent (formal) sense—in theater and film—somebody plays, portrays the role of the "manservant," another that of the "countess." Roles are distributed and one feels oneself into these *roles* without *really and truly* being them. *Julius Caesar, Wallenstein*, or *Antigone* "are" also great theatrical works. And yet!

ii) Somebody plays a *role*—this also means—he is within a circle of tasks, in an enterprise, a society and community of *great import and decisive significance*. Role—the prominent, the distinguished, an eminent position, the true being of the particular human being, not something into which he merely transposes himself (see (i)).

This characterization of *persona*—role—clearly comes out in the Roman conception, for example, in Cicero. The *persona*—the human being with an eminent *dignitas*. [125]

3. The preeminence of such a human being lies in its ability to influence, to decide, to direct and to govern, to form; it depends on what distinguishes the creature "human being" (*animal*) from the animal, that is, on *"ratio"* (*anima*). For this reason *persona* is often used in the wider sense for the *rational* animal in distinction to that which lacks rationality. Augustine: *persona hominis mixtura est animae et corporis*.

4. Within the Christian faith the concept *persona* is molded and stressed in a particular way, and this in two directions:
   a) In the doctrine of the divinity; trinity: one god in three persons.
   b) In the *doctrine of human being*, insofar as for it—as the one who is in each case individuated—his own *salvation* is what is de-cisive, not only for the hereafter, but also and especially in this "life" here; *finis vitae: beatitudo—salus*. Accordingly, from this perspective the human being is in a strong sense *his own purpose as an individual*.

5. Subsequently, medieval theology—which to a large degree works with conceptual tools from an Aristotle interpreted in a certain way—arrives at a sharper conception of the concept of person: *persona est—rationalis naturae—individua substantia* (*Thomas Aquinas*).

Person: is the indivisible (individuated) *self-contained subsistence* [*Aufsichstehen*] *of a rational being*. Of decisive importance in the notion of the person is the *subsistentia*, the *self-contained subsistence* of the *rational* animal which therefore is oriented *toward itself*—the designation of its ultimate purpose.

6. *This* medieval notion of the person is of some significance for the formation and justification of the modern concept of personality. For some time now we have known how strong was the influence of late medieval scholasticism on Descartes, the founder of modern philosophy; influence in the sense that he integrated his new foundational insights into the traditional system of concepts, though without taking these up in a blind and doctrinal sense. The same can be said of Leibniz and [126] of his school; Wolff, whose conceptual world became the "presupposition" for Kantian philosophy and then even for Hegel.

In connection with the foundational doctrine of Cartesian philosophy—*ego cogito, ergo sum*—the human being's knowing itself as a rational, thinking creature becomes the fundamental characterization of the human being and its properly understood humanity, the *persona*.

This human being, knowing itself with absolute certainty, is what is held to underlie anything knowable, and therefore any "being" is *sub-jectum*; from now on the human being is conceptualized as the "subject" and this is determined as rational self-consciousness.

The *rationality* of the human being (*ratio*) has now received an *even more* essential characteristic; the dignity and the role of humanity are now essentially situated in the realm of *rationality*.

Genuine human being—*personality*—has to be understood and characterized from its *rationality*.

7. We owe to *Kant* the first and at the same time the most profound foundation of the modern notion of personality; even the relation between "personality" and "character" becomes intelligible from the perspective of the Kantian delimitation of the essence of personality.

   The Kantian characterization of the essence of "personality" moves in two directions:
   a) The differentiation of person and thing.
   b) Personality as *one* of the three "elements" of the characterization of the human being.

   With respect to (a) all beings whose existence is not based on our will but on "nature" have merely, insofar as they are without reason, the mode of being of a *means*. Such beings are called *objects* [*Sachen*].

   Rational beings, *in contrast*, are distinguished by means of their *rationality* as beings that have to be understood as their own *purpose* and which are never to be used merely as means for something [127] else. These purposes are "purposes" *for themselves* [*zu sich selbst*], "*objective*" purposes, not first by means of the relation to "us." Such a rational being is called *"person"* (unconditional value). (Cf. *Groundwork of the Metaphysics of Morals*, 1785.)

   Therefore *person means*: the *self-dependency* that is already posited in the essence of the rational being; one's own being, the fulfilment of which is what is at stake. *The rational* being comes *to stand* within this unconditioned.

   Reason: the faculty of principles according to maxims, being able to represent the latter as such and to act accordingly.

   With respect to (b) it is only in the later work (*Critique of Practical Reason*, 1788) and especially in *Religion within the Boundaries of Mere Reason*, 1794, chap. I, num. 1, that the concept of personality is fully developed.

   The three "elements of the characterization of the human being":
   a) That of the *animality* of the human being as a *living being*.
   b) That of the *humanity* of the human being as both a living and a rational being. (Reason: the faculty (of the representation) of principles.) The human being, characterized by its humanity (ra-

tionality) is not, however, a merely "theoretical" being, since the *technico-practical* is also and already grounded only in theoretical reason. "Humanity" therefore corresponds to the traditional doctrine of the human being as *animal rationale*.

    c) That of its *personality* as a rational and at the same time responsible [*der Zurechnung fähig*] being.

        Self-dependence—as autonomy—to be practical for oneself and from oneself.

        The law—yet this law is the "categorical imperative," the unconditional "thou shalt"—to bear this in oneself as the highest motivation (maxim).

        Being as personality!

        "Act in each case as if the maxim of your action were to become through your will [128] a universal law of nature" (*Critique of Practical Reason*).

        "Act in such a way that you always treat humanity, whether in your own person or in the person of any other, never simply as a means, but always at the same time as an end" (*Groundwork of the Metaphysics of Morals*).

        Personality: the self-dependence of a living, rational being founded in and developed by its rationality in the sense of *autonomy* in "action" and in being human.

8. *Bearing in oneself the law of action as its own end.* This is the determination of the essence of personality from which the intimate correlation between personality and *character* can be clarified.

    Character:

χαράσσω —to scratch, carve, engrave, mark.

χαρακτήρ—the tool with which to do so; and *that which has been engraved*. Sign, *mark, distinguishing characteristic* of the particularity of *how* something is.

    For Kant: *Character*—the manner in which a cause (*causa*) is a cause; the *moral law* [*Sittengesetz*] is also indeed a kind of cause, insofar as it is represented as a categorical postulate, insofar as it is reasonable, intelligible, and conscious; here an *intelligible character*. (*Cause from freedom; autonomy as freedom.*) *From here*: a human being determined in this way is a *personality*, a "character."

    To determine for oneself the law of one's actions. To assume this for oneself *in its* causation, *to be responsible*.

9. The *essential consequences* of personality are really already given in this: a willingness to accept responsibility, the ability to make decisions, decisiveness; mostly the essence of personality is characterized only from the perspective of these "properties" and is often taken in a *biological* and formal sense—a *brutish daredevil* gone wild!—, without keeping the *"essential-ground"* in sight; for *Kant*,

what arises from [129] a dark driving force never has value and existence, even if it may appear "good." Only what occurs according to an ultimate responsibility for the dignity of the human being has value and existence.

10. *Personality*—while this is the essential characterization of the true being human of the individual, it is this in such a way that in such true being human, and due to its power, the ground has been furnished for the being-with-one-another [*Miteinandersein*] of human beings from belonging to the same essential task.

Personality—*not* particularization as shutting oneself off and separation, but also not: first personality *and then* also *community*.

11. Summary: in the modern conception of personality, founded on the Western determination of the human being as such, two essential determinations have been brought to an inner unity:
    a) The Romano-Christian characterization of the dignity and individuation of the *rational* "animal,"
    b) The modern characterization of *subjectivity*, of the self-certain determination of oneself as the essence of reason.

* * *

Nietzsche does not even begin to think through the essence of personality, but keeps himself to the general idea of the term as it has become common currency in Schopenhauer's philosophy, which in turn rests on Kant's.

It is for this reason that he mostly talks about derivative issues when speaking about the *weakness* of *personality*. Fundamentally there is here neither "weak" nor "strong," but there either is personality or there is not; *the Not*: the absence of the power of self-determination and therefore inability to stand up for oneself, and an inability to resist.

Faint-hearted, uncertain with no belief in oneself, being *evasive*, "a mere onlooker"; incapable—in prolonged trepidation—of holding fast to the unintelligible as the sublime. [130]

Knowing belongs—not as an addition, but as their innermost ground—to personality and character, the knowledge of the highest law and, indeed, not of the law in its universality, but of the law in its determining, regulating, and forming application in each moment of action. The knowledge of the essential domains of decisions, the knowledge of the essence of what in each case stands to be decided and in what way it does so.

"Knowing" is certainly not the opposite of character, rather it is its essential ground; without such knowing every action remains blind and arbitrary. Yet this knowing remains unreliable and weak unless it is based on the self-sufficiency of the will [*Insichstehen des Willens*].

Yet if one understands "knowing" in the nineteenth-century sense first and foremost as "science," then no opposition is *even* possible: if character, understood as the mere perseverance of the will, and science are evaluated in contrast to each other. "Intellectualism" is first, foremost, and essentially a misapprehension of knowing and only consequently an undervaluation and misinterpretation of the will. *Scientific education* is as such inessential with respect to character, but all the more essential is *knowing*; yet the latter emerges from the power of reflection and from the courage of questioning. Every will is *in itself* a knowing and is the more willing the more it knows; and yet, the more it is a knowing the less can it be affected by "science." Therefore in the modern idea of personality the force of the will goes together with a demand for rationality—an appeal *to reason, that is, to understanding* [*Einsehen*] and to an insightful knowing. Therefore here also self-evasion; the closing of one's eyes in the face of one's own situation; no *truthfulness* with respect to oneself (cf. 9).

* * *

11. c) *In what situation—in such times—will philosophy find itself?*

Why is this question suddenly posed here? We can draw an answer from what Nietzsche says about philosophy, from how he determines it. "*The most truthful* of all sciences," "the honest and naked Goddess." [131]

Why or why not "science"? To what extent is it necessary to characterize philosophy in this way? What has to be said at this moment: *highest truthfulness* (for Nietzsche this means justice): only where there is knowledge of the essence and the essential necessities of truth can there be "critique," a knowing that ranks and posits standards.

What Nietzsche says in this short section about philosophy is underdetermined and rather general; it does not at all do justice to what Nietzsche had thought during this time (1873) about philosophy, with respect both to its history and, more fundamentally, to its vocation. Understanding this is necessary for what follows (justice—truth). Cf. vol. X, p. 109, *On the Philosopher* ("Reflections on the Struggle between Art and Cognition" 1872), especially pp. 112, 186, 187; and vol. X, pp. 285ff., "Philosophy in Distress" (Autumn 1873), especially pp. 297, 299; "On Heraclitus," vol. X, p. 44; and *The Will to Power* on Greek and German philosophy, vol. XV, no. 419 (1885), p. 444f.

These reflections on philosophy are decisive with respect to Nietzsche's own future and final position in the history of Western

§53. Section V   107

philosophy. The stance that will *make* him into the *one who consummates Western metaphysics* is prepared at this time; cf. "Notebooks," vol. X, pp. 5ff.; "Philosophy in the Tragic Age of the Greeks," fragment, 1873.

Why is philosophy named here? Because *it* is true "critique" in the essential sense; because in this age of universal education where it remains the most urgent matter, philosophy is nevertheless what is most foreign to us, and thus is either disfigured into a particular kind of "scholarliness" amongst others, or is not taken seriously at all.

"The most truthful of all sciences."

"Science," formally and generally as a *mode of knowing*; [132] its character and essence not to be conceived according to the "sciences" as "positive research activity" (empirical psychology and anthropology), but according to the essence of the knowing of *truth*. "Science" (the passion for knowledge) and science (research); the "most truthful," questioning in the direction of and from the essence of truth itself, not shirking away from any question or obfuscation, without any *reservations*, the "naked Goddess." (The sciences, in contrast, already and necessarily presuppose *the truth of their domain and of its methods*.) Nietzsche characterizes philosophy in the traditional sense as the highest "science" (*in the modern sense*), *the highest certainty, truth, Kant, and German Idealism*; this is also of a contemporary necessity.

Why is it necessary—with essential qualifications—at times to call upon philosophy as the true "science"? Because otherwise *according to the reigning scientific consciousness* one will too easily interpret the rejection of the scientific character [of philosophy] as a denial of the value of knowledge as such, that is, *of questioning*; and therefore misinterpret philosophy as *part poetic, part preaching, part journalistic "confession."*

But if our age had at least the power of recognizing its own truth, then the only honest attitude toward "philosophy," toward its "idea" and "intention," would be to suppress and ban it; certainly not to "play" with it or even to make it "popular" and to recommend it as a part of a "general education."

Nietzsche's idea of the "effects" of philosophy remain insufficient, even though he knows that it is not and can never be for the people.

Despite these essential insights philosophy is here always seen only from the perspective of "life" and "culture"—"the philosopher"—and not essentially investigated in view of what in its truthfulness is properly to be questioned and known. [133]

Essential as a *transitional reflection*; but precisely for that reason thoroughly and fundamentally bound to the tradition—to metaphysics.

And for this reason dangerous in both a bad and a good sense, unless the necessity of thinking what has to be thought-out [*das zu Er-denkende*] within it is formed from this philosophizing itself.

(*The philosopher* remains essential, but in another way, more discreet, *more perseverant* [*inständlicher*], less human.)

d) The presuppositions for *enduring* "history," that is, the past as something known. "Historiology"! The *proper power* [*Eigenkraft*] and thus the reliability of choosing and deciding, of the *knowing* of what is *important*. Nietzsche—"life" (only for the individual and its intentions?). In contrast here: the "Eternally Objective" (cf. sec. VI).

e) *To close oneself off against any veritable effect and the possibilities of having an effect (being-dulled).*

Resorting to "critique" as psychology and biography and as a calculative accounting; dissolution in going backward instead of positioning oneself within the realm of decision. Analytic dissolution that reduces character to the biological. (This is fundamentally— even if not recognized as such by Nietzsche—fear in the face of what is worthy of questioning and of the perils of judgment.)

The independent activities of the individual sciences and the *review*-community, *the historiology of published books and articles about . . .*, more essential than what they are about; the latter is merely a good occasion for the former.

(Slippage into the *narrowness* of personal needs and tasks; still in the realm of educational and cultural activity, which are to be reformed; later *the liberation 1878*.)

What is here declared as a *weakness*, a lack of subjectivity, that is, "objectivity," is claimed as a strength. [134]

* * *

Still, letting himself go in this way (the tasteless ranting) was in those days an achievement and an inner necessity for a human being who already had accomplished much and heeded an inner calling. When this is rehashed two generations later, it has become both feeble and tedious; above all, it changes nothing; quite to the contrary.

Since one is "in need" of the sciences, the nagging against "intellectualism" has to be called off; instead university rectors have to appear at the party conference in full regalia, which is to affirm that the hitherto existing sciences are "fully" justified, and the result of this is simple: now more than ever any real reflection on the sciences is taken to be a superfluous and needless disruption. Now, more than ever, any will to questioning is paralyzed and is at best exposed to ridicule.

In this way, the sciences move onto that path which was long ago fittingly *allotted* to them, a path which was cleared and prescribed by the determination of truth as certainty, the self-certainty of the "I and we represent"—a determination hidden in the sciences themselves.

§54. Oversaturation with Historiology and with Knowledge Generally

is today no longer to be deplored and even where it still threatens, it is not contained by dispensing "less" through shortening and clipping teaching hours while pouring everything into convenient *handbooks and compendia*—as if into bottles. [135]

J. Concerning Sections V and VI

Truth. "Justice." "Objectivity." Horizon

§55. Life—"Horizon"

Cf. Nietzsche's later concept of "perspective" according to its traditional meaning and the word itself; *horizon*: delimitation, limitation, confinement, safeguarding, and consolidation of "life."

The horizon not so much according to its own jointure, but rather *according to life*—in view of enlivening life [*Verlebendigung*]—it makes life "strong," "healthy," "fecund" (p. 287) (from here the horizon again becomes narrower or broader!).

Later, what is here horizon becomes what has been fixed, the true, being as *necessary semblance*!

Critical question: I. What, for Nietzsche, is the *horizon*?
1. *A layer of haze and atmosphere* (which envelops and enshrouds) or
2. their *delimitation* or
3. their reduction and limitation by "thought" (p. 288) or
4. the line between light and darkness (p. 287) or
5. all this together?
   II. how does the horizon relate to the "plastic power"?

§56. Objectivity and "Horizon"

The horizon and the perspective-character of life (cf. no. 119). The projection of the horizon [*Gesichtskreisentwurf*]—its breadth and extent—, *how is this determined*? An oriented, jointed looking round and about [*gefügter Aus- Umblick*]

liberating—curtailing	enshrouding
consolidation—safeguarding	
"opaque milieu" ["*Dunstkreis*"]	

§57. Justice

Nietzsche's "doctrine" of justice stands in an essential connection with his doctrine of "truth"; yet the latter is an [138] essential part of "life," particularly of human life.

"Truth" is that *error* necessary for the securing of the continued existence of life, yet this error is nevertheless included within what is lively in life and thereby remains somewhat harmless, insofar as it does not dissolve everything into a mere erring.

This understanding of truth (cf. lecture course 1936–1937[1] and exercises 1937[2]) is metaphysically grounded in the understanding of being as beingness = constancy [*Beständigkeit*]; therefore it is rooted in the unquestioned adoption of the traditional and metaphysical fundamental position according to which beingness is determined according to the guiding thread of thinking (of "logic"); and all this furthermore on the transformed foundation of modern thinking—despite the enmity with Descartes—which only replaces the *cogito* by a *vivo* and thereby merely raises the *subiectum* to the highest level of its preeminence. (cf. vol. X, p. 212)

Early on Nietzsche had seen—instructed by Heraclitus—that his fundamental Schopenhauerian position (but also his later thought that is detached from Schopenhauer) will drive him, with respect to the question of truth, into the arms of an untenable and desperate "skepticism" or, alternatively, into a barren "utilitarianism" (pragmatism). This threat is countered by the introduction of "*justice*." Justice is the legislation of life itself with regard to truth; justice adds the "and" to the relation between truth "*and*" life.

"Justice" itself in the ambiguity of life:

1. as the legislation of life as such	(Life = Beings as a whole),
2. as the "virtue" of the human being	(Life = Being human). [139]

---

§58. Justice—Truth

Justice takes back truth (as the constant) into the becoming *of life*; at the same time it makes error, as unreliable, *harmless*.

"Law" [*das "Recht"*] and the right [*das Rechte*] of the "stronger." But wherein lies *strength*—never in success and victory—*wherein lies victory*? The beast of prey covets its quarry and victory.

    Justice—what is lifelike in truth, truthfulness.

"*Relativism*"—in relation to which *absolute*?

        (*life*—in-constancy—its essence!)
        (Being—truth)
        (Metaphysics—ground).

"*The lie is* the philanthropy of those who know." Vol. XII, p. 293.

---

1. Martin Heidegger, *Gesamtausgabe*, vol. 43, *Nietzsche: Der Wille zur Macht als Kunst*, ed. Bernd Heimbüchel, (Frankfurt am Main: Klostermann, 1985).

2. Martin Heidegger, "Nietzsches metaphysische Grundstellung (Sein und Schein)," *Gesamtausgabe*, vol. 87, ed. Peter von Ruckteschell (Frankfurt am Main: Klostermann, 2004).

§59. Life—and Horizon

On p. 379 Nietzsche speaks of "horizon limitation," of a "limited horizon".

How do "being able to forget" and "horizon-limitation" relate to each other? Are both the same? If not, how are they different? Is the horizon *limitation* the *historical in the positive sense of the word*, to which therefore also belongs the ability to forget—that is, a *limited*, eliminating kind?

Horizon—for "everything alive" (p. 287). Then horizon for animal and human being (cf. p. 338), these are correlatively (in their essence) different. [140]

§60. Beings as a Whole—The Human Being

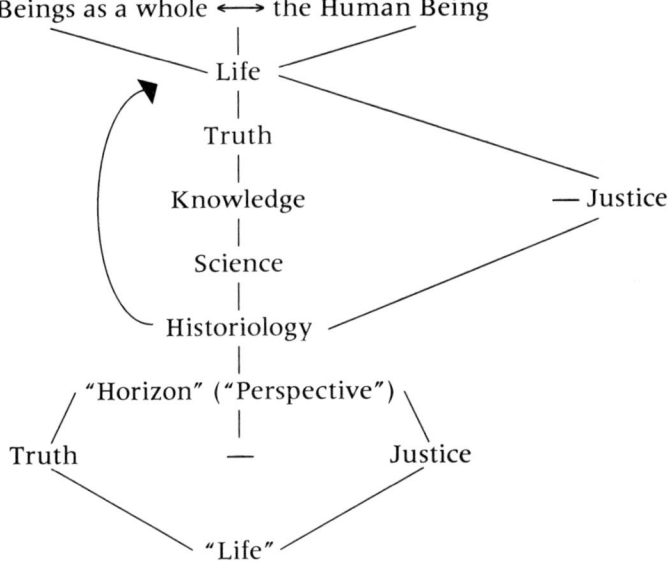

Horizon and the "un"-historical.

The unhistorical as that historial reality that Nietzsche did *not* understand as such, grounded in temporality.

Truth—cognition ⟷ "science"
knowledge
Truth—knowledge—*Da-sein*
knowledge → cognition as a consequence and as specified in "sciences."

§61. "Truth" and the "True"

Is the true skimmed off things and beings as cream is skimmed off milk—objectively?

Is the true and what something is just *meant-onto* [*angemeint*] the thing as an object and talked-onto it by means of human intentions and their views—subjectively?

Or *partly* objectively, *partly* subjectively?

Or have we by means of this presupposition finally lost any possibility of understanding the essence of the true?

Where are we to we draw the essence of truth from, what is it that guarantees us—and how does it do so—the vocation of finding this essence and preserving it?

What does it mean that we mostly call on what is present to us and our beliefs concerning it, and that we are satisfied with what is washed and swept up by our mere life-craving concerns?

§62. The True and Truth (vol. X, p. 189ff)

as the *valid*, obligatory; that with respect to which there is agreement and accord, a *re-presenting-(to-)oneself* (!), common approval; reaching agreement on what is "semblance," which, once fixed, will solidify "life" itself.

Where, then, there was individuation and struggle and dissimulation, there is now a *peace treaty* on the basis of a will *to peace* (where from?), the will *to truth* (accepting), will *to peace* as will to *community*! "Truth"—something "communal"?

And yet, in order to explain *semblance* and its reign, from out of which this agreement is meant to arise, we find at the same time:

1. the true = *the true is equated to what is adequate; "truth is therefore correctness," the adequate*, and
2. it is said that for the human being this adequation is inaccessible.

"Truths" are "illusions"; basic principle. And now the question: where does the drive to these *illusions* come from?

Will to truth = will to "believe" in truth, to imagine that one possesses it; therefore *will to imagination*.

Truth, insofar as it arises *from agreement* on the respective advantages and their apportionment [*Vorteils und Zuteilens*], therefore arises from *"justice,"* [142] and this first of all in the sense of a distribution [*Verteilung*] ("equilibrium"): *to each his own*, and with this Nietzsche wants to banish the danger of a crude and arbitrary illusionism.

§62. The True and Truth

And yet truth here, and particularly here, remains being-represented—semblance. But the question now is: how and with what intention this semblance is posited, for there is no mere semblance for itself, and it is always in the service of advantages and disadvantages *"for life."* Therefore, how life is understood, and by whom it is valued, is essential.

Because there is no *mere semblance* in itself, detached from other things, such semblance taken in itself cannot be dangerous and destructive. It becomes this in each case through *judging* life—*justice*. *"Truth" is dethroned.*

From here we need to look into the essence of the one who judges (critique); which is essentially—as with the old κϱινεῖν—not just negative, but first of all what properly *posits standards and rank*.

Justice (in distinction to truth) more originally *belongs to life* (in Nietzsche's sense), that is, it is the highest representative *of life itself as the will to power.*

But here we also find *the consummate subjectivism of unconditional subjectivity.*

For all that Nietzsche deals emphatically, insistently, and repeatedly with the question of truth and of *the will to truth*, everywhere—and, over time, more and more clearly and resolutely—it is a question of *justice*, of the positing of values, of a positing and distribution of the conditions of *the highest life*.

This "justice" is itself placed into life, and in this way the elimination of any question concerning beyng is finally complete.

Justice is the name for the reign of the *subjectum* (of life in its vitality), that is, of beings as such and as a whole, *of "nature,"* into which everything falls back.

(Every attempt, in contrast, to save *spirit and "reason"* is mistaken and insignificant, because spirit and reason themselves originate in the animality of man and lack, for themselves, the [143] essence and the power to unsettle consummate *subjectivity.*

But is not this subjectivity *able* to interpret everything that is raised as a question and as worthy of questioning immediately as "human" and anthropomorphic, and thereby to claim these for itself and to "deal with them"? That is indeed the case: the only opportunity left is the essential transformation of the human being into *Da-sein*.

---

§63. Truth and the Human Being

Nietzsche's outlook is expressed most unequivocally in the sentence: "It is by virtue of what is thoroughly *subjective* that we are *human be-*

ings. It is the accumulated inheritance in which we *all* share" (vol. X, p. 212).

"Subjective":
1. One-sided, conceited, made up—the *apparent* and its reign (a "subjectivist perspective").
2. But this only where the human being as *"subjectum,"* that is, *being represented* by *it* as the representing "I" and "we," is generally what gives the measure for beingness. Subjectivity.
3. The subjectivist perspective is *possible only* on the ground of *subjectivity* as such and in general.
4. And subjectivity has necessarily to *consummate* itself in an unconditional "subjectivism" and finally to determine itself only from this perspective.

§64. Will (Drive) to "Truth"

can be named only once "truth" is in its essence already determined and evident, at that moment, thus, when the first "truth" about the truth *is true*.

The doctrine of appearance can be established only on the ground of something *true*. [144]

Apparently Nietzsche derives "truth" from "appearance," but apparently only; because "appearance" is already determined according to a representation of truth as *its* untruth.

What of this decisive determination of the essence of truth? (When Nietzsche claims that we cannot attain such a truth (thing in itself—*adaequatio*), he lays claim to a knowledge of what is higher than it, namely its essence, on which knowing rests the explication of "truth" as obligatory illusion and illusionary obligation).

But: we are not concerned here with pointing out the "contradictions" in Nietzsche's work or instances of circular reasoning, *but with what? The superficiality and arbitrariness of his most decisive approach*, which in turn is adjusted again by the relating of "truth" to "justice"; and yet this only increases the questionableness of this approach to *"truth."*

§65. Nietzsche on the "Will to Truth"

The will to truth belongs to "life" and in *this* belonging it is precisely the will to untruth, to appearance. Because "life" is that which "becomes," flows, is *"becoming"*; yet "truth" is that which *is fixed*, "being," "being."

But according to what is the *essence of life* here understood, and how is it grounded? Is there not also a dogmatician at work here; at least a *drive. The will to pass beyond oneself,* the will to remain in *motion*. This is perhaps *one* determination of "life"; but is it that one according to which there can be a decision about the essence of truth? And does the completely empty differentiation between "becoming" and "beyng" suffice for this decision; *that is,* Platonism, the overcoming of which, or *only* its reversal and thus its preservation lies closest to Nietzsche's heart? And, furthermore, is truth everywhere where there is "life" or is truth foreign to life (plant-animal)? [145]

What Nietzsche here grasps as "will to truth"—always from the perspective of the human being—is it not simply the will to the "true," that is, to what is "fixed," and therefore precisely *not* will to truth as an essential will to the question-worthiness of the essence of the true? This "will" belongs to the essence of the human being—the will to become absorbed by and settle with available things, which always remain the orienting point of all calculation. But that is not will to truth, but rather an evasion of truth, a flight from steadfastness in the essencing of beyng, a flight that is always necessary in certain ways and within certain limits.

Because Nietzsche does not pose the question of beyng, he can quite arbitrarily understand "life" as "being," that is, as becoming, and for the same reason, in taking up the traditional concept of beyng (the "is" of logic), he can and must determine truth as fixation and securing of continued existence. [147]

K. On Sections V and VI

Historiology and Science
(Truth)
(Compare J. Truth. "Justice." "Objectivity." Horizon.)

§66. The Human Being—The Gods

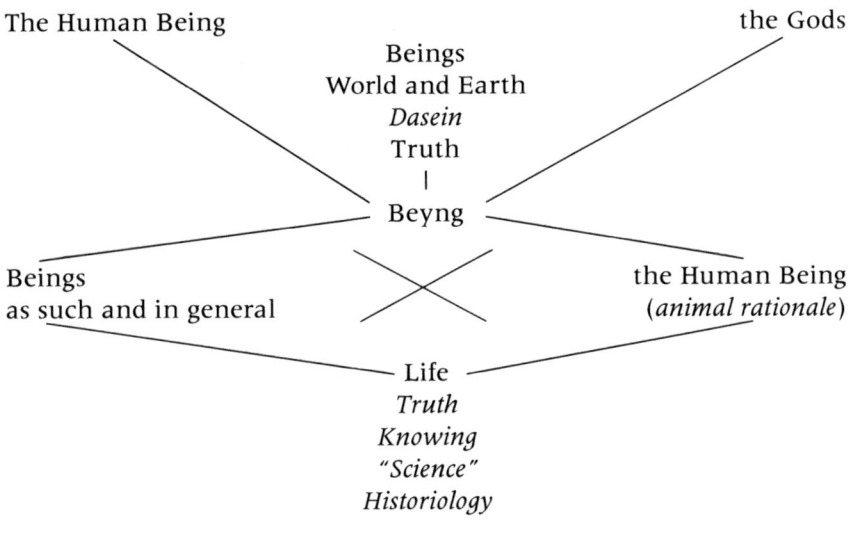

§67. Whence the Primacy of "Science" in Historiology?

1. From the encroachment of *scientificity*?
2. From a decline of historiology (of life)?
3. And where do both of these come from? From a common root?
   Modern humanity (historiology in the widest sense).
Truth as certainty.
Absolute knowledge as *the* science.
The conversion into positivism
while holding fast to "certainty": psychology—biology
                                    anthropology
"Truth" and "epistemology."
   Truth and knowledge; cognition [*Erkenntnis*] is grounded in knowledge [*Wissen*],
      but not the other way round.
         yet knowledge is grounded in *Da-sein*. [150]

§68. "Positivism"

The *renunciation* of Hegel and Hegelianism as a *conversion of idealism into realism* (that is, beingness and truth) is *not* at all a *mere* inversion, with which everything would be standing on its head or, supposedly, have been put on its feet (with both "feet" in "life" and "reality"), and that in such a way that everything would "otherwise" remain as it was. With the conversion of the Hegelian metaphysics of history into positivism it is much rather that historial truth and its perspective (perfection) are lost in favor of a crude, indeterminate idea of *progress*, which indeed "life" itself is supposed to deliver.

Everything loses its boundaries and is without an essential horizon. One abandons oneself to "development."

Nietzsche's incomprehension of the genuine metaphysics of Hegel.

§69. Historiology

Methods for determining its essence:
1. The most apt consists in going back to what, as a mode of knowing and truth about . . ., it takes as its "object," to *history*.

    But how can we determine the essence of history, given that it is not determinable as the object of historiology, which would imply only its reduction to historiology?

    History can be an object for historiology only insofar as it is recognized that before any objectivation, history is in itself a being whose being can be so little determined by historiology that it is much rather historiology, as a particular mode of representation, that must be rooted in history. But how can we conceptualize the essence of history? From the essence of the human being! And the human being? From out of its "relation" to the truth of beyng.
2. Historiology can be determined superficially as a kind of cognition [151] and even as "science" by means of differentiating it from *other* sciences, whereby its being other than the latter will ultimately only be drawn back to the difference between their respective realms of objectivity [*sachhaltige Gegenstandsbezirke*].

§70. Historiology and Science

Knowledge— as observing, assertion and accumulation of knowledge;
as leaving things for *dead,* as mummified.
Historiology— originally as science, but still *re-presentation.* remembering, making present
Or else what is it?—"Truth"

1. What is meant in the demand: historiology shall be a science?
2. Where does this demand originate?
   The origin of the claim to *scientificity.*
   Objectivity—reality.

Is "science" *as such* a disadvantage or only the way it is essentially determined and its self-sufficiency? If indeed the goal of science is to *accumulate* knowledge, this does not derive from science, but from where then?

Knowledge as something *"internal,"* which *either becomes a motive* for *"action"* and *"work"* or does not.

§71. The Impact of Historiology on the Past

The past "suffers" from every form of historiology, it loses something, is taken one-sidedly, is altered, there is no pure knowledge of the past *as such and in its integrity.*

Can something like this be presupposed at all? The pure comprehension of the past as such. And if so, in what sense?

And if not, to what extent can we still speak of "suffering" and encroachment? [152]

Is there a pure, (absolute) understanding and comprehension of the past as such? What does "pure knowledge" mean here? (Essential limitations in its projected perspective [*Entwurfsgesichtskreis*].

Conception of "truth" in *historiology?*
—"Truth" and "life,"
"Will to truth."

Aptitude for life (vol. X, p. 255). From where and how is the truth of historiology determined in its three modes?

The *true*—that which is *in each case* useful from the perspective of each particular mode. But where does its authenticity and right in each case derive from? From an essential pertinence? That which in each case appears *according* to its historical relation, therefore: *ficta*—

non facta. But if never at all *factum*, how then *fictum*? The *fingere* comes first! Seen from which perspective?

Historiology— first of all not as "science," but as the relation *in* respect to which and *in whose* service research in each case establishes itself, or (sec. IV ff.): "science of universal becoming" (p. 311). What is happening now? The relation to the three modes—independence of *which* re-presenting? Pure making present!

Historiology— as a *kind of representing*, representational explanation, *making present* in the service of remembering, becomes *self-reliant* and even overpowering in setting the standard for all historical relations (remembering) on the basis of *their* truth as scientific truth. *What is happening here?*

Historiology— as *science*. The concept of "science" (explanatory representing and producing [*Vor- und Herstellen*] (cf. lectures on modern metaphysics).[1] (Historiology and technology—cf. no. 19, p. 53f).

How "science" can acquire an essential primacy. "Art and science," *a thoroughly inappropriate equation*. What makes it possible? [153]

From both sides: the art industry   —decline
                the science industry—oversaturation

and this within the culture industry.

Mere making present of the past—*without remembering what has been, without future.*

---

§72. Truth

Aptitude for life (vol. X, p. 255). How "life" is understood is essential; the *evaluation*. Aptitude = effectiveness for the intensification of life, its securing, liberation, rigidification.

    The true = that which "truly" (effectively) is. (This also holds if after the fact truth is understood as semblance (fixation).)

---

1. Heidegger, *Gesamtausgabe*, vol. 41, *Die Frage nach dem Ding. Zu Kants Lehre von den transzendentalen Grundsätzen*, ed. Peter Jaeger (Frankfurt am Main: Klostermann, 1984); *What is a Thing?* trans. W. B. Barton Jr. and V. Deutsch (Chicago: Regnery, 1967).

§73. Historiology as Science

1. the modern conception of knowledge,
2. absolute knowledge and idealism,
3. positivistic "sciences".

The sciences are never capable of grounding the opening *relation* [*erschließender Bezug*] to beings as such. Why not?

Historiology in a supposedly *fourth* mode as science of universal becoming.

The pretension of being, by virtue of *pure objectivity* itself, the basis of any historical relation.

The reversal. [154]

§74. "Historiology" and "Perspective" and "Objectivity"

1. *Why* is all historiology as such *bound to perspective*?
2. To what extent is it this *perspective* that first determines the *objectivity* that is in each case possible?
3. What follows from this "perspectival" essence of historiology (*of all* cognition of beings)? Perhaps the endeavor to harmonize and aggregate all "perspectives" into *a* singular, correct and complete one? *What does this mean?*

   Is the "past" affected, for example, in its being in-itself, if all kinds of historiology (e.g., Nietzsche's three modes) are joined together?
4. "Objectivity" and "justice." Justice and the three modes of historiology.

* * *

Truth and justice and "objectivity" (cf. sec. VI). [155]

L. SECTION VI

(Justice and Truth)

§75. Section VI

With this section it is necessary to recall the guiding concern: Historiology—Life, now: *Truth* and Life, that is, *beings as a whole*.

How is the essence of truth determined? *What* truth "about" beings as a whole? What does the interpretation of beings as a whole *as* life mean? In what sense of "truth" is this interpretation *true* (philosophical truth)?

Thoughtful thinking,	Though different, these three all have
Scientific thinking,	to be enacted—"practically"!
Everyday thinking.	Higher "praxis."

For as long as self-reflection [*Selbstbesinnung*] and clarity is to govern the university, everyone should know in each case when and how to "think"; instead there is a random mishmash of opinions only differentiated by their particular "matter."

(No empty "reflection," no mere seeking practical benefit.)

The relationship posed in the guiding question is that of *Historiology and Life*.

We have grasped this relationship more fundamentally as one between *Truth and Life* (accompanied by the constant and obscure role of the question of the "human being"). But *truth* is thought in its connection and identification with *"objectivity."*

That truth is grasped as "objectivity" is decisive for *modern thinking*.

This means at the same time: only from the *perspective of this* conception of truth as objectivity is it possible to understand why and in what sense Nietzsche, when asking the question of truth, comes upon the question of *justice*.

Therefore, if we seek first of all to clarify the idea of "objectivity," we will inevitably be led to an elucidation of the question of truth.

Objectivity—character of the *object*; object essentially related to the subject—*subjectivity* and consequently: subject-object relation. [158] Accordingly, we find first of all a triple sense of "objectivity" (cf. p. 133).

§76. Section VI (Paragraphs 1–7)

The oversaturation with historiology brings about the emergence of the idea that one possesses a higher *justice* (cf. §79; p. 141ff.). The fact that the question of truth in general stands under this heading is decisive for all modern, and thus for all contemporary thinking.

1. *The age of scientific objectivity* (see para. 3) considers itself in possession of such higher justice (this holds generally for the age of the scientific worldview, grounded on the sciences).

   Is this *objectivity* caused by a heightened need and *desire for justice* (see §77) or is it something completely different that *drives* us to such *objectivity and its demands*: an evasive tendency, *imagining* that one possesses virtue, an illness that is close to madness . . .; with the conceited claim to possess justice one becomes for the most part always worse and "more unjust." Where does this conceit arise from? (Does it arise from the oversaturation or is this only a motive and the path of its reinforcement?)

2. What is *justice*? The following paragraphs (2–7) respond to this question by bringing to light the relations between truth, Will to Power, objectivity, and justice; these headings always name both the essence and the un-essence of what is meant and therefore remain ambiguous, giving rise to apparently contradictory assertions.

   A constant feature of the text is the distinction that Nietzsche was working out more and more determinately at the time: the distinction between cognition and art and the struggle between the two; even though all this is not yet grasped in relation to "being" and "becoming," as it will be later (Will to Power). [159]

   The main concepts are here delimited rather than defined; what they name is appraised and a decision is made concerning the *comportment* toward them.

   The timely perspective is contrasted with the untimely, and the latter is placed in the position of judgment.

---

§77. "Objectivity" and "Justice"

1. Is *objectivity sought because of a desire for justice*, that is, is it sought not simply as a possession, but as something that in its *essence* is first to be determined as the *highest virtue* (as enabling us to be human beings in the proper sense, that is, enabling a comportment in the midst of beings as a whole and as such)? Does justice remain something that *in its essence* has to be striven for, as the most difficult to attain and as motivating the will to essential struggle [*Wesenskampf*]?
2. Or else has "justice" already been claimed and taken into possession, in such a way that it is essentially determined as *acceptance* [*Geltenlassen*]? And thus is objectivity consequently taken to have already been decided and elucidated as true and self-evident (precisely as imagined), and therefore is what drives us a desire to take refuge in *security* and *complacency*?

   The essence of *"objectivity"* is determined according to these possibilities.

With respect to this concept we have to draw out some fundamental issues and first of all point out an ambiguity relating to it (*objectum-subjectum*: the originary meaning opposed to its contemporary, that is, modern meaning).
1) Objectivity as characterizing the subject (the human being); the representing [*Vor-stellen*] remains unexplained! (Comportment).
2) Objectivity as characterizing the object (toward the object); (as essential persistence [*Wesensbestand*]).
3) In each case the root is given in the subject-object relation (modern humanity). Objectivity as *property* of "cognizing," of "cognition."

Concerning 1): An "objective" human being, a reasonable human being (i.e., a [160] "truthful" human being), who accepts the validity of the *state of affairs* (instead of accidental opinions, moods, or valuations), who accepts how things are and who understands "the true" as the purely self-determining "object." (But how could the ob-ject be this, when *in itself* it stands over and against the subject?) Therefore

Concerning 2) objectivity: what makes the object an object. The *Kantian* conception of *objectivity* [*Gegenständlichkeit*]—*not without the subject*, but *how*? The true, what truly and really is in beings, beingness.

Concerning 3) But on what does the subject-object relation *rest* and how? Where can we find the ground of objectivity in the first and the second sense? (In the understanding of truth as certainty.)

Here we find *three internally related* and therefore *often confused* conceptions of objectivity:
1) Objectivity as a comportment of the *human* subject, (of the human being as subject).
2) Objectivity as essential definition of the object *as* object, (*objectivity*).
3) Objectivity as property of the subject-object relation, (which for this reason can also be called "subjectivity"). (Objectivity of the sciences, that is, of their truth as validity.)

In Nietzsche these three conceptions are confused, and the direction in which he is thinking, without clearly signaling the limits of the different determinations of objectivity, has to be understood in each case according to the context. (The individuals who are concerned with "objective" sciences; "objectivity"—the sciences themselves.) (Here as everywhere the fatal consequences of Schopenhauer's *superficial inter-*

pretation of Kant. (Why in Kant are objectness and objectivity everywhere *the same*?))

In a certain sense one might say: all objectivity derives from *subjectivity*; while *subjectivity* itself is, *as subjectivity*, in each case marked by its relation to an *object*, and finds its essential tenor and ground within this relation. [161]

To formulate this point more clearly: "subject" and "object" cannot be thought "in themselves"—in this way they would be nonconcepts, by means of which one would try to understand in itself that which *is* precisely only insofar as it is *for* its "opposite." One might understand this "not-without" in comparison to "privations" discussed earlier: death-life; forgetting-remembering; to be silent- to speak; unhistorical-*historical*?

Subject — that which represents and has a *"consciousness"* of something and *is* such consciousness [*Bewußt-"sein" ist*].

Subject — that with respect to which the re-presented (object) is what it is.

Subject = *ego* as *ego cogito* and this *as ego cogito cogitatum (qua* certum, verum, objectum*)*.

Object — that which stands-in-opposition to the subject understood in *this* way. *Objectum, cogitatum*—the *cogito* as ego *cogito.*

It is for this reason that there is a "subject" and an "object" only insofar as there is in some way an *open/opened* re-presentation of something as something *for* a representing being. This Open [*das Offene*] is the ground of any possible representing relation of something represented to and for something representing. And within this realm of possible relations, the Subject-Object relation is a particular dispensation with a particular stamp that marks out an essential moment of Western history. Thought rigorously, it is thus not simply the case that the relation is prior to the *relata*. It is rather the Open, experienced first of all as disjointed and indeterminate, that gives to the "relation" its particular stamp, and that thus at the same time prefigures the *relata* as subject and object.

The Openness of this representing relation is then called "consciousness," *cogitatio-perceptio*. More precisely, the Open is not apprehended, and still less understood, as the essential ground of the relation; it is much rather consciousness, and consciousness alone that first of all creates this *relation*. Such an understanding of the subject-object relation is facilitated by the belief, which has existed for a long time and was already there at the beginning, that the representing relation of the human being to beings as such has been adequately [162] clarified and explained as following naturally from the essential determination of the human being as *animal rationale*. The human being is a present-at-hand animal, and this animal has something like *ratio*—νοῦς—in the same way that a tree has branches. The human being is *endowed* with this faculty and it uses it just like the hand uses a "tool" (organ).

But how is it that this apprehending, representing relation of the human being to beings as such takes precedence in the form of the subject-object relation?

It occurs when the *representational relationship* (of the representing to the represented), and thus beforehand the "relation" itself, is constituted in such a way that the representing human being is distinguished as *subjektum*, and this initially still in the traditional sense of the word. When the human being becomes this distinguished *subjektum*, the concept of the *subjektum* comes to receive a new meaning from what particularized it (the *human being* as *ego*), and at the same time what is differentiated from the *subject* and thereby contrasted to the human being within the representing relation is determined as "object." Why *ego*? Because being related *back* to the human being, the "I" says and "calls" "itself" I.

The transformation of the representational relationship of the human being representing beings into the subject-object relation originates from a *change in the essence of truth*. Despite "alterations," truth has been and is still understood as *adequatio intellectus ad rem*. Correspondence to; correctness in the sense of being directed to and measured against something. Truth as *correctness* is still, and still will be sought and required as absolute *certainty*, established in itself *for* and *by* the human being; this is to say, as a mode of representing in which what is represented can establish itself as indubitably present, in such a way that everything else representable is grounded absolutely and securely *on* it. The crucial aspect of correctness is now the *unconditioned surety* of representation and, in fact, a surety which the representing human being can secure, at each moment, from "out of itself" (ambiguously). As soon as *correctness* changes *into certainty*, [163] that is, as soon as certainty becomes essential to correctness, then, first of all, the directing-itself according to [*das Sich-richten nach*] becomes a directing itself *toward and back onto itself*—a directing itself toward itself [*das Sich-richtende*]; the "I" as relational ground is now, more than ever, essential.

What is unconditionally given conjointly and in advance for all human representing and in any representing, what is thus secured is that the *ego* as *res cogitans*, as the *certissimum*, is at any moment the foundation of every representing—the I, which represents. This is to say, that in the context and the domain of all that is representable, the *ego* (*res cogitans*) is the paradigmatic ὑποκείμενον, the paradigmatic *subjectum. The* genuine *subjectum is* and is now called *ego*, which is to say: the *Ego*, the I and egoity give a new sense to the *subjectum*; now "subject" = the consciousness of what is represented and known that is certain of itself. "Subjective" now means to belong to the I, to be proper to the I, "to be of the character of consciousness."

This determination of the human being as subject in the sense of the *ego cogito* is in no way "egoistic" in the sense of the I, contingent and isolated in each case, and of its opinions; on the contrary, the subject is I in the sense of "egoity," in the sense of what is essentially binding for any *I as I*.

This is thus not a coarse, licentious, and haphazard egoism, even though here the self-determination of the human being gains a new status, since now the human being has become the determining center of all beings as such. That the human being henceforth *liberates* itself from its former ties to authorities in the interpretation of beings (e.g., church doctrine), is the inner consequence of the conception of the human being as *subjectum* and not *vice versa*. The true conception of "liberalism" is *self*-determination, being responsible for the *self*, whereas the *false* conception is *arbitrariness*, accepting anything as valid, indecisiveness. This conception of the human being, by means of which and with which modernity begins, is grounded in a transformation of the essence of truth. Correctness becomes *certainty*, "surety." "True" is what secures for the human being its being human within beings as such, and is therefore what furthers this securing and is of use to it. [164]

But from where does this alteration of the essence of truth from correctness to certainty, surety, and assurance originate? Who determines the essence of truth? The human being and its free, arbitrary will [*Willkür*]? What and who is the human being? Is it not rather the case that the human being, and particularly the human being, is dependent on an essential determination of truth, a determination which thus lies outside the realm of its authority?

(Truth is essentially the truth of beyng; *beyng itself* decides on the essence—how? "E.g."! in the mode of self-refusal [*Verweigerung*], in such a way that it leaves the human being to itself and to its pursuance of beings and its securitization in the midst of beings as such and, therefore, abandons beings; abandonment of being [*Seinsverlassenheit*]).

In contrast, in the first beginning, φύσις, emergence [*Aufgang*] and how it decides the essence of ἀλήθεια and its necessary groundlessness (non-grounding), which issues in a collapse and the emergence of correctness. (cf. winter semester 1937–1938[1]).

---

1. Martin Heidegger, *Gesamtausgabe*, vol. 45, *Grundfragen der Philosophie. Ausgewählte "Probleme" der "Logik,"* ed. F.-W. von Herrmann (Frankfurt am Main: Klostermann, 1984); *Basic Questions of Philosophy: Selected "Problems" of "Logic,"* trans.

§77. "Objectivity" and "Justice"

The shocks of eventuation [Ereignung] and the refusal of beyng—the ground and abyss of all history.

We have to insist on this time and again: truth understood as "certainty" is founded on the notion of truth as the *correctness* of representation: *adaequatio. This* interpretation of "truth" is the foundation of the possibility of an *elaboration* and domination of the subject-object relation. And it is therefore *not* the case that this *subject-object* relation is what comes first and could be understood as the framework within which the essence of truth would first have gained its determination and justification.

Our modern habits of thinking mislead us into thinking that the subject-object relation is to be taken as fundamental (so that we would historically trace it back into classical Greek thought!), even there and then, where and when it is not thought *"idealistically,"* but *"realistically"*; even there and then, where and when one does not think "epistemologically," but "episto-metaphysically." [165]

(In contrast the wholly different projection [*Entwurf*] on the basis of the understanding of being: the human being as *Da-sein* and this in this first instance as being-in-the-world.)

The conception of the human being as a "subject," as well as the earlier and persistent interpretation of the human being as a *present-at-hand* (living) and reasonable animal, *equally* stand in the way, mutually reinforcing each other, of a more originary questioning of the essence of the human being and humanity from out of its assignation to Being itself. "Idealism"—notwithstanding its "proximity" to this interpretation—remains at the greatest distance from this originary questioning, because it considers itself as carrying it out already.

In a strong sense, "subjectivism" is any interpretation of the human being positing it as *the* paradigmatical *subjectum* so that beings are determined as such in being grounded back on this subject (beyond "objectivism" as its opponent). Here the *subjectum* human being can be understood as consciousness, as personality, as "living body," as "life," and this again as "I"-hood or as *we-hood*, individual, community. Everywhere subjectivism is not only preserved, but is amplified and exacerbated; the determination of the human being as I-consciousness is only *one* special case of subjectivism. Subjectivism—*the mere turning around itself of the human being as that being in relation to which everything else is determined in its being.* "Anthropomorphism" in the metaphysical sense of the term.

It is essential to note that Nietzsche's concept of *objectivity* derives generally and particularly from the subjectivity of the subject "life,"

Richard Rojcewicz and André Schuwer (Bloomington: Indiana University Press, 1994).

"human life." In no way, thus, has Nietzsche overcome subjectivism. One often claims that he has by appealing to the fact that Nietzsche turns *against Descartes*; and yet Nietzsche only replaces the subjectivism of consciousness with a subjectivism of *"life"* (cf. vol. I, p. 378: "vivo, ergo cogito"—*vivo*! What is that about? *ego*! vivo). What Nietzsche says already in 1873 holds for the whole of his philosophy: [166] "We are human beings on account of that which is well and truly *subjective*" (vol. I, p. 212). (The subjective—that which is brought and held together within the *human being* as *determining-center* [*Bestimmungsmitte*]). Human being = *this* being-the-center, being-the-*ground*. "Life" (*as belonging to itself*) understood from the perspective of the *human being* (animal). What is "subjective" is "life" as *"human life,"* and that is again, as *rational*, even though "reason" is here taken back into *animality*, the *"blond beast"*: "the blond beast of prey, the magnificent *blond beast* avidly prowling round for spoil and victory."[2]

1) For this reason it becomes necessary in each case to ascertain which subject and which *comportment* of the subject serves as the origin of objectivity. *Objectivity*—truth—as *validity* and *obligation*:
   a) a merely representing [*vorstellende*], "purely" cognizing having-before-oneself of the given (cognition),
   b) a formative shaping (art) that produces [*her-stellen*], brings-forth and generates.
2) With respect to the question of "objectivity," "cognition" and "art" enter into *negotiation*, which is to say: which of these two human faculties gives rise to *true* "objectivity"? How do these two relate to each other in terms of their rank?
3) Objectivity—as the essence of the objective, of the true; objectivity = truth. Therefore:

   The question of truth from the perspective of *cognition and art*. The two *struggling* with one another. *Are these* fundamental and constant questions of Nietzsche's later and most developed philosophy?

"*Objectivism*" is the opponent of subjectivism—that is, though opposed to each other, they are of the same nature—and its ultimate essential consequence. The "human being" as the *subjectum* of the determination of beings as such and in general is simply relinquished, that is to say, it is, as this self-evident "*subjectum*," relocated into the [167] "*objectum*" ("nature," "life"), in such a way that one has now simply forgotten that the *objective* is determined as such by the subject; and that everything is grounded on the subject-object relation.

---

2. Friedrich Nietzsche, *Nietzsches Werke* (Großoktavausgabe), vol. 7, *Zur Genealogie der Moral* (Stuttgart: Kröner, 1921), 322; *On the Genealogy of Morals*, ed. K. Ansell-Pearson (Cambridge: Cambridge University Press, 1994) 25.

§77. "Objectivity" and "Justice"

The subject now is a fugacious accident, something incidental to the *object in-itself*, which itself is determined only on the basis of the *subject*. (As readily as subjectivity is accepted by all, as quickly is it *salvaged* in the form of the "objective.")

From here we can understand the ambiguity of the fundamental concept "life" and the mutual relation of the two concepts of life: 1) as human life (subject), 2) as being in general (object). The name "life" covers at the same time the (objective as such) and the *subjectum*. The subject as the *relational center* is now displaced into beings as a whole, without any question remaining of how its truth can be grounded as long as the *subject* is simply suppressed.

The exclusiveness of the relation *to* the subject and the inclusion [*Einschlag*] of the object into the subject in subjectivism corresponds to the exclusiveness of the inclusion [*Einbezug*] into the object and the *suppression* of the subject [in objectivism]. In other words, everywhere and more decisively than ever before the subject-object relation remains as unquestioned and taken for granted.

As soon as subjectivism has become sufficiently broad in its meaning, intelligible and unquestionable, it degenerates into an equally unquestionable objectivism, which, assured of itself, determines beings as a whole in their essence and has them *before itself* as present-at-hand; in such a way that the "self" passes into the objective and that everything takes place as *one process*, within which any subject runs its course.

The self-certainty of the *subjectum* thus becomes necessarily *and at the same time* the absolute thoughtlessness of objectivism, that is, the self-certainty shores up the thoughtlessness while the latter lets us forget the objectivism. And this omnipresent assurance and tranquility allows and calls for the calm conscience of *being in possession* of the truth, thereby passing off any reflection as devoid of sense and any will to such reflection as vanity. One [168] is in possession of "the truth" and the only remaining "question" is to convert this "without remainder" into "reality" (whatever that may be).

The *forgottenness of being* on the part of the human being and the *abandonment* by being of beings as a whole attain here, and without even a trace of self-awareness of themselves, *their common triumph*: "*life*"!

Now, after this first elucidation of the essence of objectivity and truth, we have to ask: *why and how* is Nietzsche, in the context of the question of scientific objectivity, led to *justice* [*Gerechtigkeit*], and what does justice mean?

What first attracts our attention is the ambiguity, even the inconsistency, in the determination of the relation between objectivity and justice.

In this early period, which was critical for everything to follow, Nietzsche's thought had not yet attained complete clarity in its presentation because, though already formed according to the attitude and direction of reflexion [*Besinnung*] and "critique," it did not yet *master* these questions *in a way proper to thinking* (Schopenhauer!).

Consequently, the *Meditation* at this crucial point (sec. VI) also exhibits something iridescent, something ambiguous in the characterization of the relation between objectivity, truth, and *justice*. This can be brought out with two phrases:

1. Paragraph 2: the pursuit of truth (objectivity) has its root in justice (the most essential integration of truth (objectivity) and justice). (To judge from the position of superior force).
2. Paragraph 4: objectivity and "justice" have nothing in common (the most adroit exclusion of objectivity and justice).

These two sentences seem incompatible; and yet, Nietzsche is not contradicting himself, for he uses the words "objectivity" and "justice" in each quote with different meanings. This difference in their meaning is not arbitrary; but in one case objectivity and justice are meant *according to Nietzsche's* [169] *own understanding of their essence*; and in the other according to their generally *perverted sense* [*Unwesen*]: the first sentence understands *justice* in its *essence*; the second sentence in its impropriety (the eternally "objective"—"proper neutrality").

The first sentence understands objectivity in its *essence and un-essence*; the second sentence in its essence (artistically).

---

§78. On the Structure of Section VI as a Whole

From the first paragraph (from the inadequately developed either-or, whether justice is sought or simply claimed, *i.e., if it is essentially question-worthy or taken for granted*, which is to say: from the outset sensed as decisive) and in conjunction with the apparently contradictory sentences concerning truth and justice, that is, concerning their relation, in the second and fourth paragraphs, it becomes clear:

1. that *"truth"* is not something ultimate or originary, but something derivative [*nachgeordnet*],
2. that justice is somehow the *ground* of truth,
3. that since "truth" has been *placed* into the subject-object relation, or is at least meant in this way (certainty-obligation), while this subject-object relation is rooted in a *subjectivism*, whose consequence is the most radical objectivism, we necessarily have to think of *justice* in a *double* perspective (according to the ambiguity of "life"):

a) "subjectively"—as "virtue,"
b) "objectively"—as appearance "of" life as such (δίκη)

§79. Nietzsche's Question of a "Higher Justice"

The phrase already suggests that in question is a justice *different* from what one usually understands by the term, different not merely *by degree* but rather in kind. [170]

This "higher justice" is nothing less than the root and ground [*Wurzelgrund*] of the *"plastic* powers" of human life and of life generally (which is to say that historiology is also rooted in this higher justice and that holds especially for the threefold, genuine historiology!).

But justice always stands in an *essential relation with truth* (objectivity). It is not quite clear yet what this means and how it fits in with the preceding argument.

Previously (up to the characterization of the structure of section VI) we tried to clarify *in what the understanding of truth as objectivity is grounded*. This modern understanding of truth; not as historical "excursus," but as historial meditation on ourselves.

But with this we have not yet expounded what Nietzsche himself explicitly thought about truth (at this time and in his fully developed philosophy).

Therefore, in order to understand "higher justice" as the *root of truth*, and as the root and ground of life as such, and consequently to understand the relation between life and truth (life and historiology), the following becomes necessary:

1. A preliminary characterization of justice *as such* and of "higher justice" (by following the structure of section VI),
2. A delineation of Nietzsche's understanding of truth and of *its origin*. (A short account of the essay: "On Truth and Lie in an Extramoral Sense" (vol. 10). It is only thus that we will be sufficiently prepared for a more independent reflection (cf. §83).

    Following this first, intermediate examination of "objectivity" and "truth," we will attempt to gain an overview of the structure of section VI. However, a true understanding of the essential subject matter of this section will only be possible through the more independent reflection on Nietzsche's thought of justice that follows. We have already dealt in detail with section I (cf. §77). [171]
3. *The description of justice as "virtue"* (cf. §82).
    a) Justice is the *fundamental virtue*, the "unfathomable sea, in which all virtues flow together"; *therefore*: the "rarest," even an "impossible" virtue (third paragraph: "severe and terrifying").

b) *The just*—the "most venerable exemplar of the human species," the *most human* since it consumes itself, tragically, with respect to *one impossible virtue*; its "dreadful profession" (seventh paragraph) only assigned to the few [*die Einzelnen*] and the rarest [*die Seltensten*] among them.

c) Truth and justice; justice as the "root" of truth; the "noblest core" of the so-called drive to truth [*Wahrheitstrieb*].
Truth
i. as the mere correctness of a mere taking notice and registering (calculation of and with the present-at-hand, and of whether something "results from it" (for "life" or not?)).
ii. as *judge* (the authority to *move* boundaries; new limits, new areas).

d. Justice as the *power of judgment* (not only the "wish" and will to be just, but the *faculty* of an *originary act of judgment*, that is, legislation, and not the mere *application* of what is valid. The ambiguity of judging:
i. Application of laws, preservation of rights;
ii. *Establishing the law.*

4. *The contemporary and traditional representation of "justice"* is clearly realized and particularly visible in the idea of "historical mastery" [*historisches Virtuosentum*]. The ability to empathize with everything; to understand everything, a comparing rendering everything equal with everything else: an *"echoing passivum."* Far removed from the *"severe" and "terrifying" virtue of true justice*. Particular degrees of the common idea of "justice"; (but genuine justice is not gradually but infinitely different from this, whose frequent possession as a virtue corresponds to its effortlessness). [172]

Magnanimity (already scarce) added to this *strength* (superiority, that is to say, strength in relation to *oneself and others*).

Tolerance (connivance), but still holding oneself out into . . .; transition between magnanimity and mere acceptance.

Acceptance (weakness) [*Geltenlassen*] (to participate).

Embellishing (the equalizing self-adjustment without harsh accents; seeking to please everyone and therefore providing something pleasurable to everyone).

Mere indolence (inertia) and cowardice: the "avoidance" of any decision as a simultaneous affirmation of everything, and above all of all that is already valid, is *impropriety* [*Unwesen*], the most extreme opposite of genuine *justice*; therefore not *in-justice* (which itself belongs to the *essence* of justice as denying the *impropriety* of justice).

It might seem as if acceptance is the most genuine access to that which is—a letting-be of beings, of what and how they are—, but letting-be is ambiguous:

§79. Nietzsche's Question of a "Higher Justice"

a. as letting oneself go within what is commonly and presently available,

b. *as letting-originate the essence of being,* within which every being as such first comes into the realm of a decision (cf. *The Essence of Truth,* 1930).[3]

5. *The essence of objectivity* (cf. 6) in its highest sense still implies an act of the imagination.

The highest objectivity is artistic, and therefore the relation to the work of art, whereby the latter is understood aesthetically and this in the sense of "disinterested intuition." To put-in-front-of-oneself, to re-present the object in-itself, without adding anything: *pure receptive apparatus* (whereas in the relation to the work of art we find the *highest interest*! *In what?* Certainly not in enjoyment! (*stimulans*)). Here Nietzsche, as he always will, misunderstands *Kant's doctrine* in the wake of Schopenhauer! For Kant, "disinterest" does not mean being indifferent, but keeping oneself aloof from any hasty [173] setting of purposes and any *general* conceptual *determination*! (cf. "Exercises on Kant's *Critique of Judgment*").[4]

6. True artistic forming as *unfolding and continuation of poetizing* [als Aus- und Weiterdichten], *as self-enacting creation* [selbsttätiges Schaffen].

Art against *cognition* as a pure gazing, and art against *justice* in its impropriety. Acceptance.

"Artistic" and "historical" (in the bad sense of the word) truth; cf. already Aristotle's *Poetics*: poetry as "truer" than "historiology": καὶ φιλοσοφώτερον καὶ σπουδαιότερον ποίησις ἱστορίας ἐστίν (*Poetics* 1451.b.3).

(More knowing *with regard to the essence and Being* of beings, and "more earnest," more concentrated, that is, *more decisive;* "the permanent"! What is higher.)

Cognition of law (science of nature) and creation of symbols (historical human sciences) (cf. *"art"* and *"culture"*).

Aristotle refers to the *naming* of poetry as ποίησις! (the *free composition*!): ἀλλὰ τοῦτο διαφέρει, τὸν μὲν τὰ γενόμενα λέγειν, τὸν δὲ οἷα ἂν γένοιτο (*Poetics* 1451.b.2).

a) to document and to retrace what has happened and has come to pass;

b) make visible (freely) *inner possibility and essence.*

---

3. Martin Heidegger, *Gestamtausgabe,* vol. 9, *Wegmarken,* "Vom Wesen der Wahrheit," 177–202; "On the Essence of Truth," trans. John Sallis in *Pathmarks,* ed. William McNeill (Cambridge: Cambridge University Press, 1998), 136–154.

4. Martin Heidegger, *Gestamtausgabe,* vol. 84.1, "Seminare: Kant–Leibniz–Schiller," ed. Günther Neumann, (Frankfurt am Main: Klostermann, 2013).

7. True objectivity (artistic) and *false* objectivity (that one is not concerned by something). The flaunting of a calmness that is nothing but boredom and emptiness; *passivity* rather than a force gathered and retained [*gebändigt und verhalten*].

    The tremendous profession of the just (cf. 3). *The standing aloof!* But how? *Having arrived later is no guarantee for standing higher and above matters*, "youth" as youth is not yet a proof of truth.
8. Like can be recognized only by like—τοῖς ὁμοίοις τὰ ὅμοια γιγνώσκεσται the great only by the great, for the great is the capacity of *becoming greater*; the small, in contrast, the compulsion to make everything smaller. (*Science* is neither something great nor small). [174] The ability to say what is known to all as something unheard of (cf. the lectures on Schelling).[5] *Simplicity*.

    And yet no contempt of *the carters and handymen* (the mere historians and thinkers of history [*Historiker und Geschichtsdenker*]).
9. The past can be understood only through the perspective of the master builders of the future and of those who know the present. *Only the one who builds can be judge*, as he is entrusted with establishing a measure (critical and monumental historiology). *Leaving to mature* (and with this seed and growth, origin and terrain), rather than domineering what is still callow.

    The hundred-strong group [*Hundertschaft*].

    To mature—to grow up into the ownmost necessity of decision making and into its knowing mastery.

* * *

Nietzsche is circling here around the essence of justice, with an assured intuition of it, but this more from opposing its impropriety than by attempting to achieve a genuine comprehension of it; and this notwithstanding the fact that in the context of his reflection on the nature of philosophy at this time he comes to see these matters more clearly than he seems to in section VI.

Here already it becomes clear that justice, although introduced as a virtue, is not thought so much in "moral" terms as in the sense of a fundamental ability to posit goals, boundaries, and standards; for this reason justice cannot be judged through *"morality" in the ordinary sense*.

---

5. Martin Heidegger, *Gesamtausgabe*, vol. 42, *Schelling: Vom Wesen der menschlichen Freiheit (1809)*, ed. Ingrid Schüßler (Frankfurt am Main: Klostermann, 1988), 137–141; *Schelling's Treatise on the Essence of Human Freedom*, trans. Joan Stambaugh (Athens: Ohio University Press, 1984).

Nietzsche's concept of morality:

1) *Broader* than its usual conception. *He understands this term as any kind of positing of an "ideal."* "Ideal"—something desirable, an *organizing point of view, "perspective."* Nietzsche, the immoralist, as the bringer of a new morality. This conception reaches so far that he grounds all positing of ideals as a positing of ideas on *morality*, therefore [175] also *metaphysics* ("morally"—"biologically"), insofar as the latter posits what goes *beyond the sensible* as fundamental in one way or another.

2) Often Nietzsche understands by "morality" the narrower idea of Christian morality in the sense of a doctrine of a denial and repudiation of life, wherein this world is seen only as a passage to the afterlife, "a valley of tears."

"*Extramoral*" = Beyond good and evil = beyond Christian morality. But precisely for this reason a new *creation of values*, yet this time for the intensification of life.

Justice—truth *in the extramoral sense*, that is, from the position of an intensification of life and of its utility for life. The relation between morality and metaphysics (cf. 3.c).

§80. Morality and Metaphysics

Because Nietzsche thinks in a modern way, that is, "*subjectively*," he believes that morality is the ground of any metaphysics. Nietzsche begins with the subjective evaluation and positing of ideals, and he does not see that at its root lies an interpretation of being, namely the *metaphysical* interpretation in general (beingness as a priori). This is because an ideal—whatever it may be—can first be posited, can first reach *the dimension of such positing*, when something like "ideas," when something like *being as beingness* has been posited as the πρότερον. But *this* position derives from a fundamental interpretation of beings as such, from a fundamental experience of being and truth; and what is this? Being itself or merely human wishing! ἰδέα—ideal; but ἀγαθόν as ἐπέκεινα! *Precisely in this* lies the moralization of metaphysics, why? Beingness → Beings—*non-being* [*Un-seiendes*]. This is why Nietzsche can never move toward an *overcoming* of metaphysics—not only because he fails to see the preconditions and the originary, preliminary questions for such an undertaking, but above all because he has to presume that with the inversion of morality, and with his reclamation of the extramoral, *metaphysics* has already been *overcome*; whereas he is, on the contrary, ultimately so ensnarled in the groundlessness of [176] modern metaphysics that he simply takes over the originary metaphysics of the Greeks in its coarsest form (becoming—being) without any reflection and hesitation.

§81. Justice—Truth—Objectivity—Life

The significance of the thought of "justice" shows itself in Nietzsche's thought very early on, and one can see here the relation to Heraclitus, which is to say: "justice" is thought not "morally" in its Christian sense, nor juridically, but from a "vital," "metaphysical" perspective; and it is precisely in this more profound account that we can find the essential *limit* of Nietzsche's thinking (cf. §82): "justice" as "virtue." It is only very slowly, in progressively disentangling himself from his ties to Wagner, Schopenhauer, philology, and science, and generally by abandoning the precipitate, youthful hopes of a *cultural renewal* by means of Wagnerian art, that Nietzsche arrives at greater clarity concerning the essence of justice. And yet this clarity reaches only as far as the *fundamental metaphysical position* that Nietzsche always maintains. Insofar as this—in spite of everything—remains dependent on a *historical tradition* that remains unmastered in the higher sense of a critique, the thought of justice is *merely* built into the metaphysics "of life," and into the determination of beings as "living." "Life" here retains the determining role in accounting for beings as such. Being is "becoming," and even though justice is brought into an essential relation to "life," from out of itself "justice" as such never suffices for the determination of beingness in its essence, nor for the destruction of the metaphysical determination of beings as such, nor for the sublation of our fundamental experience of "life," in order to force on us the necessity of an essentially *different* experience.

The necessary consequence of this is that Nietzsche, here and later on, understands "justice" from the position of the human being [177] (human *life*), just as early on—despite his metaphysical, Heraclitean insight—he conceives it as "virtue," albeit as a non-Christian and anti-Christian virtue: "justice" shares an essential ambiguity with the fundamental concept of "life." (Not here meant in the sense of the difference between essence and un-essence).

§82. Justice as "Virtue"

"Virtue" appears here as a higher and broader determination incorporating the essence of justice.

§82. Justice as "Virtue" 147

But: Nietzsche's interpretation of the essence of justice leads precisely to another conception of "virtue" in general, or rather, the latter changes in step with this development, that is, with the "critique" of morality; according to the latter "virtue" and its essence are derived from "justice."

Virtue — aptitude, efficiency—ἀρετή, for example, ἀρετή κλέπτον—*the proficiency of the thief.*

ἀρετή: τελείωσίς τις; ἕξις—προαίρεσις;
στοχαστικὴ τὸ μέσον (πρός ἡμᾶς).
σπουδαῖον ποιεῖ. ἄριστον. (*Nichomachean Ethics*).
solemn—stern—*concentrated*

virtus: *perfectio; bonitas;*
bonum et laudabile in humanitas actibus et passionibus dispositio perfecti ad optimum. "Ideal" is not a "disposition" (propensity, inclination), but an anticipatory composure.

virtus: *bonum reddit actum humanum et ipsum hominem bonum facit.*

bonum: habens *completum ordinem ad summum finem summus* finis: Deus.

Virtue:
1. Moral, that is, related to a pregiven "ideal" and its purpose and ground. Faculty of keeping hold of and realizing such "ideals." [178]
   Christian "subordination"—"sancta simplicitas."
   The greatest *vice* [*Untugend*]: "pride."
   Evil: rebellion, self-"righteousness" [*Selbst-"gerechtigkeit"*].
   the "Good": integration into the order of things.
2. In the sense of an aptitude to posit a measure [*Maßsetzung*]; extramorally. This does not overcome the moral virtue in favor of an immoral virtue, but rather: *Beyond Good and Evil* (1886). This is not to speak, against what is often assumed, of the naked, dissociated arbitrariness of accidental moods and drives, pretensions, and whims, but conversely of *the highest commitment to an originary legislation*; a decision in favor of commitments that cannot be calculated according to the advantage and interest of individuals or even of groups, and which therefore cannot be justified by invoking the endorsement they might offer. This means: not seeking shelter in a pregiven ideal; beyond good and evil; outside of, but therefore already within the still-to-be-established realm of decisions concerning "good and bad" ("bad"—not apt for a furthering of life). Yet this in relation to "life."

To believe that *life* would be justified in its mere enjoyment as if one needed only to take one's foot off the brake holding back the pressure of the directly present and simply be given "life" and "lived experience"; this, against what many among his supposed "apostles" hold, is not what Nietzsche intended.

Certainly, from another perspective: Nietzsche himself did not manage to advance toward the highest legislation and is easily misinterpreted; the "beast of prey" because he remained captive to the metaphysics of "life"; and his "thought" of *justice* comprises the highest *effort* to accomplish a *new legislation*, but this within the *old domain* ("life"—justice as the highest representative of life itself!). Nietzsche has failed sufficiently to question the fundamental presuppositions of morality as such—"metaphysics," which is to say, the determination of beings as such and in general, of truth, of the human being. [179]

§83. Justice—Truth

Nietzsche thinks "justice" in an essential connection with "truth"; but he was unable to move the question of truth beyond its essentially limited treatment as wholly bound to judgment and cognition ("logic"), unable to *problematize* in a sufficiently determinate fashion the essential nexus, even the essential unity of truth and justice, to say nothing about the absence of any insight into the essential relation between truth and being, or about the absence of a reflection on "justice" from the horizon of the *question of being*. The "absence" of these questions is not a "mistake," for Nietzsche still thinks wholly metaphysically and performs even with *respect to "justice"* an equally crude and uncritical step backward into the beginning of Western thought as he does with respect to the distinction between being and becoming.

Here we will attempt to get Nietzsche's determination of the essence of justice into view from, so to speak, the outside, by means of contrasting it with the traditional conception; in this way its essential origin will become clear, as will the way it belongs to the fundamental determinations of his metaphysics (life—truth), without it being necessary to expose in detail this metaphysics before we start; on the contrary, *this* reflection on *Nietzsche's* conception of justice is for us a way to understand his fundamental metaphysical position.

1. *The literal sense of the word "justice"* [Gerechtigkeit]—that which is right, just, *rectus*; the right is that which is "straight" and "direct," fitting, suitable; to make something "bite-sized," so that everyone can *consume* it; "to be straight in *any* saddle [*in alle Sättel gerecht*]," that is to say, at ease, *integrating* oneself, able to assimilate; "up-right"—*corresponding* to an upward direction.

   In what is "right" and "just" [*im "rechten" und "Gerechten"*] the relation to standards and goals, in the sense that something is *suit-*

§83. Justice—Truth

able or adequate or adapted to something else (thus: measure and jointure [*Maß und Fug*] are given in *advance*).

2. "Just": a) what corresponds to the measure, the rule, the law. [180]
    b) to do *this* and to fix and judge and demand and to insist on its realization, to decide *according to* the law, *judging* and *appraising*.

Justice: the attitude and ethos of such judging:
1) Justice in the (juridical) sense of legislation (legality).
2) Justice in the moral sense (the moral law), in *a guiding role* (morality).
Generally: to let each have *his due*, to apportion what is due to each, adjustment, *equitableness*.

| Everyone! *quisque!* | Taking demands into consideration, but this according to the guiding thread of adjustment: *equal rights for all*, because *all are equal before the law*; interpreted in the Christian, moral sense: everyone is equal before God—infinitely different: |

"Ratio vero iustitiae consistit in hoc quod alteri reddatur quod ei debetur secundum aequalitatem." (Thomas Aquinas, *Summa Theologica* 2–2, question 80 article 1.)

Justice: the power of adjusting, of allocating according to the law, according to the supposition that all *are equal*. "Virtue."

Yet at the same time, *justice* is thought metaphysically (cf. Aristotle, *Nicomachean Ethics* 1) as the *rectitudo ordinis* in the faculties of the human being—subordination of those lower under those higher up; hierarchy.

Christian: the subordination of the body to the soul, soul to spirit, spirit to God; eternal salvation—the *hereafter. Negation of the here and now—the worldly.* Renunciation of "life"; difference between "Life" and "living" [*das "Leben" und "Leben" verschieden*].

This is already Nietzsche's interpretation. From it, that is, from his critique of morality as such (the primacy of the supersensible over the sensible), his wholly different conception of justice becomes *intelligible*. [181]

From this perspective, justice as previously characterized is the impropriety of justice, the power of passing judgment from a tribunal stool opposite the *accused*. Yet at the same time authorizing, doing justice to all, equalization, *leveling, destruction of all hierarchy*.

3. *Nietzsche's Conception of Justice.*

This will be clarified with reference to a few central passages from that time in which the new essence of justice impressed itself most clearly on him. This is the time of *Zarathustra* and the transition to the preparation of his planned, major work (1882–1885). These are not mere "quotations," for Nietzsche himself only spoke about "justice" in such sentences (the *"last* virtue," now discovered for the first time):

"Justice as a constructing, eliminative, destructive way of thinking, from out of value judgements: *the highest representative of life itself"* (vol. 13, p. 42 [1884]).⁶

Justice—"a way of thinking from out of value judgments." Pronouncing value judgments, appraising values in relation to each other, preferring some, rejecting others. Positing values as conditions of life (intensification of life).

"A way of thinking"—which sets *conditions* for life itself, conditions according to which it can be the highest and most complete life; representing, setting up those conditions of "life" in the sense of an augmentation of life, *"constructing"*—therefore:

a) Not appraising something present-at-hand and approving and confirming its right after the fact, but bringing "life" to its high point. *Erecting* this high point first of all, by "deeper" conditions being posited for it.

b) Not valuing from a present, valid system of values. *"Eliminating"*—that which constrains life and denounces life; in such eliminating the most decisive of the new conditions must be kept pure and free. [182]

"Destructive"—*no longer letting be a condition*, eliminating that which drags life down beneath itself and makes it flat.

The *constructing*—destructive positing-of-value; "judging"—κρινεῖν.

This *"thinking"*—in which *life* presents *itself* in its highest vivacity; not as "substitute" or "façade," only exposing its surface, but within it life itself appears and *is* in its highest essence, because "life" is a *living-beyond-itself, the disquiet of a constant outstripping of itself,* not the mere flowing and And so on. Life in itself judges, builds, destroys.

Here always together: justice:
1) "a way of thinking," that is, *human life;*
2) *representative*—"life itself" (beings as a whole).

Life—"will to power"—wanting-to-go-beyond-oneself as an overpowering of oneself.

A second, nearly contemporaneous passage characterizes this "way of thinking" and therefore "life itself" even more clearly according to the perspective from which Nietzsche understands

---

6. Friedrich Nietzsche, *Nietzsches Werke* (Großoktavausgabe), vol. 13, "Unveröffentlichtes aus der Umwertungszeit" (1882/83–1888) (Leipzig: Naumann, 1903).

"life" generally. Here emerges, at the same time, the beginning of an insight into the essential relation between justice and truth (*perspective—horizon*):

"*Justice*, as a function of a farsighted power able to look beyond the narrow perspectives of good and evil, and that therefore has a wider horizon of *advantage*—the intention of preserving something that is more than this or that person" (vol. 14, p. 80 [1885]; Between Zarathustra 3 and 4).[7]

"A farsighted power": that which judges; wider horizon, that is to say, one that goes beyond the perspectives of good and evil, that is, of Christian morality and its desirables (all variants of socialism are variations of Christianity). To move furthest out toward something, which is ahead of and an *advantage* for all. [183] Aiming to preserve the intensification of life as such. The positing of *its* conditions; no "skewed perspectives" [*Winkel-Perspektiven*] (vol. XIV, p. 385). An all-surpassing looking ahead toward what is superior to all the little advantages and disadvantages and personal fortunes and plans; therefore precisely not an adjustment of what is present-at-hand, but a pre-scription of what towers above everything and therefore a disregarding of any minor benefit. Justice "as function," the *executive* of this power is the actual *overpowering itself*. Therefore the *fundamental condition of justice*: "*Prudence derived from broad insight*" (vol. XIV, p. 386 [1885]).

Profound knowledge and an *ability to evaluate* are therefore essential; and these *without regard* for what is already available, valid, and valued; creating *the horizon* in an essential *sense*, not *negotiating skills* and ownership of. . . , but a leaping *over* toward what is *still-to-be-evaluated* and only thus a true affirmation of and affective bond to that which is.

Not a mere arbitrariness and recklessness, but *love*, yet not the love that blinds, but the love which always was and remains in possession of a keen eye. This decisive character of justice as knowing and insight is best and most simply expressed in a word from *Thus Spoke Zarathustra*! 1 "Of the Adder's Bite" (1882–1883): "Tell me, where is the justice which is love with seeing eyes to be found?" (94)

Justice is love—and love? (The will that the loved *be* what it essentially is and can be). φιλοσοφία—"love of wisdom"!

---

7. Ibid.

But justice is love with *seeing* eyes. The seeing of what the loved one has to be, so that it may be what and how it *is* in its essence.

Justice is this knowing donation in advance of essence, of that within which alone something can be essential.

Justice only donates. She cannot receive or accept anything, because she always looks ahead of herself, [184] looks beyond any kind of possession and fulfillment and repose and stasis within the self, beyond any rigidification of oneself.

Insofar as "lovers" search in a certain sense only for the latter, justice is for them an unsolvable riddle, if not even anathema.

"Those who are truly just cannot receive anything: they give everything back. It is for this reason that they are anathema to the lovers" (vol. XII, p. 291; *Sprüche und Sentenzen* [1882–1884]).

Therefore Nietzsche sees the danger of *in-justice*, of the cordoning off of a horizon, of rigidification and solidification, wherever something comes to rest, to a stand, finds a foothold and seeks support. Therefore:

"In veneration there is more of the unjust than even in contempt" (vol. XII, p. 297).

This is because contempt has to move on and has to dare to enter into the open in order to posit a new and higher value. Veneration (the danger of merely looking for protection and shelter).

An earlier remark from the time when the essence of justice first becomes clearer to Nietzsche goes in this direction. (cf. *Human, All too Human*, vol. I, no. 636 [1878]; vol. II, p. 411).[8]

Here justice is understood as a genuine form of "genius," next to the philosophical, political, and artistic: justice is "an enemy of convictions" (cf. *Human, All too Human*, f. no. 637; "Opinions grow out of *passions*; *inertia of the spirit* lets them stiffen into *convictions*," vol. II, p. 412. This as a stolid abidance in a presumptuous questionlessness of everything essential.).

Justice is the free, anticipatory, and offensive fore-sight and the seeing pre-scription of decisive "values."

The opposite of justice—in-justice—is not an improper and disproportionate distribution, preferring this and [185] rejecting that, but the *evasion* of this anticipatory and offensive positing, *cowardice* (cf. vol. XII, p. 290)

---

8. Friedrich Nietzsche, *Nietzsches Werke* (Großoktavausgabe), vol. 2, *Menschliches, Allzumenschliches* (Stuttgart: Kröner, 1921). *Human, All Too Human*, trans. Reginald John Hollingdale, (Cambridge: Cambridge University Press, 1986).

§83. Justice—Truth

Acceptance of everything and apportioning justice to all, each to their own in the sense of everyone receiving the same, everyone being equal!

Therefore, in Nietzsche's thinking, the opposite of justice is the customary *concept of justice*, which for Nietzsche does not contain the essence but *the counteressence* of justice, and which, therefore, cannot be "the highest representative of life," insofar as justice in the essential sense *directs and commands* life into its orders of rank.

In fact, justice—adhered to in its counteressence—brings about chaos in the sense of a confusion of all orders, *mishmash*. From here we can understand another sentence, which first of all might sound uncanny, as it does not make clear on its own terms how the word *justice* is to be understood within it. This sentence clearly attempts to let the word *justice* shine in the ambiguity of its essence and counteressence:

"Giving to each what he is due: this would be to seek justice while attaining chaos" (vol. XII, p. 291 [1882–1884]).

Suum cuique—that is the guiding idea of justice, and it also contains something pertinent for the *essential* concept of justice, as long as everyone is not equated with everyone else; but at the same time, merely apportioning in the sense of binding oneself to pregiven claims, of being considerate with respect to all and everyone, becomes the counteressence of justice, a renunciation of looking further ahead toward *the* advantage that is forbidden from taking individual fortunes into consideration.

The *truly just*, that is, the one who posits values and laws, rather acts according to the maxim: I give to each what is mine; that which is mine, that is, that which has to be posited ahead of everything, in whose horizon *each individual* can first of all accede to his *proper* determinability, with his *proper* entitlements. But this *justice* is not "self-righteousness," is not a hardening into *one's convictions*, but a being resolved to decide [186] and, that is, to every coming moment of the necessity of a new *judgment*; there is here no pretension to have settled all accounts once and for all.

Any belief that reward and punishment lie already in the consequences of a deed are based in the predominance of the thought of *justice* (in its counteressence) as apportioning of reward and punishment.

Of this idea Nietzsche says (vol. XIII, p. 315 [1884]): "that reward and punishment are already lying in the consequences of our actions—this thought of an immanent justice is fundamentally wrong. . . . *All* kinds of such ideas about "immanent justice," "the order of salvation," reconciliatory "transcendental judgement," are today circulating in *every* head,—they contribute to the *chaos* of the modern soul."

Nietzsche wants to say: everyone and every group and every party sees in the adverse consequences of the actions of an adversary a punishment and a confirmation of its injustice, while seeing in the beneficial consequences and successes of one's *own* actions a form of recompense and that reconciliatory justice ("providence") has proved one right—a form of thinking that, according to Nietzsche, is rather lacking in "nobility." This is chaos in the sense of disorder, for it is always possible that what is essential and great appears in its "consequences" as the adverse (the downfall). Everything great perishes, that which is small remains forever.

Nietzsche here demonstrates at the same time that he ought not be counted amongst those who take something for justified and true on account of its "success" and its benefits. But the essence of justice first becomes visible in its relationship with truth.

4. *Justice and Truth*

Nietzsche's conception of justice does not arise from a "philosophy of right" or a "moral philosophy," but rather from the question of *truth* and its connection with "life"; from the very beginning the question of truth itself becomes, for Nietzsche, that of the [187] relation between *art and knowledge* (science) and their "significance" for "life." (cf. "Exercises," summer term 1937[9]).

In this, Nietzsche understands *truth* from the outset in the sense of the tradition of metaphysical thought as a determination of *knowledge*, of the "intellect," of judgment, λόγος—"logical." He understood the "logical," however, as a manifestation of life and his questioning turned toward its relation to life, so much so that he thought he had encountered the essence of truth in accounting for this relationship. What we have not yet seen, though we have had an indication of it, is how this question of truth, as the question of the relation of the intellect to "life," should have led Nietzsche toward *justice*.

For the following clarification of the relation between justice and truth, and for the concomitant essential determination of both, we need to remember two guiding thoughts that have emerged from the characterization of justice so far:

---

9. Martin Heidegger, *Gestamtausgabe*, vol. 87, "Nietzsches metaphysische Grundstellung (Sein und Schein)," ed. Peter von Ruckteschell, (Frankfurt am Main: Klostermann, 2004).

§83. Justice—Truth

1) Justice is the positing of the widest horizon emerging *from* evaluating life and *for* life.
2) *Justice* is the root of the will to truth.

But first we require a brief presentation of Nietzsche's concept of truth; and this will, in a way corresponding to our presentation of justice, take into account Nietzsche's thinking at the time of the *Untimely Meditations* as well as in the period when he was dedicating himself to his major work.

From the period of the *Untimely Meditations*, we find in the posthumous work a treatise with the title "On Truth and Lie in an Extramoral Sense" (vol. X, p. 189ff., [Summer 1873]). For Nietzsche's notion of truth at the time of the *Will to Power*, compare the Lectures 1936–1937,[10] exercise 37.[11] [188]

This brief presentation needs to be organized so as to clarify how and in what way Nietzsche is led to *justice* through the question of truth.

Two guiding statements concerning Nietzsche's conception of truth (cf. §89, pp. 192–193):

1) From *Zarathustra* vol. II (1883), summer, following a disappointing stay in Rome, "for the poet of the Zarathustra the most indecent place on earth."

"Of the Priests": "their folly taught that truth is proved by blood. But blood is the worst witness of truth" (Z 116) (in the sense of a*n intensification and transfiguration* of life).

2) *Will to Power*, vol. XVI, p. 19, no. 493 [1885]: "*Truth is that kind of error* without which a certain living species [the human being] could not exist. The value for life is ultimately decisive." "A belief can be a condition of life and *nonetheless* be *false*" (vol. XVI, p. 12, no. 483 [1885]).

However, this doctrine concerning truth should in no case be associated with a coarse and cheap American pragmatism, even if this is derived from Nietzsche—from a misunderstood Nietzsche.

---

10. Martin Heidegger, *Gesamtausgabe*, vol. 43, *Nietzsche: Der Wille zur Macht als Kunst*, ed. Bernd Heimbüchel (Frankfurt am Main: Klostermann, 1984).
11. Martin Heidegger, "Nietzsches metaphysische Grundstellung (Sein und Schein)."

§84. Truth and Art (cf. Lecture)[12]
(Cognition)

Will to Power, vol. XVI, p. 248, no. 822 [1888]: "We possess *art*, lest we perish *of the truth.*"

"That art is *worth more* than the truth" (vol. XVI, p. 273, no. 853, IV, [1887–1888]).

"But truth does not count as the highest measure of value, even less as the highest power. The will to semblance, to illusion, [189] to delusion, to becoming and change (an objectivated delusion) here counts as a deeper, as more originary, 'more metaphysical' as the will to truth, to reality, to being:—the latter is itself nothing but a form of the will to illusion" (vol. XVI, p. 272–273, no. 853, 3).

§85. On Nietzsche's Treatise "On Truth and Lie" in an Extramoral Sense" (vol. X, p. 189 ff.)

1. How does the will to truth arise from the will to justice (in its impropriety)?
2. What is Truth? Obligation—Validity.
3. Scientific Cognition—*one kind* of illusion.
4. The relation to "life"—"*art.*"

§86. Truth and "Intellect"—Justice

1. The intellect as a means of preserving the individual. The intellect deceives itself (why? on account of its flexibility?) about itself and therefore about life.

    "Dis-simulation" [*Ver-stellung*]—pretense—deception—theater play—fluttering around the flame of vanity.

2. How does—in the intellect—a *pure will* to *truth* arise?

    The human being—thought as a single individual!—*can*not (from an external necessity) and does not want, for fear of boredom (from an internal necessity), to be on its own. It therefore has to come to terms with others, to achieve mutual understanding, to come to agreement on *obligations*, validity.

---

12. Martin Heidegger, *Gesamtausgabe*, vol. 43, *Nietzsche: Der Wille zur Macht als Kunst*.

3. Truth—in advance! For that reason *thought* as bindingness and *universal validity* (Schopenhauer-Kant!)?
    Truth—*preserving the status quo of communal, social life*.
4. Here already—though still in the form of its impropriety, of acceptance—*justice* is the root of *truth*. [190]
5. How this thought is then grasped in an essentially deeper sense:
    a) From the position of justice—broadening of the horizon—positing.
    b) Truth as the *fixation* of a "perspective."
    (cf. sec. VI, §88)

* * *

The guiding principles characterizing Nietzsche's fundamental position:
1. The human being as *"subject"*
   in the sense of *the isolated consciousness in the form of an I, on the basis and on the back of animality*. Animality is what supports and envelops. *Human life*, and this again in the universe of life and of the cosmos.
2. Truth as universal *validity*,
   valid for the commonalty, the community. *Validity*, because obligatory; *obligatory*, because *necessary* (useful) for the continued existence of the communal life of human beings. *Validity* not as an essential consequence of objectivity, but as the immediate consequence of the *subjectivity* of the "we" and the demand for a securing of togetherness.
3. Truth at the same time as *adequatio*.
   Adequation to beings; the question is whether this is possible or not. *Metaphor* as substitute, the one instead of the other. Enhancement, augmentation; protection.
4. According to 1–3 "language" is *construed* as *"tool,"*
   the interpretation of the "logical" is connected to this; compare later (Will to Power).
5. "Nature" as "life."
   The "real as such"; inaccessible and given only in "signs" and imaginations. (How can this "as such" be known?—in contrast the Kantian "thing-in-itself.") [191]

§87. Truth and "Intellect"

From where does the "intellect" gain "its importance"? Its imposing character derives from its ability to move "freely," from dis-simulation and de-ception *(imagin-ing)*, a variant and perversion of the "artistic force."

Nietzsche here still wavers between Schopenhauer and his own, proper questioning.

---

§88. Nietzsche's Conception of Truth
(Determined from the Ground up by Western Metaphysics)

1. Truth as that which is permanent—A *is* b—, (what has been fixed *against* becoming, life), as "being" (being as permanent presence: οὐσία / φύσις; the fixed.
2. Truth as obligatory (the fixed *for* human (animal) life). Obligation as universal validity, that which secures, *secure-certain*. Certainty → toward correctness → *correctness* → unconcealedness → ἀλήθεια → φύσις → ? (what fixes and grants permanence).
3. Truth as what has been *fixed against* life *for* human life (what rigidifying, solidifies and inhibits). Truth viewed wholly from the perspective of "life"; *the essential determinations* of obligation and surety (permanence), no longer conceived in their re-presenting–reproductive relation to "beings" as such, *no longer correctness and even unconcealedness*, but solely as *belonging to life and being in accordance with life* (life as intensification of life, usefulness).

   But insofar as "life" = "becoming," all *truth* as *stability* and rigidity is semblance and "error." "Error"—not *incorrect, false*, but in the sense of what is adverse to life, what *inhibits becoming*, and yet what is adverse to life *is still required by "life."*
4. *Justice as the constant liberation from truth* in the service of the enhancement of life. [192]

---

§89. Justice and Truth (cf. above pp. 187–188)

Truth is a kind *of error* required by the human being (as a living species); does this determination of truth as error presuppose the idea of an *adaequatio*? (cf. below, pp. 92–93). An error, insofar as that which endures is taken to be exemplary for beings, whereas it is only semblance, insofar as becoming is the "real."

But the complete and outright surrender of life to becoming would not only make life *un-stable* in the sense of continual change, but would make it lack any stability at all. *The fixation by means of the fixed is necessary, but so is the overcoming of rigidification.*

§89. Justice and Truth

Justice is more originary than truth, for it *adjusts* itself to life—which desires, as a constant becoming, to go beyond itself—and it *adjusts* itself by intensifying and transfiguring life as it has been fixed at any given time, by means of a new setting of goals.

Justice is *suited to life* in the sense that it is compliant with life, in that it is the *judge*, the legislator of life, pro-jecting a wider and the widest horizon onto life. Therefore within life there is a constant struggle *concerning standards*.

* * *

With "blood" (Nietzsche here thinks of the martyrs) one proves something that has been fixed and made final, arresting life, cutting it off from new possibilities, and thus one can only prove what truth itself is: "error" and semblance; and therefore blood is the worst witness of what actually "*is*," namely becoming for *the* truth, from which Nietzsche knows himself to be *banished* as "only a fool, only a poet."

Truth as "error"; thought in this way it means: truth is un-truth. But then how are we to understand the truth that is *denied by the "un-"*? Is this again the old *adequatio*, commensurate to the real, to that which is in the proper sense, here to *becoming*! which adequation is only possible in art by means [193] of "transfiguration," which is neither adequation nor "truth" as correctness.

Nietzsche's conception of truth is—with regard to the inversion of metaphysics (that is, the twisting out of it) enacted by him—also merely an inversion, that is, the ultimate taking over of the metaphysical conception of truth as the correctness of representations. For this does not mean that truth conceived as error is un-truth in the sense of a deviation from truth (correctness), that is, from *error*. In the end, it does not have to deviate from error, but rather has to *be it*. Error means incorrectness and therefore signifies *rigidification*: *restriction of life*. The true as that which is rigid *has* to be *incorrect*—when measured against becoming, but this in-correctness as a lack is the advantage of *what is rigid*.

Nevertheless, Nietzsche does not understand the "erroneous" nature of truth as a mere noncorrespondence, as incorrectness, but as the *rigidification of becoming*. Not only an inappropriate reproduction, but a constraining *intervention* into becoming in the sense of a *rigidification*, and this as permanent existence is precisely "the true"; truth is "being" (permanence) in contradistinction to becoming; the "semblance" belonging to it! while Platonically speaking "becoming," is only a degraded reflection of "being" (ὄντως ὄν).

§90. Truth, and Science Conditioned by Worldview

Science as a true representing—cognition—is an *error* belonging to life.

Science, as setting the standards of objectivity, necessarily misses and masks what is objective in the sense of the real, that is, in the sense *of life*, and denies *becoming* to it.

The disadvantage is not *incorrectness*, that it is only ever a *perspective* and that it attains *objectivity* only on the basis of *certain presuppositions*, but rather that it generally and necessarily *fastens*; in fact, it is that this necessary fixation becomes rigidification and that the latter becomes the sole and unique standard. [194]

This conditioning of "science" by life and *for* life, as *Nietzsche* understands it, has nothing to do with the now-common petit-bourgeois demand for a science "close to life"; it is precisely *"close to life"* that science *cannot be* and that it *ought* not to be, because it cannot cozy up to "life," but rather has to build something constant into it; in this way it "serves" life. But if "life" is to *intensify* itself, that is, to be *life* according to the "natural" determinations of *hunger*, preservation, and excretion, then the relation to life has to have its source in prescientific relations. But science (historiology) itself—for the very reason that prevents it from instituting originary relations—is necessary in order to fix any project as realized at a given time, and to build it into "life." *Therefore* we have the Imperial Institute of Historical Research. The decision concerning the question of the essence and the limits of historiology is grounded in the understanding of "life" according to the ambiguity that we have pointed out (cf. below, N, "Life").

Therefore one *cannot* do justice to the essence of science by recognizing its presuppositions in each case, by contenting oneself with these, and by bringing to bear a new philistinism on this assumed shadowy realm. Doing justice to the essence of science is here only possible by means of experiencing a higher objectivity and by daring to assume the virtue of justice, and by recognizing that undiscovered and unexhausted horizons still remain to be torn open. That is, a science bound by worldview is as little allowed to invoke Nietzsche as is Catholic theology. The mere adoption of statements and demands from his writings amounts to a falsification of his thought.

In the play of the world (in the sense of beings as a whole) being and appearance are mixed together, that is, "truth" in Nietzsche's sense and "transfiguration" in Nietzsche's sense. *Stabilization* of life and its *elevation*. "Science" as a kind of securing of a continued existence (not as a *cognizing* of the real) is necessary *for* "life" (of the human being) on the basis of the *essence of life*. [195]

§91. Truth and Science

Truth as the securing of the continued existence of the present "horizon" of life is what first of all grants the directives for the essence of the sciences, and for Nietzsche, this means for their relation, as a kind of cognition, "to life."

"Proximity to life" is not at all decisive! But is that not exactly what Nietzsche demands of *historiology*?! Yes and no! Proximity to the *essence of life*, certainly, but *precisely not proximity* to what at any given time is customary, familiar and well established! Not what is immediately of use on the day, not what is intelligible to everyman, and no "solidarity with the people," no currying favor with everyday common sense and its standards.

Proximity to the *essence* of life, that is to say, indispensable to life, that is, *necessary* for life, to which belongs a horizon that is in each case fastened but never rigidified; this securing of the horizon is achieved by the sciences by means of their "rationality," by means of their *conceptuality*.

Only where there is constancy and at the same time the *ability to overcome* what is fixed can there be *becoming*. Life as self-intensifying demands "steps" and thus rigidity, constancy, not *dissolution* and sheer unraveling. Neither "close to life" nor "far away from life," but *essentially fitting* with respect to the *essence of life*!

For historiology *as a science* this means: historiology itself as a science cannot institute a relation to life as "becoming," though within the "natural" relation of "historiology" to life it is the necessary form of its development, consolidation, and of the granting of its continued existence.

§92. Historiology → Science → Truth—Justice

Nietzsche's doctrine of justice and truth is contained in one of Heraclitus's fragments.

Fragment 28: δοκέοντα γὰρ ὁ δοκιμώτατος γινώσκει, φυλάσσει [196] καὶ μέντοι καὶ Δίκη καταλήψεται ψευδῶν τέκτονας καὶ μάρτυρας. (Cf. summer semester 1939, lectures.[13])

---

13. Martin Heidegger, *Gesamtausgabe*, vol. 47, *Nietzsches Lehre vom Willen zur Macht als Erkenntnis*, ed. Eberhard Hanser (Frankfurt am Main: Klostermann, 1989).

For it is only the apparent that is understood (what shows itself at the moment, the appearing); this is recognized by the most famous (the one who appears more than most and enjoys the highest esteem), and he holds fast to it (takes it to be that which is solid). Yet verily justice will also know how to get hold of the carpenters and the witnesses of calculation (falsehoods) and (reifications) (it will get to grips with them from above and subject them to it, which is to say, it will overcome them).

It is *decisive that* Nietzsche *looked back* to Heraclitus in the first place and that he saw a connection between Δίκη and the δοκέοντα. This is not to say that Nietzsche simply gleaned his ideas from him; *between them lies*, of course, *the whole history of Western metaphysics*; nevertheless there is here (and this is also and still more obviously the case in the doctrine of "being" and "becoming") a characteristic looking back on Nietzsche's part of which he is quite aware; *Heraclitus—his* philosopher.

"Philosophy, in the only form that I myself can still accept it, as the most general form of historiology [!]: as the attempt somehow to describe Heraclitean becoming and to abbreviate it in signs (to *translate* and to mummify it, so to speak, into a sort of apparent being)" (vol. XIII, p. 23; [1885–1886]. Indeed, even the new setting of goals in Nietzsche's most proper philosophy is Heraclitean: *"the having turned out well* [*Wohlgeratenheit*] *of the human being,"* the "essence" of life (the admixture!) as being suitable, but not just for *any* form of *praxis*. To be sure, there are only indirect references, above all to fragment 2.

Nietzsche always and everywhere denies the possible possession of truth, because he, as much as any Scholastic, naively believes in truth as *adequatio*, and takes this, without fully or clearly being aware of it, to be the measure for anything that can be understood about truth in its essence. [197]

Only judging by this standard can he say that all truth, which means at once everything valid and binding, is an "error," a going-astray and a not-corresponding to the "becoming" that is taken to be authentic "being."

The naïve adoption of such a standard, the concomitant conception of truth as bindingness and the interpretation of being as "becoming" arise in particular from the fundamental experience of "life" as what is genuinely "actual," from the *ego vivo*; it is an appeal to what is taken for granted, and also to truth as *adequatio* (compare equally Kant's remark concerning this determination of truth and also *Mindfulness*, truth as clearing[14]).

---

14. Martin Heidegger, *Gesamtausgabe*, vol. 66, *Besinnung*, ed. Friedrich-Wilhelm von Herrmann (Frankfurt am Main: Klostermann 1997), 313–318; *Mindfulness*, trans. Parvis Emad and Thomas Kalary (London: Athlone, 2006).

§92. Historiology → Science → Truth—Justice

This extreme biological Cartesianism is thus also consistent enough to demand the necessity of the highest rationalization of science, instead of slipping and lapsing into a superficial "irrationalism" and supposed "anti-Cartesianism."

The intensity and continuity of Nietzsche's opposition to Descartes is then due to Nietzsche's judgment that Descartes is not yet sufficiently *Cartesian*, because he thinks subjectivism only from the superficial perspective of the "I" and not from the embodied life of the human being as *animal*. [199]

M. Nietzsche's Metaphysics

Elucidated from the verse:

"Welt-Spiel, das herrische,
Mischt Sein und Schein:—
Das Ewig-Närrische
Mischt *uns*—hinein!. . ."

"World game, the ruling force
Blends false and true
The eternally fooling force
Blends us in too!"

§93. Nietzsche's Metaphysics

Nietzsche's metaphysics interprets *beings as a whole* as life, the *human being* as animal (the thinking beast of prey) and truth as "justice."

Justice constitutes the horizon in going beyond what is, and thus grounds the possibility of a fixation that life as becoming needs, a fixation that is determined as "truth."

"Justice" is thus no longer a title for a "moral" property, and "truth" is no "epistemological" or "logical" property, but rather both name the essence of "truth" and of the just, that is, of *beings as a whole* and of the human being.

Justice and truth are metaphysical terms that, from the perspective of the basic words of metaphysics, can be named as "being" and "appearance," but this depends on grasping the full content and amplitude [*Schwingungsweite*] of these metaphysical concepts.

Nietzsche's metaphysics is said in the simplest way possible in the following verse:

> World game, the ruling force
> Blends being and appearance
> The eternally fooling force
> Blends us in too!

To understand this verse means to draw near to Nietzsche's fundamental position and to grasp it as the completion of Western metaphysics, that is, as the concealed necessity of an unknown decision (cf. the confrontation with Nietzsche's metaphysics in terms of the history of beyng).[1] [202]

That Nietzsche "writes poetry" and must, as a thinker, "poetize" like nobody else before him in the history of modern philosophy, means: Nietzsche divines more profoundly (but at the same time vaguely and inchoately), that the *projection* of beings as a whole is of a different nature from the knowledge proper to "science" in the widest sense; philosophy is a "type" of "art" and yet it is not art itself.

Nietzsche is not capable of knowing or even of questioning what philosophy is in *its* essence, because he does not break through to *what* is given to philosophy to think—*being* and its truth—and to think this

---

1. Martin Heidegger, *Gesamtausgabe* vol. 50, *Nietzsches Metaphysik*, ed. Petra Jaeger (Frankfurt am Main: Klostermann, 1990). This was a Freiburg lecture course announced for the winter semester 1941–1942, but which was not delivered.

in such a way that it is thought in and from itself and from the abyssal ground that it calls for.

Nietzsche's poetry is also not a kind of "philosophical poetry," but rather always *a thinker's struggle with metaphysics*. (cf. above, §53, para. 11)

---

§94. "Life" in the Two Senses of World and Human Being

viewed from the perspective of human life: *knowledge and art in their conflict*; envisaged from the *whole* of beings (world): in conflict is what knowledge and art propose and deliver in each case to the human being: on the one hand, that which is constant and constancy itself (fixity)): *being*; on the other hand, what surpasses and transfigures what has been fastened: *semblance*.

"Life"—constantly requires the securing of its continued existence, and yet it ceaselessly surpasses the latter and thus ultimately *repeats itself*.

Nietzsche's fundamental conception of "life" is expressed in the most beautiful fashion in the last verse of a poem from the "Songs of Prince Vogelfrei," published as an appendix to the second edition of *The Gay Science*.[2] [203]

The poem: "To Goethe."[3] An antiphon to the end of the second part of *Faust*; for this reason it is at the same time an upturned affirmation, arising from the inversion of Platonism, of Goethe's world.

> World game, the ruling force
> blends false and true
> the eternally fooling force
> blends us in too.

Guidelines for an Interpretation of the Verse

World-Game: the world as a game; Heraclitus fragment 52: αἰὼν παῖς ἐστι παίζων, πεσσεύων.

---

2. Friederich Nietzsche, *Nietzsche's Werke* (Großoktavausgabe), vol. 5, *Die fröhliche Wissenschaft*, "Anhang: Lieder des Prinzen Vogelfrei," (Stuttgart: Kröner, 1921), p. 349; *The Gay Science*, trans. Walter Kaufmann, (New York: Vintage, 1974), p. 351.

3. Cf. also *Friedrich Nietzsches Gedichte* (Leipzig: Inselbücherei, 1923), no. 361, p. 14.

§94. "Life" in the Two Senses of World and Human Being   169

The ruling force:	the *mastery* belongs to the game, ibid. παιδὸς ἡ βασιληίη.
Blends:	the blending—world—as a mixing bowl; not just crudely and arbitrarily mixed together, but the inherent belonging-together and that which constitutes the world.
Being and appearance:	what always, in an ambiguous way, reciprocally brings together at each time the securing of existence *and* its surpassing.
The eternally fooling force:	the foolish; the *overflowing* of life—*the mask*—laughter; that which poetizes eternally: determining from the ground up.
Blends *us*:	explicit, decisive emphasis on the belonging of the human being (life) to the *world*—*we*—our essence wholly derived from it.
in too!:	at the same time as a *counter*-determination to Goethe's "elevating us"—in the sense of the "ideal"—no longer morally and bound to Ideals, but rather belonging to the world; thus also not "down." [204]

We are able to think through the verse as a whole only when we understand the two fundamental metaphysical words, *being* and *appearance*, and think what the "foolish" is metaphysically.

"Being" as constancy is, on the one hand, stability and fixity in opposition to becoming as that which is genuinely "real" (i.e., beings). Therefore being is appearance in the sense of semblance and lie; but, at the same time, constancy also refers to what *becoming* "is" in its becoming, since "becoming" is not simply "nothing," but, on the contrary, genuinely existing overcoming.

Appearance is an *illumination* of the unknown and of what goes beyond and transfigures all present things (beings); it brings the fixed in its fixity back into becoming, and consequently it is what is genuinely actual, belongs to becoming; on the other hand, when limited to the fixed, it means what is merely apparent and deceptive.

"Being"	is	*appearance and*	appearance is	*being*
(Permanence as rigidity)		(error) (transfiguration)		(permanence as presencing = the essencing of becoming)

Thus "being" is *in itself equivocal*; it is its own mask, one thing stands for another, essentially a blend; the same holds for "appearance"; being and appearance are always *intrinsically* blended together and, as such, in their blending are essentially related to each other. The blending itself of what is already intrinsically blended is what first constitutes—even preceding it—the "playing" of the world game.

The ambiguity of "being" as permanence in the sense of fixity and constancy and as permanence in the sense of the presencing of becoming is nonetheless grounded on the undifferentiated univocity of "being" as permanent presence, wherein the "truth" of φύσις is interpreted according to a determinate "temporal" sense, which itself remains ungrasped. The equivocal manner in which *Nietzsche* uses the word *"being"* is consequently only the un-mastered re-presentation of *the way in which* the whole of metaphysics thinks and must think its fundamental word. This is in no way a [205] game of multiple significations thought up by Nietzsche alone. Nietzsche is himself blended into the game of metaphysics.

The same holds for "appearance," whose two senses both go back to appearing as self-*showing* (cf. summer semester 1935, *Introduction to Metaphysics*).[4]

Being as rigidity is the *debased* fundamental meaning; being as presencing is the un-mastered and at once unavoidable sense, for in the end being has always to be taken into account, even if as becoming; but the decisive question is precisely that of knowing what such unavoidability means and in what it is grounded.

Yet because we are long accustomed to seeing here only an empty signifier of the emptiest concept (instead of experiencing the abyss of all beings and of beingness, thus taking this abyss as ground), we pass by the question of the unavoidability of being, and find such passing by to be "perfectly" in order. This is the order that the dominion of metaphysical thinking has long made familiar to us.

The game, however, is the *eternally fooling*. The "fooling" is that which is constantly "foolish" and only that; what does *foolish* mean here? *Foolish* is here ambiguous according to its essential and inessential senses. *Foolish* in the inessential sense is mere exuberance, the fact of leaving behind all that is commonplace and dull, but which can fall and degenerate into "vulgarity," "tastelessness," and coarseness; and which in its complete abandonment can even lose its own ground (cf.

---

4. Martin Heidegger, *Gesamtausgabe*, vol. 40, *Einführung in die Metaphysik*. ed. P. Jaeger (Frankfurt am Main: Klostermann, 1983); *Introduction to Metaphysics*, trans. Gregory Fried and Richard Polt (New Haven, CT: Yale University Press, 2001).

§94. "Life" in the Two Senses of World and Human Being

the "raving madman" as Zarathustra's "ape," vol. VI, p. 298ff., "On Zarathustra's Passing By," part 3).[5]

Foolishness in an essential sense is a continuous overflowing, but from *wealth*, from contact with its own ground, and in developing the latter; it is a "knowing" superiority that *laughs* even at itself as a matter of the utmost seriousness. [206]

The *foolish* is the sign of *self-surpassing*, of the basic character of *"life"* (in Nietzsche's interpretation).

The foolish is here at the same time the masklike, which in surpassing itself at the same time *conceals* and deceives, and by means of and in this deceiving and self-effacing play [*täuschendem Sichüberspielen*] properly plays *its* game, the world game.

Therefore in the foolish there lies a double relation to, on the one hand, what has at each time been *surpassed*, the fixed and unfoolishly "sober," that is, to being, and, on other hand, to the ec-centric [*das Aus-gefallene*], the wholly other and yet also self-concealing, to *appearance* in the twofold sense of the term.

The foolish is called "eternal"; yet with this Nietzsche does not merely mean that the foolish constantly endures, but rather he wants to say in a more philosophical sense: the *eternal*—what the genuinely and always existing being is—has foolishness for its essential characteristic; the eternal—"the world"—is therefore continually outstripped and masked, for itself, by itself, and on account of its essential semblance; it continually overcomes "truth" in the sense of the fixed, but it cannot persist in its *overflowing* without securing at the same time the means of existence for the new appearance, which in turn will overcome it. And *what* does all this mean? That the world excludes itself from truth, where truth is now after all understood as the pure correspondence of representation to the real.

Therefore whoever is condemned *to think* beings as a whole must be a fool and can "only" be a poet: "The wooer of *truth*?. . . . No! Only a fool! Only a poet!" (cf. *Thus Spoke Zarathustra*, part 4, "Song of Melancholy," pp. 431 ff.).

Zarathustra himself: "Scorched and thirsty / With one truth: / . . . *That I am banished / From all truth, / Only a fool! / Only a poet!*" (ibid., p. 437 f.). The wooer of truth is also the one who is "just," the one who must make an impossible virtue possible.

We obtain in this way a preliminary interpretation of the last line: "blends *us*—in too." It provides the essential interpretation of the place

---

5. Friedrich Nietzsche, *Nietzsches Werke* (Großoktavausgabe), vol. 6, *Also sprach Zarathustra* (Leipzig: Naumann, 1904); *Thus Spoke Zarathustra*, trans. Reginald John Hollingdale (London: Penguin, 1961).

of the human being in this world game. We should therefore not think that [207] the human being first of all exists for itself and is only from time to time mixed into the blend, but rather: the question who *we* are—without having been posed—receives the answer: the human being "is" the one it is only insofar as it is what has already been blended in and remains thus blended in, and *this is why* it, in its essential relations, must keep itself in existence as a creator (art and philosophy (knowledge) in this admixture), and why it has by necessity to become the struggle between art and knowledge (appearance and truth). The more essentially the human being says yes to this being blended *in*, the more it is "in being," the more purely does it belong to the world game as a participant, who itself plays and is played. Every falling out of the game, every form of wanting to leave it turns into a negation of "life" (in the sense of beings as a whole); every positing of an ideal that in any way points beyond and away from life is a denial of reality. This is why there is nothing eternal that would "draw us up"—up and away as an "ideal"—, rather *we* are "ourselves" *blended "in"* for there is nothing other than this (cf. *Will to Power*, vol. XVI, 401f., n. 1067 [1885])

Here we find conceived in an implicit manner the thought of the "eternal return" as the fundamental *mode in which* beings are as Will to Power. But it cannot be grounded on the Will to Power, nor can it be drawn from it, but rather must itself remain the broader project. [209]

N. "Life"

§95. Nietzsche's Projection of Beings as a Whole and of the Human Being as "Life"

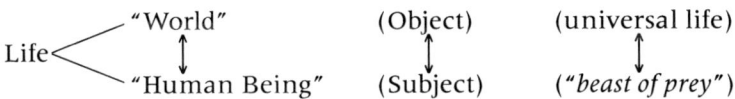

The truth of this "translation" of "becoming" as "life" (in the sense of "being").

The confrontation with Nietzsche's *metaphysics* in terms of the history of beyng.

§96. Disposition

1. The interpretation of the two guiding propositions about truth (see above, §77)
2. Truth—justice—science—historiology.
   Science—in accordance with the *essence* of truth, is *not* "close to life," not "distant from life," but rather *necessary for life*, corresponding to the essence of life-intensification (see §91).
3. Heraclitus, fragment 28 on Δίκη and appearance (see §92).
4. The interpretation of the third verse of the poem "To Goethe."
5. *Life* as domain, measure, and enactment.
   The truth "about" "life" (*Will to Power*, no. 1067).
   The *position* on life—"genuine needs"—organizing the chaos (sec. X).
   The question of the human being—"anthropomorphism."

§97. Recapitulation According to the Basic Questions

The thought of a higher justice is the center from which Nietzsche's thinking radiates, a center that was still hidden from him at the time of the *Untimely Meditations*. Justice first of all appeared [212] as the root of truth (of objectivity). Only in relation to *this truth* is the essence of historiology as a science, indeed as a knowing relation to the past in general, to be determined. This means that the triple, "natural" relation, a relation adequate to life, of the human being to the past, is borne, driven, and guided by higher justice as the form of enactment of this constructive, eliminative, destructive power that is farsighted and projects horizons in advance. This higher justice ruling over the human being as a living being is *life* in an essential sense, beings as a whole, *world* (will to power). Justice is the *root* of truth *only because* it is a "function" and "representative" of *life itself.*

The question concerning the truth of historiology and consequently the question of the essence of truth has led us via historiology in general and via truth to justice and thus to life itself, and to what we characterized at the beginning as the domain, the measure, and the enactment of Nietzsche's thinking.

The *Untimely Meditation* on historiology moves in this domain, takes it as a criterion for any evaluation, and seeks to effect its enactment. The question whether and with what right "life" has to be taken, and can be taken in any sense, as domain, measure, and enactment is here not posed at all.

The attitude of the *Untimely "Meditation"* is certainly reflective and meditative, but it is at the same time *immediately* and *exclusively motivated* by the desire *for a renewal of German culture*; this is why the positing of "world" as "life" and of the human being as "life" is generally not properly questioned or grounded. The will to a creative intervention bringing about immediate transformation is manifest everywhere, particularly in section X. In accordance with the "critical" attitude as one that liberates, the *Untimely Meditation* ultimately has to pose the question: if the excess of historiology hinders and destroys life, what is to be done about it? [213]

Nietzsche formulates two demands:
I. "to reflect on one's genuine needs,"
II. "to organize the chaos within."

In *both* demands there is an appeal to *life,* namely that life itself, as the fundamental domain and the measure of everything in its genuine needs, illuminate the path and goal of life-preservation and enhancement, and that life shall attain its goal through its self-ordering.

We would, however, have to ask here, quite independently of the appeal to life as such (in relation to I):
1. How is the genuineness of needs determined, and what is artificial within them? Is every need already genuine insofar as *it expresses itself*? If it does not, what condition must it satisfy?
2. Nietzsche will retort: the need must point toward the furthering of life and its intensification and its heightening. But in what does the *height* of "life" consist? Is it simply present within life? If not, through what and how does "height" emerge? In what direction does this heightening go? *Who* determines what height is?
3. Nietzsche responds: the genius; but who is a genius? Within, for example, the lineage of German thinkers: Meister Eckhart or Leibniz or Kant or Hegel or Schopenhauer? Each one of these understands

§97. Recapitulation According to the Basic Questions

the height "of life" in fundamentally different, although always metaphysical, ways, presuming that all of them, which is questionable in the extreme, posit "life" as the fundamental determination of beings as a whole, even if only in analogous senses.

Who decides which genius is to become the one setting the standard? Can this be *decided* by means of reflection on the *genuine needs*?

4. Does a return to the needs of life truly belong to mindfulness, or is it not rather a flight *from* mindfulness and a flight *toward* the animal, which simply by the fact of living is already "in the right" and "just"? What if "higher justice" were only the self-justification of the animal as a beast of prey? [214]

(In relation to II): "to organize the chaos within oneself":
   a) What does chaos mean here? The mere confusion of evaluations or the gaping of an abyss as the origin of new decisions?
   b) Is modern chaos merely the deep but nonabyssal hotchpotch of mindlessness and *brutalitas* (cf. *Überlegungen* XI[1])?
   c) Does the "organizing" lead to "life" or only to the confirmation and completion of the already dominant higher "mechanism,," which has already assimilated and absorbed everything biological?

* * *

Nietzsche does not here justify or question the positing of beings as a whole as life and of the human being as the animallike *subjectum*.

This position remains unquestioned not only here but throughout the whole of his later philosophy, in such a decisive manner that it is taken for granted *all the more* within the unthinking development of the interpretation of the will and of the human being as "life."

"Life"—not only what *conserves itself*, but *what drives beyond itself to life*, and it is this that requires first of all the securing of existence (of perspectives). *Beings as becoming (the question concerning the fundamental experience)*.

This "life" comes into its own in the human being as animal, in such a way that the human being grasps itself as the *subjectum* of any determination of the whole as living; (not *ego cogito—(ergo) sum*, but *ego vivo—ergo cogito*). The *ergo* is grasped in this way by Nietzsche as a natural consequence; this is to say that the *ego vivo—much more so*, and more crudely than in Descartes—is in essence a wholly unclarified,

---

1. Martin Heidegger, *Überlegungen VII–XI*, GA 95, ed. Peter Trawny, (Klostermann: Frankfurt a.M., 2014).

but still fundamental experience. *Ego vivo*—the yes to the beast of prey (cf. below); not simply recording the fact of *being-alive*! Everything else is merely an *expression and consequence* of this life and is justified only as such. [215]

How do matters stand with the *truth* of this interpretation of the world and of the human being (of the whole) as "life"?

We speak of "interpretation" and understand this in the sense of an anticipatory projection; something that, for example, constitutes the ground of every science.

But truth, according to Nietzsche, is fixation; is not *this* project then also such a fixation, if not exactly scientific? It is no mere transposition of "biology" as a science onto the whole world, but the transposition *of* the projection, on which biology as such rests, onto the whole of "beings." This is no mere "biologism," for sure, in the crude and almost impossible sense of an extension of contemporary biology to all domains of what can be known and evaluated, but it is still *biologism* in the essential sense of adopting the foundations of biology as the fundamental determination of beings as a whole. We have not overcome biologism in explaining that the positing of life is not an extension of biology as a "science"; it is still more essentially biological, because it takes over *its* fundamental position. And this without any justification! According to what "justice" is this widest horizon posited? What decision lies at the ground of this position?

When we reflect on these questions, *one thing* becomes clear: the essential aspect of this project is not that beings are posited in general as "life"—as opposed, say, to the *lifeless*—but rather that "life" is posited in advance as *life-intensification*, as the consuming desire for victory, spoils, and power, which in and of itself means: *always more power*. For power remains powerful only in the intensification and expansion of power, that is to say, in the deployment of violence as a means of power. This *always more power*, which constitutes the essence of powerfulness, governs all rights; that is, violence and predation are not consequences and modes of exercise of legitimate "rights," but the inverse is true: predation is the ground of the justification of all rights. We still know little of the "logic" of power, because [216] we continually color it with *moral* considerations and because the affirmation of power itself in its power-interest works with "moral" grounds and goals (cf., for example, the English *cant*[2]).

---

2. With the parenthetical "der engl. cant z.B.," Heidegger seems to refer to the few times that Nietzsche plays with the homonyms "Kant" and the English "cant," meaning hypocritical talk or moral hypocrisy. In these passages Nietzsche often blames the "English" interpretation of Kant for the general European acceptance of Kantian morality. Thus the following quotations: "Kant: oder cant als intelligi-

§97. Recapitulation According to the Basic Questions 179

The essential decision concerns the self-affirmation in the intensification of power, the interpretation of the thinking animal as *"beast of prey,"* and it is *this* decision whose inner consequence is the preservation and the assertion of "life." "Biologism"—if we are to use such an empty term—is the necessary *consequence* of "dynamism," if here δύναμις is understood as force, and force, in turn, is understood as power.

Vivo—not only says *that* I live, but rather that *my* "being," human being (!) is "life" and that "life" means above all: willing to go beyond oneself; but not away from oneself into a beyond of life, but rather *beyond oneself* as something always and necessarily fixed and subject to fixation: going *beyond* oneself in order to come all the more back to oneself and *only to* oneself.

At the same time it means: to me and to humanity belongs the living body and consequently the "soul," "thinking" being only a *particular* and indeed very ambiguous manifestation of it (living body—spirit—soul): *in this way* spirit is retained within "life," particularly "spirit" in the sense of thinking consciousness.

Vivo—is the "yes" to the interpretation of the animal human being as the *beast of prey.*

"Beast of prey"—the phrase designates what attacks, what *lusts after victory and spoils*, aiming at the assertion of life in the form of aggression and the deployment of power; but "beast of prey" does not signify what is merely rapine or wild, what is merely assailant and rapacious; Nietzsche thinks at the same time of what is "noble" in the "beast of prey" in opposition to mere cattle. The "noble" is thought together with the idea of "rarity" (eagles produce few offspring, those of sparrows are countless).

Nobility and *rarity* are nevertheless determined from the perspective of animality and according to animal kind. Nietzsche did not elaborate the sense of either, and consequently he did not think through the essence of the "beast of prey" proper to his thought; if this had happened, then he would have had to come to decisions [217] bringing the power-character of beings as such (of "life") into question.

Here again Nietzsche's conception of the human being (the "beast of prey") as the already fixed and determined animal "operates" essentially superficially, and in accordance with the spirit of his time, in the sense of the intensification of power on the part of this being determined by force that the human being is [*Kraftwesen Mensch*]. Nobility and rarity remain—in a genuinely metaphysical way—merely

---

bler Charakter" (*Kritische Studienausgabe*, vol. 6, p. 111); "der verfluchte englisch-europäische Cant" (Ibid., vol. 11, p. 73).—Trans.

accessory and tolerated "ideals" that are essentially unable to make visible and questionable the machination-character of power.

The decision that Nietzsche himself brought to the fore, a decision that was not grasped and questioned as such, is consequently first and foremost this: whether "being" (in the sense of the preservation of life as life-intensification (i.e., as becoming) or "not-being" (loss, decline, and degeneration into weakness).

Such a decision for "being" is a decision for the "being" of *the human being as subjektum, for the securing and development of that subject*, which increases its beast-of-prey character toward the boundless and absolute by means of the positing of beings as a whole as "life" in the sense of an elevation of the power of life beyond itself [*Lebensübermächtigung*]. Life as human life thus integrates itself into and appears to fall "under" life in general; but this "integration" grounds power and empowers it into the exertion of power, precisely because "being" as such has and must have precedence over not-being. The individualism of the individual subject is eliminated *only* for it to reappear and prevail in the form of the limitless tyranny of the *subjektum* in the sense of universal life, the people and that which is common to all.

"Being" here means that beings, and what is taken to be such, *be* what is "actual" in "life," that is, that they become. Precisely to the extent that he apparently elevates "being" (denigrated beforehand) to "becoming," Nietzsche remains wholly imprisoned within the metaphysical thinking of being as the beingness of beings.

Nietzsche does not and cannot know anything of a more original decision than that between being and not-being in the metaphysical sense; for this would require putting metaphysics as such into question, and [218] a fortiori its *inversion*, and to overcome it in an originary way.

The most extreme forgottenness of being (for which the truth of beyng can never become a question) reposes on the most extreme abandonment of beings by being, in that the machination of beings themselves (still camouflaged here as "life") justifies the raid by the animal human being on that which is as a closed totality of power, and in this way comes to complete the *subjectivism* of the *ego vivo*.

But the decision between *beyng and beings* is essentially different— and of an abyssal origin; in this decision the question of whether I am, or whether we are, falls back into indifference with respect to the one point, namely that *beyng* in its truth shall come to presence and tear the essence of the human being away from animality; not in order to make it inoffensive, stolid, and satisfied, not in order to transform the beast of prey into a domesticated animal taking its abode in a questionless drifting along, but rather in order to show the human being the other, quite different summits of his essence as *Da-sein*, in which the human being finds itself given over to the highest resolution, that of the guardianship of the truth of beyng, within the urgency of which the encounter of the divinity of the Gods and of the humanity of the human being is required for the gifting of its essence.

But with this Nietzsche is not "refuted," but rather only situated in what will remain unique to him: that *in his un-thought* he forces a decision about metaphysics as such, while remaining *inaccessible* for any exploitation by "worldviews" and "literary" enterprises, inviolable for any historical importunateness; from beginning to end a thinker worthy of questioning, never requiring fame or glory.

§98. Concluding Remark

Our reflection on some of the fundamental concepts of Nietzsche's text has been carried out with a constant eye to [219] what he means by "life." This word encloses—more essentially than anything else—*three essential decisions*:
1. about beings as a whole (within the decision concerning the fundamental interpretation of being)
2. about the essence of truth and its ground—"*Metaphysics*,"
3. about the essence of the human being.

The three belong essentially together: the human being—standing within truth (and untruth)—comports itself toward beings as a whole. Beings as a whole sustain and govern in their truth the essence of the human being.

The sciences stand within this triple decision—*as one that has already been made*. The "sciences" are incapable by their own means of seeing, posing, leave alone deciding this question in any direction. "Worldviews" are also grounded—even if in a different way from the sciences—in these metaphysical decisions. They derive from this their inclination to ground or, at least, extend themselves scientifically. Pointing out the worldview-related "presuppositions" of the sciences is both possible and necessary; but can in no way reach into what underlies them both; *the decision or the decisive understanding* of being, truth, and human being.

But in such exercises, which can amount only to preparations for mindfulness, such decisions shall not be taken, and hardly even be named; for it all too easily appears that they can be formulated and decided in the way of dialogue and thinking proper to such a preparatory exercise.

We must instead put ourselves to the test: whether now and in the future we will read the texts and words of the genuine philosophers *in a different way* than we have previously; placing higher demands on ourselves, with an enduring will to *question*, and with a presentiment that there is something *knowable before* and beyond all science; we have to put to the test whether we have learnt to read. *If* we can affirm that we *want* to read in a different way and more meditatively, then we have done enough for the moment. [220]

§99. Nietzsche's Early Characterization of His Own Thinking as "Inversion of Platonism" (cf. summer semester 1937, exercises[3])

Platonism: "thinking" in the manner of Plato,
the "doctrine of ideas"
means: determining the being*ness* of beings; κοινόν, and this as ἰδέα—νοούμενον νοητόν.
what is re-presented in "thinking," that is, representing something in general (generally καθόλου): "house"—human being—"truth."
The non- and suprasensible.
That on account of which beings are what they are, and for that reason ὄντως ὄν. The suprasensible as genuine being.
The *sensible* as the μὴ ὄν. (Later (in modernity) the sensible: the living, life, nature (Nietzsche); the suprasensible: spirit).

The inversion: the *sensible*: life—nature: (avarice, will, and drive)—what properly is;
the *nonsensible*: illusion—atmosphere—*horizon*, necessary for life as before: ἰδέα for ὄν—μὴ ὄν.

The inversion: *without the question* of what is actually in question (beyng); *without the question* of the domain of the turning. What occasions the inversion.

Platonism in the form of Schopenhauer's philosophy. Schopenhauer turns away from this world here, but he still admits nature as a fundamental actuality while negating the will to act.

Nietzsche—life affirmed in its cruelty and senselessness. [221] Art—thinking—[. . .]*—completion of this world as belonging to it. Great individuals as high points of history justify *"life."*

Life itself is, however, not only a wild flux, but rather: *"justice"*—δίκη; in *this* it presents itself in its highest essence.

---

3. Martin Heidegger, *Gesamtausgabe*, vol. 87, "Nietzsche: Seminare 1937 und 1944," ed. Peter von Ruckteschell, (Frankfurt am Main: Klostermann, 2004).

*[an illegible word]

§100. "Life" (*ego vivo*) (on sec. X)

Reflecting on "genuine needs." *Whose? Is* the human being merely something present, something ascertainable?

What is the human being? And *how is* it? What is the point of appealing to "needs," if the essence of the human being remains undetermined, if it does not even feel the need *to question* its essence?

The essential presence of the human being derived from an *essence-attunement* [*Wesenser-stimmung*]. But the latter from the pro-priation in the event, from being assigned to beyng.

§101. The Philosophical Concept

The steadfastness within the truth of beyng, as questioning, deciding, knowing. Correspondingly: the essence of the *word* [is] the event of beyng itself.

The concept—*conceptually* [*inbegrifflich*], that is:
1. grasping beings as a whole from the perspective of beyng.
2. incorporating the one who understands (the human being) by way of its transformation.

No mere representing of something universal.
Not the mere means of a calculating mode of orienting oneself.
The projection of being.
Grounding of the truth of beyng. [222]
On the fundamental critique of the *Second Untimely Meditation*, cf. *Überlegung* IX, 101–102; 104–105; 116–117.[4]

§102. On the Critical Meditation

"Truthfulness"!   yes, but truth (cf. Nietzsche's later doctrine).

"Life"!   yes, but *beyng*.

* * *

Given the urgency of the situation, Nietzsche does not question in a sufficiently originary fashion. Yes, even the *distress* itself he sees pre-

---

4. Martin Heidegger, *Gesamtausgabe*, vol. 95, *Überlegungen* VII–XI (*Schwarze Hefte* 1938–1939), ed. Peter Trawny (Frankfurt am Main: Klostermann, 2014).

cisely in the horizon of *the* metaphysics (of life) that is (by means of the primacy of beings as such over beyng) its most hidden ground. That is to say, Nietzsche is an end and a final transition, but *not a* beginning.

§103. Decisive Questioning

1. Beginning with *"life"*—fundamental metaphysical position (*guiding question*).
2. *History* to be determined neither from the perspective of "life" nor from "historiology," neither "ontologically" nor "epistemologically," but rather from out of the *essence of beyng* itself, and that means at the same time *Da-sein*. (cf. *Überlegung* X, 35)[5]

§104. "Life"

From where does "life" draw its "heights" and "depths"? What are these? Does this not mean that "life" is not merely "more" life, but rather *something other* than "life"?[223]

---

5. Ibid.

O. THE QUESTION OF THE HUMAN BEING:

"Language." "Happiness."

Language

(compare §15, "Forgetting" and "Remembering")

§105. Language as Use and Using-Up of Words
(Not the Mere Occurrence of "Words")

Language as *use of tools*; what is implied in this interpretation of language; (λόγον ἔχον).
"Word"—Collection of letters as a sign for. . .
    —Sound image   as a sign for . . .

§106. Word and Meaning

"Meaning"—what is "meant"?
    —the being re-presented and being?

§107. "Happiness" and *Da-Sein*

"Happiness."
"Why ever should as many people as possible live for as long as possible? Is their happiness a justification of all existence? Is it not rather something contemptible?" (vol. XII, p. 277 [1882–1884]).
"In your calculations you have forgotten those to come; you have forgotten the happiness of the greatest number" (ibid.).
"Happiness"—"Unhappiness" in the sense of *being-happy*, "having" happiness.
"Happiness"—as granted and coming to one from the outside.
Happiness—as being happy. The *self-supporting existing* [In sich stehendes Bestehen] of the being *that one* is and has to be. Character of de-cision. Openness and being closed *to oneself, holding oneself in this— abandoned in the midst of beings.*
This is why—in the comparison of the possible relations to the past—the question of "happiness" immediately arises. Because *this relation essentially belongs to the living being—belongs* to it, which is to say that the living being never lacks it.
The living being—why "happiness" here? What is "happiness"?— ambiguous [226] question: (a) essence (being-such); (b) whether it is within "happiness" that "happiness" is to be *sought*!
Life—a being which is *in such* a way. *Which way?*
    "*Life*" and "life"—   (endurance [*Beständnis*])
    How we take "life," how we "endure" it,

It thus has to be "taken"—"for what reason"? "Holding oneself within it."

Thus: How the *relation to the past* relates itself to the *enduring of life*, for this relation to the past, in a certain manner, goes in the *opposite direction* to the flowing and rushing onward of life. Endangering the endurance.

Why speak of "happiness"? Because of "life"? To what extent? "Life," *how we endure it*, which is to say? Yes—No.

"Life"—the *way* of enduring *life*, has to *be* "happiness."

---

§108. "Happiness"

"Happiness" and "life":
1. The *concept* of "happiness" as such; εὐδαιμονία already an interpretation? (Nietzsche's determination (vol. VII, p. 218): "a feeling of an increase of power").
2. In what it consists *in each case* and *wherein* it is placed—"feeling," "disposition" [*Befindlichkeit*].
3. Why can it receive different possible determinations?

Twilight of the Idols, vol. VIII, p. 62: "If you have your *why?* for life, then you can get along with almost any *how?*—The human being does *not* strive for happiness; only the English do that" (as contentment, profit).

Happiness—the *pacification* of life?

>The condition in which and from which one says yes to "life." What is "life," such that this is possible and necessary?

Happiness—"what retains the living being in life and urges him to live" (vol. I, p. 285). The "yes" to life! (In the "yes"—the "over and above.") Why "securing" and "urging onward"? [227] Because of obstacles, falling behind and going under. Whence and in what way? And why this? *The hidden ground—the relation to being* [?] (going beyond oneself as coming to a stand within oneself).

Being happy also in *remembering*.

(Cf. vol. X, p. 294): "that for him [for the human being] there is somewhere an *indisputable* truth," thus *a form of pacification*, a final inviolable appeal. Always again: the *secure hold* and the *yes*.

"Life" and "happiness," the extent to which the essence of life is determined from this! Being *carried* and impelled *by* life *to maintain oneself in existence*.

§108. "Happiness"

What, then, is *"life"*?

For example, the *concept of the human being* (in section 2). Here already the question, what is the human being? Who is the human being?

The who-question—positing the human being as such; the one who *is*, insofar as it is *itself. Self—selfsameness* and *singularity*. [229]

P. The Fundamental Stance of the *Second Untimely Meditation*

§109. The Guiding Demand of the Meditation

Know thyself, *your genuine* needs.
1. Which are the ownmost needs—the self?
2. Which are genuine?
3. What type of truth (cf. sec. VI, pp. 327–330: history as the core of the drive to truth) belongs to this cognizing?
4. In what does truthfulness consist (truthfulness and *"justice,"* sec. VI).
    Relation of "cognition" and "life" (cf. the concluding remarks in sec. X).
    What conception of the human being is directive here?
    What is the interpretation of beings as a whole from which this interpretation of the human being arises?
    What metaphysico-historial fundamental position determines this interpretation of beings as a whole?

§110. Guiding Stance

The right and the task of *youth*.
Nietzsche's concept of youth (both "biological" and not "biological"), cf. *Überlegungen* IX.[1]
"Where with profoundly sustained emotion one holds fast to the unintelligible as the sublime" (p. 320).
To gain an overview of the whole by means of a first reading. Then a fundamental working through of the individual sections. The structure of the text is *not* everywhere equally rigorous and clear. First contact with Nietzsche—what is first in philosophy. It is essential that we ourselves learn to question. [232]

§111. Concept Formation in Philosophy and the Sciences

Intention: reflection on science, its historial, modern necessity. Philosophical concept formation considered not as a philosophical technique, but as an indication of something completely different, something that does not exist on the same level as the sciences (philosophy and art).

---

1. Cf. Martin Heidegger, *Gesamtausgabe*, vol. 95, *Überlegungen* VII–XI (*Schwarze Hefte* 1938–1939), ed. Peter Trawny (Frankfurt am Main: Klostermann, 2014).

194   P. The Fundamental Stance of the *Second Untimely Meditation*

Path: by working out a determinate and at the same time for us decisive question. The essence of history, and thus at the same time and first of all the question of "historiology," consequently the relation to "science"—not merely the relation to the "science of history" [*Geschichtswissenschaft*] in the narrow sense, but generally to the historical human sciences. Furthermore: if technology is the historiology of nature (ἱστορεῖν), then the natural sciences are also included here: indeed, all essential sciences.

Means: moving along this path of reflection on history and historiology with the help of already existing considerations (Jacob Burckhardt, *Reflections on History* and Nietzsche's *Second Untimely Meditation, On the Advantages and Disadvantages of History for Life*). Both of these, not only because they are bound together chronologically and deal with the same subject, but because they are *historically* essential.

Process: always directed at essential meditation and essential provocations; but at the same time without neglecting exact knowledge and craft.

§112. "Life"

Philosophical concept formation—"life," ambiguity of the concept and the word.

Thinking in the highest sense of the thinking of thinkers; what is thought within it, beings as a whole—being. [233]

Hence within the interpretation, an immediate focus on what corresponds to this in Nietzsche's thought: "life"—beings as a whole; *at the same time*! "life" = human life.

This suggests that maybe in the thinking of beings as a whole, in the thinking of being, reflection on the human being is quite essential (but not in an anthropological sense). Why and how? this remains obscure (in contrast to "sciences, for example").

Bearing only *this correlation in mind*.

A sign: the *ambiguity* of "life." Not overlooking this sign is already an essential step.

§113. "Life"

can mean:
1. the *whole* of the living.
2. the way of being—of *a* living being and of living beings as such.

3. this way of being itself as a determination of the "genus" and "species" to which the individual belongs.
4. the whole of beings in general.

The lifeless —what stands outside of the possibility of life (2.) and hence even outside of the possibility of "dying," and does not result from a loss of life.

The dead —a *form* of the living; what exists in having lost its life, beings.

The unliving—(what lives, but is weakened).

§114. "Life"

requires —being able to forget.
 —*but not remembering* (as shown by *the animal*).
"life" —the *unhistorical power.*
support —*what flows through it—what envelops it.*
"animal" —as "en-souled" in general (ζωή).[234]
"life" —*as fundamental actuality* for "nature" and "culture," the "natural aspect" of life is decisive, φύσις.

From what fundamental experiential stance is this conceived? From an aesthetic and cultural-political one. Where does this come from? From the characterization of life as natural: Schopenhauer—German idealism—Leibniz—Descartes's *ego*—human being.

  World (*cosmos*) as "macroanthropos," not the human being as a "microcosm."

Culture —*an "improved physis"* (vol. X, p. 313; vol. I, p. 384).
 "im-provement"; where and how?
Art —as ("physis").

§115. Nietzsche's Fundamental Experience of "Life" and Opposition to "Darwinism"

The plastic power—"art"—"genius"—"culture."
1. Life—a formative force coming from the "inside," which *utilizes, exploits, and incorporates* the "given."
   Not: "adaptation."
   a) But how and on what basis is there something like "inner" and "outer" and the "given"?
   b) What form does this take in plants and animals and how is it present in the *human being*? Understanding of being (for Nietzsche, on the contrary: "thinking" only as *"function of life"*).

2. Life as developing force, growing beyond and above itself, accumulation and enrichment, intensification.
    Not: *Struggle* for existence [*Dasein*] as presence-to-hand, as remaining and mere preservation of the genus and species. Consequently, no purposes or goals.
    "Will"—*Instinct—spurring on to intensification*.
3. Life as the becoming dominant of the stronger (and destruction).
    Not: "selection"; which only achieves preservation, and not a higher formation. [235]

§116. Life

life—"the purpose"
life—what *"dominates"* and *leads*.

§117. "Life"

how this gradually emerges from the different sections.
Cf. sec. I.
Sec. II, para. 1: threefold "life."
  Para. 7: on different soil and climate.
Sec. III to *beget* life (p. 307).
  Life = to be unjust (p. 308).
Sec. IV para. 1: goals, forces, needs (*of* life) of a human being, of a people.
    Life as past, present, and future.
  Para. 3: *What is alive does not know the opposition of inner and outer* (p. 312ff., 319).

§118. "Life"

is, for Nietzsche, the name of that polymorphic existence that is not merely present-at-hand and that cannot simply be attested to and justified by bare "life."

That it requires justification, and to what extent this is the case.

Life is never just "life" (in the sense of what one generally calls by that name, on the grounds of various and possibly even correct reasons).

"What is not fit for life is not genuine historiology. Admittedly, this depends on the more or less elevated, more or less debased idea of life that you have" ("Meditations from the Horizon of Bayreuth," vol. X, p. 255, n. 40). [236]

§119. "Life"

"Life"— *the plastic power* (pp. 286, 378),
the ability to forget (pp. 285, 295),
the *horizon character* (pp. 287, 338) (Leibniz),
field of vision, opaque milieu, atmosphere, the protective illusory mood, "love" (pp. 339, 342),
the unhistorical and the suprahistorical (p. 379),
the "genuine needs,"
"life" and *"happiness"* (εὐδαιμονία).

The living	1. acting and striving
	(monumental historiology)
as such and	2. preserving and venerating
	(antiquarian historiology)
"culture"	3. suffering and the need for liberation
Cf. §19, p. 43.	(critical historiology)

Where does this characterization derive from? Perhaps from historiology and its present forms?

"Goal" of life: mere preservation and "continuous existence"? (Or else: precisely what does not have the ability to question, but is rather only this drive itself (cf. p. 308, p. 310)?)

§120. "Life"

"That dark, driving, insatiably self-desiring power" (p. 308).

"Itself"—but what is itself and what can it be, what are its genuine desires and needs (cf. later *Will to Power*)?

This and the *ordinary wanting to live*. [237]

§121. "Life"

The "organic"—that is, that which grows from itself in the sense of creating itself by raising itself up (to where?) on the basis of an overflowing and exuberance in self-enjoyment.

Fundamental form of "life" as being: relation of the *"creator to his material"* (vol. XIV, p. 81; cf. p. 276).

(The wheel rolling out of and again into itself)
Life—*"an unhistorical power"* (Vol. I, p. 294).

§122. Life and "Adaptation"

Adaptation is certainly thought in an inadequate fashion, if a "living being" is taken to "live" by itself first and *then* also to *adapt itself*.

The expression is misleading.

The living being is in itself—*as milieu—captivated, integrated*; "it" does not adapt itself, but deploys "itself" by means of the *enactment* of its integration and *within* the latter *masters* the "given" *or else withdraws from it*.

In this integratedness lies—confront*ation* [*Auseinandersetzung*]—whereby it is precisely in the latter that the force of life gathers momentum [*der Lebensschwung schwingt*].

§123. Life—Health and Truth

Nietzsche later clearly sees (*Gay Science*, §120ff. and §110) that what is necessary to "life" does not yet thereby prove its truth. But what is truth exactly? Does Nietzsche not determine it as what life requires, as that which has been fixed and as that which fixes? But it is appearance that does so.

This means that life is *not at all* an "argument," because at bottom it does not admit such "argumentation" or any such "truth," for life itself is being *as such*.

Who says what health is? The healthy. But who are they? [238]

§124. Life as *Dasein*

The Question: Is life worthwhile? (Schopenhauer). What sort of question is that? Life as a "business."

If yes, what is it that makes it worthwhile? (Nietzsche)

By means of its justification in and by means of its highest possibilities. Where do the latter come from and why precisely these? What are they and how are they determinable?

"Life"—as the life of *the human being*? or as *beings in general*?

§125. "Life" and "Death"

From a well-known work concerning "general biology" (*Contemporary Culture*, 1915),[2] I noted down some twenty years ago the following propositions of a renowned zoologist:

"We do not know what life in its most profound sense is, and there is little hope that we will soon come to know. But the essence of death, that we do know."

It is: "the irreversible loss of life of a living individual, in which the living organism is transformed into a corpse."

Death: transformation of something living into a corpse (that is, something dead).
1. Why is this nonsense (though it may be correct)?
2. To what extent is this researcher unable to "think"?
    Because he thinks it possible to know the essence of death without knowing anything of the essence of life.
Yet, the greatest secret of life itself is precisely death.

Death belongs so essentially to life that the latter is thought most profoundly when we grasp the living being as that which is capable of suffering death (to die death—as an "act" of life itself). [239]

---

2. Carl Chum, and Erwin Baur, *Allgemeine Biologie. Die Kultur der Gegenwart*, part 3, sec. 4, vol. 1, (Leipzig: Teubner, 1915), p. 190.

Q. ANIMALITY AND LIFE

Animal—ζῷον

The "living body"

cf. winter semester 1929–1930 lectures[1]

---

1. Martin Heidegger, *Gesamtausgabe* vols. 29–30, *Die Grundbegriffe der Metaphysik: Welt–Endlichkeit–Einsamkeit*, ed. Friedrich-Wilhelm von Herrmann (Frankfurt am Main: Klostermann, 2004); *The Fundamental Concepts of Metaphysics: World, Finitude, Solitude*, trans. William McNeill and Nicholas Walker (Bloomington: Indiana University Press, 1995).

§126. Milieu and Environment (World)

Milieu—the scope [Um-*fang*]—the range [*Umkreis*] of what *captures* and captivates.
    Being-taken [*Um-nehmung*] *into captivation* [*Benommenheit*].
    A *captivating* and thus at the same time *enclosing* openness in such a way that what the animal is captivated by and *related to* cannot be experienced as a being.
World—environment, where beings as such are opened "as a whole" and where they *reign*:
    The *human being* as *being-in-the-world*.
    The stone: occurs within and amongst beings.
    The animal "has" no "world," because it is not determined by the mode of being that is *being-in-the-world*.
    Animal-being is not world-forming.

§127. Soul—Living Body—Body

Not: living body [*Leib*] and soul—with living body and bodying forth [*Leiben*]—for this is already and precisely "soul." At most: body [*Körper*] and soul.

The *"bodily limit"* necessarily ambiguous:
- adumbration of the living material body [*Leibkörper*]
- extent of the range of *captivation*, milieu

1. The living body is not simply a corporeal thing, but *as* living body is the *limit of a material shape* in the sense of a *spatial shape* (*to stroke the coat of an animal*); living body—body; a material thing that *is a living body*.
2. The limit and enclosure proper to *bodying forth, the reach of the living body* and that wherein it *bodies forth*; the limit proper to the living, to the animal. [242]
3. *The "limit" of the bodily form* [*Gestalt*] *is nothing in itself*; it belongs in 2) and is thus precisely not the limit of the living body or the limit of the animal, but rather only the *adumbration* of the *living material body*; but even so it is to be distinguished from the surface of a body (the "lizard").
4. Bodying forth *"in"-corporates* [*einverleiben*] not merely through *ingestion*, but rather by *integrating its environment. Taking the measure of space* [*Raumdurchmessung*], not merely taking up space with a material living thing.

"Living body"—no mere material thing with something else added, but rather *something absolutely original: living body*. Life *bodies forth insofar as it lives; it lives insofar as it bodies forth* [Das Leben *leibt, indem es lebt; lebt indem es leibt*].

§128. Embodying

Life (as a mode of being) has affixed the living body within itself—in terms of the vibrancy of its *milieu captivation*—and pulsates through "it" in such a way that the living body *is* only insofar as life pulsates through it.

Every living body can be considered as a material thing. No *material thing* is a "living body." ("*Body*-structure and character" [*Körperbau und Charakter*].)

(The "living body" as "animated body" [*beseelter Körper*], and "soul" as what constitutes the material thing as a "living body.")

§129. The Animal Has Memory

insofar as it "retains" in certain ways; but it does *not* have "memory" in the sense of re-membrance.

Accordingly "forgetting"—to *lose out of sight, out of mind*, or a mere slipping one's mind; no longer occupying oneself with it!

Retaining: the dog—the place where it has buried its bone.
   The bee—the "location."
Retaining and instinct. Larva of the stag-beetle (male—female).
   Migrating birds (*time and region*). [243]

§130. Animal (Questions)

Is the animal happy?
Can the animal forget? (Can the stone die?)
The *joyful welcome* of the dog.
Its dejection when left at home.

Human empathy?
Domestic animals?
The *"eagle"*—the dog.
Can the animal remain silent?

Critical question:
What and how can we know about the animal?
It cannot communicate anything to us.
Therefore: empathy—transposing ourselves into it.
How, on what basis and how far?

The *similarities*: 1) between the sense organs and such like
                  2) of comportment.
But in spite *of all this* there can be an abyssal *difference*.

---

§131. Delimitation of the Essence of "Life" (Animality)

In *Being and Time* (*Sein und Zeit*), p. 58, it is said: the constitution of the being of life—the structure of this mode of being "can only be determined in a privative manner" (on the basis of the interpretation of *Da-sein*).

This sentence has been crudely misinterpreted to mean that the living is only the "privation" of *Da-sein*—crudely put: that the animal is only a defective and inferior human being!

No, the animal is never a human being, but rather an "animal." But the question remains of a possible determination of the animality of the animal *by the human being*!

It is precisely because this being is absolutely original and because it is closed off to us—and this in a different way to the stone, which has neither milieu nor world—, [244] that the question of the projection of the structure of the being of animality is extremely "difficult"; profound reflection is required in order to find sufficient guiding threads. But we have to do this from the perspective of *Da-sein*, which still needs to be projected, and which in *Being and Time* had still been grasped in a way open to misinterpretation.

---

§132. Animality

Cf. *Second Untimely Meditation*, sec. I (the animal and the everyday drifting along of the average human being).
Animality and Embodiment—"living body" and "body"
                      "animated" body.
                      "soul" understood from the living body
                      as *living* material thing?
                      cf. Aristotle: ψυχή. [245]

R. The Differentiation of Human Being and Animal

(cf. O. The Question of the Human Being)

§133. The Un-historical and the Historical

What is the ground and consequently the essence of the distinction that Nietzsche introduces at the beginning between the un-historical and the historical? (In relation to beings as such. Language, its essence. *Language and Beyng*).

It is not because the animal forgets that it does not say anything; but rather since it cannot *say* anything (lacking a relation to being), it has to "forget"; but if it "forgets" in some sense, does that mean it can retain *something as something*? What does *"forgetting"* mean here?

§134. The Unhistorical—(of the Human Being)

Cf. sec. X, p. 379: "the art and power of *forgetting* and of enclosing oneself within a limited *horizon*."

The human being is not unhistorical insofar as it is an *animal*, that is, it is not *unhistorical like the animal*, but as a *historical being* even more un-historical.

The animal "forgets" "by itself," if it can be said at all that it forgets. The question arises:

In what is being able to forget grounded?
What determines the limitation of the horizon?

§135. Animal and Human Being

The question of their differentiation moves on the ground of an essential determination of "life" as such. To what extent?
Animal   —living being—*animal*—("plant")
Human Being—living being—*animal*—*rationale*
                            —*reasonable*
                            —*"sensible"*
How is the human being viewed here? ὄν—ζῷον. [248]

* * *

The question of the demarcation between animal and human being—does this distinguish animals in the usual way from the human being as a "particular" animal, or is it such that the human being cannot in any way be predetermined as an animal, in such a way that the difference between human being and animal is an abyss covered over precisely where the human being is posited as the rational or "historical" animal?

The distinction between the unhistorical and the historical.

The distinction between animal and human being.

These two distinctions do not coincide; because human being as *animal* rationale—a living being—life.

Can the unhistorical-historical distinction at all facilitate the distinction of *animal and human being*?

Or does the borderline between them run elsewhere? How? (The question is important with regard to the determination of the essence of "life.") [249]

S. "Privation"

(Cf. Manuscript: Beyng. ("Negativity"))

§136. What Happens to us as "Privation"

death—life
forgetting—retaining
being silent—speaking
poverty—possession
unhistorical—historical

What has been deprived is not merely the "object" of deprivation, but rather its ground. The deprivation *is* in having deprived what has been deprived, precisely by virtue of the deprived element itself. This means that the deprivation in not opposed to what has been deprived, but, on the contrary, that it genuinely belongs to it and to its essence. But what does this mean? Where does this originate?

Privation and *negation*
Negation and the not
Not and nothing
Nothing and being
Being and beings as a whole ("Life")

§137. "Privation"—Inter-ruption

Negation—
a) not only negation, exclusion
b) rather, the exact inverse: invoking *the yes* and being rooted in it in order to say it in the essential possibility of its loss and in this way to determine it essentially ("Death").
c) Therefore not even as negation is it what is lowly in an evaluative sense; language is often very *poor* in its naming power.
d) The different possibilities of inter-ruption.
e) Inter-ruption (in a metaphysical sense) and *abyss*. [253]

T. Structure and Composition of the *Second Untimely Meditation*

§138. On the Advantages and Disadvantages of History for Life

The text is not rigorously structured. It is more of an appeal and interpellation; it does not yet possess the form of a definitive reflection, still less is it the site for explicitly essential questioning. "Life"—to *awaken* and *save creativity is the essential* intention.

* * *

Title—*Content and Key Concepts,*
only then: *to what extent an "untimely meditation."*
At the same time: *reflection on history—Da-sein—*beyng.
Always: enactment of the difference between scientific reflection or explanation and philosophical thinking.

* * *

The principal question underlying Nietzsche's *Second Untimely Meditation* is not that of the disadvantages or advantages of historiology, but rather that of justifying the positing "of life" as fundamental actuality in the sense of a biology of culture.

How sections VI, VIII, and IX essentially deal with what arises from the lack of justice understood as a faculty of the power of judgment (cf. sec. V, para. 2). [257]

Addenda

I. Seminar Reports
Winter Semester 1938–1939

Introduction to Philosophical Concept Formation
(Nietzsche, *On the Advantages and Disadvantages of History for Life*)

Seminar exercises for beginners. Three-hour sessions

Report on the Seminars of November 7 and 9, 1938

There are three provisional aims of the seminar:
1. It aims to give an introduction to philosophical concept formation, that is, to thinking. But not to thinking in just any sense, but rather to thinking in the manner of thinkers, to what they think about, precisely in distinction from all sciences and arts.
2. This will be shown by means of a particular text, namely the second *Untimely Meditation*, *On the Advantages and Disadvantages of History for Life*, which was written in Basel in immediate proximity to Burckhardt and bearing the influence of his lecture "On Historical Greatness."
3. Interpreting this text from 1874 means at the same time entering into Nietzsche's philosophy. This represents an end in the sense of the completion of Western philosophy, and therefore a return to its origins. From this emerges Nietzsche's quite particular relation to philosophy, that is, to its beginning in the pre-Socratics and in particular to Heraclitus.

Nietzsche's true philosophy is to found in what he held back, in his notebooks. The published works are, so to speak, a cry for help. Just as important, at least in part, are his letters, [260] which, emerging from his thinking, form an inseparable unity with the whole of his work.

In turning to our chosen text, let us look first of all at the title, which gives the theme of the text as a whole, and ask: What is this theme? Historiology, and precisely its relation to the advantages and disadvantages for life. Advantages and disadvantages are thus calculated. Under what conditions does such accounting occur? Every calculative account requires a setting of goals, and the measure, according to which this accounting occurs, is life. If historiology and life in their interrelation are to be subject to investigation, then this relation must be located in a definite realm in which it is grounded. And the realm where the calculative account [*Verrechnung*] takes place is the human being.

On the Advantages and Disadvantages of History for Life. Now, what do we understand under the heading of "Life"? First, everything that lives, that is, the whole of living things, a determinate region of beings, that does not include all things; the stone, for example, is lifeless, that is, it is in a way that life is not. But nobody can deny that the stone is. So life here can no longer signify simply everything that lives, rather it is here meant as a state, as a manner and mode of being.

Having differentiated the regions of the living and the lifeless, we now ask: where does the dead belong? It cannot belong to the lifeless, for only what is alive can suffer death (the stone, for example, has never lived, is therefore not able to die, and because it is lifeless it never has the possibility of life). So death belongs to life. The result of this analysis shows us that life is often used in two senses:
1. As the whole of living things, a determinate region of beings.
2. As the mode and manner of how the living being is as a living being, as a way of being.

In considering this double concept—life as the whole of living things and as a way of being—we have seen that next to [261] the living (to which also death belongs) stands the realm of the lifeless. We have also seen that the first concept of life in the sense of "everything that lives" does not include "everything that is." For Nietzsche, however, life signifies being as such.

If we ask, what is life? then we must first of all delimit the concept, that is to say, provide a definition (the Greek ὁρισμός) of it. How are we going to deal with such a question? Which science is able to provide information? Let us consider first of all the science of life, biology. βίος means life, whereby we must observe that βίος in the proper sense means individual life, and often also the course of life, whereas ζῷον in the narrow sense signifies the animal. The sciences of life that are biology, zoology, and anthropology provide information about living beings, and these disciplines take it upon themselves to deal with plants, animals, and human beings respectively.

To the question of what life is, all these sciences provide a univocal response: a function, an operation. Yet plants, animals, and human beings are not only a function, but rather living beings.

This shows that before dealing with life the sciences must already know what life is. The concept of life is the prior ground of the individual sciences, and this grounding representation of life constitutes the domain in which they move. But they can never provide an answer to the question of what life is. This question goes beyond them. Because there is no longer any philosophy, there is no longer any general doctrine of life (biology). For this reason the sciences are no longer philosophical, but rather technical.

I. Seminar Reports

Concerning the question, what is historiology? it is evident that Nietzsche means historiology and history in one and the same sense. The two terms are confused in his work. We want to distinguish them.

Historiology derives from the Greek ἱστορεῖν = to recount, report, inquire. And in fact inquiring about something that is present-at-hand. In the course of its evolution, the concept gained the sense of an inquiry concerning something already there before us, and finally of an inquiry into that which is already past, and it has maintained this [262] sense. Through the centuries this inquiry into the past became a science, which, as a science, elaborates specific technical procedures in order to bring back what is past. This is what characterises historiology. Passing into the field of general culture it becomes an element of "education" [*Bildung*].

History—in opposition to historiology—is in no way an inquiring, but rather the mode and manner in which something is. History is the actuality of what occurs, and is thus the object of historiology. The historian always already presupposes what history is. Always having in advance a determinate guiding representation concerning the essence of its domain is what characterizes, as we have seen, every science.

The scientific realm in which Nietzsche's text moves must be determined and delimited, for Nietzsche did not himself do this.

Looking at the structure of the text, we discover ten sections, the first of which embraces in a certain sense the whole of the realm that grounds the text. It begins with a comparison, that is, with the human being's view of the animal: "Consider the herd grazing before you. . . ." After two examples of comparisons (comparing the number three with the Prince of Homburg, a motorbike with a primrose) the task was set for us to find in Nietzsche's comparison the relation, that is to say, the perspective, that guides the comparison, and to find the inner organization of the text.

Rolf Neuhoff

Report on the Seminar of Monday November 14, 1938

We began with asking once again what we had gained from the elucidation of the title *On the Advantages and Disadvantages of History for Life* and from what had followed this elucidation.

In our text historiology and life are taken into account. The standard, the measure for this calculation is, [263] again, life. Consequently life has a superior value with respect to the calculative account. But the calculation is a need, demand, and necessity of life, and the carrying out of this necessity belongs, once more, to life itself.

In order to take a position in relation to the text it is essential to know in what context the text finds itself. The realm is that of a determinate—in fact, the Nietzschean—conception of life. On this point it is essential to recognise that "life" for Nietzsche, as we have already said, is a plurality of concepts.

We then began to identify the internal organization and articulation of the first section of the text. As a whole, the section deals with the unhistorical, the historical and the suprahistorical. It clarifies what historiology is with reference to the unhistorical and the suprahistorical. In this way the section makes apparent the essence of the historical.

It begins with the animal. In the first two paragraphs it is said that the animal is unhistorical, whereas the human is historical. We said that it is essential to be attentive to this opposition, for this particular manner of speaking is demonstrative of the particular mode of questioning at work.

The third paragraph says that forgetting belongs to action, and that the human being consequently must also exist unhistorically—in action.

For the human being, therefore, the unhistorical and the historical belong together, as the fourth paragraph states, in such a way that the ground on which they stand is the plastic power. This plastic power is hence the fundamental determination of life.

The fifth paragraph gives primacy to the unhistorical over the historical.

The content of the three following paragraphs is: when the human being considers the unhistorical, it raises itself to the level of the suprahistorical. However, the stance taken with regard to the historical and the unhistorical can be twofold:

1. It is possible to be *solely* historical.
2. It is possible to deny the historical, and this [264] *either* by being historical in the extreme—whereby the historical itself becomes the impulse for an active, that is, unhistorical future—*or else* just by the suprahistorical.

In the ninth to the twelfth paragraphs historiology is equated with knowledge, and the question concerning its relation to life is now a question: What relation do knowledge and life have to each other? Is cognition a consequence or presupposition of life? And so we ask once again what is compared in the comparison of human being and animal, wanting to gain an understanding of the region in which the essence of historiology is situated.

Karlheinz Funke

I. Seminar Reports

Report on the Seminars of November 21 and 23, 1938

I. Two Provisional Considerations:
What do life and historiology mean for Nietzsche?

1. *Life* in Nietzsche means first of all "beings as a whole," and second, the way of being, and ultimately—once life becomes the ground for the calculation of the advantages and disadvantages of history—the human way of being, human life.

    Life has this last meaning in a passage from Nietzsche's notebooks, vol. X: "What does not serve life is not true historiology; this depends, of course, on the more or less elevated idea of life that you have."

    Here it can only be a question of human life; for only the human being is historical and only the human being can have a low or elevated grasp of its life.

2. *Historiology* from ἱστορεῖν (the root ϝid is contained in the Latin *videre* and the German *wissen*) originally means an enquiring, not only relating to the past, but also to the future and to nature. In Heraclitus's fragments we find: χρὴ εὖ μάλα πολλῶν ἵστορας φιλοσόφους ἄνδρας εἶναι (fragment 35). Philosophers have to be, [265] before anything else, human beings who know a lot, and this not in the sense of πολυμαθίη—this *reason* does not teach (νόον ἔχειν οὐ διδάσκει), as stated in fragment 40—but rather in the sense of νοεῖν, of an *apprehension* of the essence of things. Thus ἱστορεῖν is for Heraclitus inseparably bound up with philosophy, that is, with the passion for essential knowledge of things. ἱστορεῖν is the necessary path of this passion. This suffices for the original sense of the word. For *Nietzsche*, historiology is first of all the general, that is, unscientific relation to the past.

II. The Comparison

Nietzsche's text begins with a comparison of animal and human being. The *perspective* underlying this comparison is the relation to the past: forgetting and remembering; *both* as relations to the past. The *objects* compared are animal and human being. Comparing presupposes an equality of the objects compared, and, for it is here a question of a determination of their *essence*, we look for an equality in *what* they *are*.

The question arises of whether this presupposition of equality in Nietzsche is necessary or accidental. To the extent that Nietzsche is a Western thinker, it is necessary; for the Western human being has defined itself as an animal for more than two thousand years:

ἄνθρωπος	ζῷον λόγον ἔχον
homo	animal rationale
human being	the rational "animal"

are the philosophical terms which, although not identifying human being and animal, still assert the equality of the generic domain of animal and human being, that is, animality.

We must ask ourselves whether the positing of the human being as ζῷον is so self-evident, whether *human being* cannot be defined more essentially. The answer to this will be a decision *for* or *against* Western thinking, and consequently also against Nietzsche's thinking. For according to him [266] the human being is the "not yet determined animal," a type of animal; consequently he has to be *distinguished* from the animal by means of a comparison with the latter. This is the sense of the first paragraph: the search for and the setting up of the line of demarcation between animal and human being.

III. The First Paragraph of §1

The human being considers the animal: he sees how it moves, what it does; he sees that it does not speak. From this he concludes that it "continually forgets," that it does not know "what yesterday is, what today is," that it is absorbed in the present.

What does this observation mean? Does it say something about the essence of the animal or is it not rather purely superficial? Consider a zoologist: he examines the animal much more precisely, he dissects its visible form, he observes its inner organs. Does he come to know in this way the interior of the animal? Is an animal nothing more than its body? What is the living body? An *animated body*.

We briefly touched on the question of the distinction between body and living body: every living body is a body but not every body is a living body. While the essence of a body lies in its visible exteriority, the essence of a living body goes beyond its external boundary. So too the essence of the animal as a living body; in other words, the animal relates to the *"milieu"* in which it moves, and it is first of all this relation that constitutes its own interiority.

Hence it is appropriate to include this relation in any reflection on the essence of animality. Nietzsche's statement that the animal is absorbed in the present is consequently essential; for it means that the animal is considered in its *particular* relation to its milieu; in particular this means at the same time that this relation is *not* proper to the human being. The *animal* is continually captivated by the present, such that it is never able to experience the present as the present. The *human being*, on the contrary, has a knowing relation to time, to the past and to the future. Between these two different relations to time, the [267] conscious and the unconscious, or, as we can also say, the unhistorical and the historical, lies for Nietzsche the line of demarcation between animal and human being.

We must here again pose the question whether this relation to time is sufficient to draw the line of demarcation between animal and human being.

K. L. Hampe

Report on the Seminars of November 28 and 30, 1938

We took the designation of the animal as "organism" as our starting point. Ὄργανον means in Greek the tool; yet the animal is no mere sum of ὄργανα, its unity is not the result of an assemblage of organs. We could say: the animal is a whole, thus: the unity of the animal is the *ground* of the development of a plurality of organs. But that is hardly a solution, it is rather only an introduction to a new question concerning the ground of unity itself, concerning how the "whole" is here to be determined with respect to its more genuine concept.

If we say: the animal is an organism, then its unity is, first of all, everything that belongs to this animal and indeed primarily to its living-body [*Leibkörper*]; beyond that, it relates itself to other things, such as food, predators, sexual partners. This relation to the outside belongs to the essence of the animal itself; *every living thing has its own range* [Umkreis]. Uexküll names this range the environment [*Umwelt*]; a poor terminological choice for what is better named "milieu" [*Umfeld*].

In order to characterize the animal's relation to space, we must draw two boundaries: the first is given though the adumbration of the living-body, while the second delimits the realm of its milieu, to which the body, through and beyond its own adumbration, relates itself. There is, of course, a difference here: the body as a corporeal thing certainly fills space, but it also [268] takes up space, thus disposing of it. How exactly the animal takes up this space, and whether it is not rather captivated by its milieu, is another question (for example, whether a hawk traverses space *as space*). Here the risk of anthropomorphism is never far away.

If we turn back to our treatise from the question of the animal's relations to space, we see that Nietzsche, beginning with the distinction between the historical and the unhistorical, situates the frontier between animal and human being within their *relations to time*. With his determination of the historical Nietzsche counterposes two limit cases. The human being appears as the extreme case of the historical:

he is an *imperfectum imperfectibile*: that which is follows him constantly from behind.

The animal, however, is unhistorical: it is always something present, for it does not have anything behind it, and it is at the same time a *perfectum*, for it is always and at each moment complete.

The animal is thus determined through a continual and immediate forgetting, whereas the human being is determined though the "was,," a not-being-able-to-forget. Forgetting therefore plays a central role.

Nietzsche begins his *Meditation* with the animal, using human concepts as a guiding thread and attributing these with certain restrictions to the animal. Here arises once again, as it did above concerning the relation of the animal to space, the danger of anthropomorphizing the animal, because Nietzsche, even when he begins with a reflection on the animal, really starts with the human being; for "forgetting" is a human concept that he transposes onto the herd.

The interpretation, precisely because it starts from the human being, is dependent on how the human being understands itself. The human being has a "vegetative" and "motor" nervous system. Insofar as it is composed of determinate substances, it falls under the domain of chemistry. It is thus plant, animal, and still something beyond that: human being. Everything belonging to the cosmos is unified in it; it is a microcosm. Conversely, the world can be [269] grasped as human being writ large, as a macrocosm (as macroanthropos).

Forgetting and remembering, we said, play a central role in relation to the distinction of the historical and the unhistorical. In §1 Nietzsche describes the "unhistorical" as a "continual and immediate forgetting"; in §10 it is the "art and the strength of being able to forget." Only the human being is capable of the latter, for the animal surely does not need it; as it is "bound to the stake of the instant." It is not free, only the now is given to it. (This difference, that is, the double determination of the unhistorical, will be important for our approach later. Here it is to be remarked that, in this first paragraph, the "forgetting" of the animal is ambiguously determined: on the one hand, as a complete absorption in the present, as completely without any relation to the past. On the other hand, it is said that the animal *sees* "every present sink back into the fog and night," such that in this "just now" there is a relation to the past, however slight it may be).

In order to delimit the concept of "forgetting," we would do well to begin with the word itself; we will do this by reflecting on the meaning of the term, not simply in a philological sense, but rather with a questioning attitude to the matter at hand.

The root of the word is linked to the Middle High German *"gezzen,"* which still survives today in the English word "to get." "Forgetting" means therefore "not holding onto something," that something escapes me, such that it has *gone*.

In Latin forgetting is *oblivisci*, from *oblino* = to wipe away, to smooth out (in the sense of what was written on a wax tablet having *gone*).

In Greek ἐπιλανθάνεσθαι has the root λαθ = hidden, which is also to be found in ἀλήθεια = the unhidden, truth. Accordingly ἐπιλανθάνεσθαι then means "placing oneself in the hidden with regard to (ἐπί) something," such that what is occluded has *gone*.

In each of these three fundamentally different perspectives what has been forgotten has *gone*, has not been retained, it has escaped, it has gone from the immediate proximity of available things. [270]

This determination is negative, in it something is negated—as in, for example, a definition of death as "no longer being alive." What is negated is the presupposition of the negation. There is forgetting only where there is retaining. Hence forgetting, as a particular mode of retaining, can be determined only on the basis of the concept of the latter. This has two consequences:
1. If there are several possible forms of retaining, then there will also be several possible modes of forgetting.
2. Where there is no retaining, there is also no forgetting.

When I retain something, such as a number, I can always represent the number to myself, I can *make it present* [vergegenwärtigen] to myself again and again. I can also make Strasbourg Cathedral present to myself, the thing itself, and not only an image of it. I can make present something to myself, that is—even the cathedral—, but beyond that something else, namely, what was, and beyond that still, what will come to be. Making present means, therefore, bringing something that is not present but that is still a being into the vicinity of that which I am presently related to.

Another mode of retaining is "remembering." I do not remember Strasbourg Cathedral, but rather that I was there, that I have seen it. I can remember something that has been only *as* something that has been, and indeed in such a manner that in this thing that has been there is a relation to me. Language is here imprecise, for I do not draw what I remember (*das Erinnerte*) back into an inner sphere, but rather place myself in what has been as having been alongside it.

Making something present to oneself and remembering are thus fundamentally different ways of retaining, to which different modes of forgetting must also correspond.

By way of conclusion, we elucidated these modes in considering the concept of "memory" [*Gedächtnis*] and established that it meant first the capacity for making present.

In order to elucidate the second sense of memory, we took the example of a war memorial. Here "memory" ("to the memory of the dead") means to think about, remembrance, and the relation to us is given through it [271] in that *we* think of ourselves as having to remember the dead.

Wolf Lohrer

Report on the Seminars of December 5 and 7, 1938

The question now concerns the essence of historiology. The realm in which the question moves is, for Nietzsche, prescribed through the distinction of human being and animal as two limit cases of the historical and the unhistorical. Unhistorical-historical are determined with regard to historiology as a relation to the past, and signify continually and immediately forgetting, and not being able to forget as always having to remember.

In accordance with the given question the two concepts had first of all to be clarified and determined univocally. Here, for methodological reasons, we remained within the realm of the human being. Concerning the conception of forgetting, which was introduced according to Nietzsche's starting point, it emerged that forgetting is a not-retaining. The essence of forgetting, as a negation of retaining, must be determined on the basis of retaining. We worked out the essence of retaining. It appeared in a twofold form:

1. Being able to make something present to oneself as bringing it into the present;
2. Remembering as a situating of oneself back into something past as such.

These correspond to two modes of forgetting:

1. Not being able to make something present to oneself. This occurs when something escapes us. Here the act of forgetting is no longer at our disposition.
2. No longer remembering, that is, no longer being able to situate oneself in what has been as having been. In this the human being is at the same time cut off from its own having-been.

In both forms of forgetting there is something [272] impersonal and passive: something can escape us and we can be cut off from what has been without our willing this. This leads to another form of forgetting that is opposed to the two others: no longer wanting to remember as a voluntary turning away from what has been as such, in which one turns oneself away from that which has been.

Corresponding to this, on the side of retaining, is what Nietzsche calls not-being-able-to-forget; positively, always having to remember.

This is not to be understood as continually having to have something present to mind (as it occurs in certain forms of mental illness), but rather as continually having to remember. The necessary nature of this "having to" is here not a constraint to which human being is submitted, but rather emerges from a decision with respect to what has been, to which the human being has subjected itself, and which means that it cannot bear to detach itself from what has been.

Retaining and forgetting were two possible modes of relating to the past, although they do not concern solely the latter. But it is this relation to the past that characterizes historiology, which was the focus of our questioning. It is necessary, therefore, to seek out what unites and is common to retaining and forgetting in their different modes. The differences between the different modes will be clearly determined on the basis of what is common to them.

Of what nature, then, is the relation to the past? Let us begin once again with retaining. Within it, as a making present, we are related to something as present, a present being, to a being as present. In retaining as a remembering we are related to what has been as having been, that is, to it in its having-been, to beings as having been.

Thus: in retaining we are related to beings as beings in a particular mode of being; to beings as present in making-present; to beings as having-been in remembering. The essential difference between the two ways of retaining resides in this. [273]

Such a self-relating to beings as beings is named comporting oneself toward. . . . This "comporting oneself" is an eminent determination of human being, and signifies the relation to all beings in which the human being stands, and in which what it relates itself to, that to which the relation is related, is given and manifest as a being. All other animate and inanimate beings stand in a wholly other, and in each case different, relation to the rest of beings.

Retaining (remembering, making present) is a relation having the character of a comporting oneself, that is, a relating oneself to a being as a being. From this perspective forgetting (as a negation of retaining) has to be not relating oneself to a being as a being. Here the negation affects not the relating, but rather what we are related to, and this not in an indeterminate fashion but rather in a particular respect. In other words, forgetting is still a relation, and indeed a relation to beings. If what was forgotten, that to which forgetting is related, were not, were not a being, then the forgotten could not return to us in remembering. But in forgetting the being as a being has gone; that is, it no longer shows itself to the one who has forgotten it. Insofar as they are, beings are only within a particular relation to the human being. If a being exists no longer as a being, this changes nothing in the being itself, but the human being enters into a different relation to it. This relation to beings can be described as an un-relation. But the being still stands in the region of that to which man has the possibility of relating himself. Hence this un-relation is of a wholly different type from, for example, the animal's lack of a relation to mathematics. This must be determined as a simple absence of relation.

This un-relation within forgetting must be characterized more precisely.

In forgetting what is forgotten has gone, has gone as well in its having been forgotten. But this means the forgetting is also forgotten. This most characteristic aspect of forgetting, that not only what is forgotten but also the having-forgotten are involved in the state of forgetting [274], we name the vortex-character of forgetting. It is with respect to this characteristic of forgetting that we say that the human being stands in the state of forgetting. But he stands in it not because he can forget, but rather forgetting as the falling away of both what is forgotten and the forgetting is possible only on the basis of forgottenness [*Vergessenheit*], in which the human being must always and already stand if it is to be able to forget. This always and already standing in forgottenness proper to human being indicates the passive character that we have already encountered in our earlier account of forgetting.

Retaining and forgetting were characterized as relations in the sense of a comporting oneself toward something. This meant to relate oneself to beings as such. What else lies in this characteristic in which they both share?

In his comportment the human being takes up beings as beings, in each case in a particular manner and in the guise of a particular being; for example, objects as something present-at-hand and this, say, as a blackboard. But in order to be able to take up something as a blackboard, as something present-at-hand, it is necessary to have a prior understanding of what blackboard and being present-at-hand mean. Only on the basis of an understanding of whatness (τί ἐστιν, *quidditas*), of being-present-at-hand, and consequently of being as such and in general, can the human being take up something as something, as something present-at-hand, as a being.

The fact that an understanding of being is a condition for beings to be apprehended as beings emerged only after long questioning. But the following became clear: in every relation to beings we follow and understand being, though for the most part we do not think about this understanding of being, and still less do we have a clear concept of what we understand in it. "We never and yet continually think being."

Being and the understanding of being generally remain in forgottenness, a state of forgetting that nevertheless includes something that must always be retained in order for us to be able to relate ourselves to beings as such; in order, in other words, for us to be able to be human.

This state of affairs points toward the pivotal role played by retaining and forgetting in the determination of the essence of human being. [275]

The reflection turned back to Nietzsche's question of historiology and the form in which he poses it.

Historiology was, according to Nietzsche, a characteristic determination of human life in opposition to animal life. Nietzsche works out this conception on the basis of a guiding statement about life: "without forgetting it is quite impossible to *live* at all" (vol. I, p. 286). Positively: forgetting, and being able to forget, necessarily belong to life. For Nietzsche, the unhistorical is rooted in forgetting, but the extreme case of the unhistorical is the animal. Consequently, the historical as a particular case of life is here determined from the perspective of the unhistorical: the historical is a not-being-able-to-forget. Insofar as being-historical is the essential characteristic of human being (vol. I, p. 289), the human being is here determined in its essence from the animal, and this through a restriction of the essential determination of animality: being-unhistorical.

The pertinence of this starting point and the procedure for such a conception of the historical, and consequently of the essence of the human being, needs to be investigated in order to attain a clear delimitation of the region in which the question of historiology has to move.

Both of the guiding concepts for this question are given to us through Nietzsche: retaining, forgetting. These have been clearly determined in their different senses. Moreover, an essential reflection has shown that there is forgetting only on the basis of retaining.

On this basis, and in relation to what Nietzsche himself provides to ground his claims, we must now decide whether it is justified to posit the difference between the unhistorical and the historical in the form of the difference between animal and human being.

Hence we ask: is the animal unhistorical? In other words, can an animal forget in any way? In order to be able to forget, it would have to stand in the realm of the possibility of retaining. But it is unable to retain. This is not to say that it is wholly delivered over to the state of forgetting, but rather: retaining is a relating oneself to beings either as present or as past. [276] But to this belongs an understanding of being-past and being-present. According to Nietzsche's own characterization, however, the animal does not know "what yesterday and today are" (vol. I, p. 283). So the animal cannot retain; and so it is also unable to forget; "unable" in the sense that the animal stands outside of the possibility of forgetting because it stands outside of the possibility of retaining. This shows also that the proposition advanced above, according to which forgetting belongs to all life, is, at least in its generality, unjustified.

What is said here against Nietzsche is only that the animal is unable to relate to beings as beings; neither does it need to do so in order to be an animal. Nietzsche aims at something essential, while his presentation of this point is inadequate. It was determined by us as the animal's being captivated by what surrounds it, a captivation from which it can never be released; instead it is always held and let go again by some particular thing. What surrounds the animal and that in which it moves was named the animal's milieu.

It can now be seen why we speak of the "milieu," and not of the "environment" [*Umwelt*], as one does in modern biology. The expression "world" means that "wherein" the human being "lives," in that he understands being and thus relates to beings as beings. Hence there is world only where beings are manifest as beings. The animal, though, can in no way relate itself, in our sense of the terms, to beings as beings, for it has no understanding of being. Consequently it cannot have an environment, and we must rather speak of its milieu.

Now if the animal cannot retain or forget (in the sense given above), then it can neither be historical nor unhistorical. For only what is historical in its essence can suffer a lack of historiology. The animal, with regards to historiology, is without historiology.

From this it emerges that the differentiation of the historical and the unhistorical does not coincide with the difference between human being and animal. [277] The question of historiology rather moves—even and precisely when its starting point is the historical-unhistorical distinction—wholly and exclusively in the region of human being. But if historiology is precisely what makes the human being the being it is (vol. I, pp. 288–289), if the human being is, therefore, essentially determined by it, then such a determination of the essence of the human being does not need to be referred back to animality; it rather moves purely in the domain of human life. In this way we repudiate the classical approach to the question of human being by means of the *animal rationale*.

With the question of the essence of the human being, we thus question *the* human being; that is, we question the essence of the human being, the essence of the humanity (Kant) of the human being. Nietzsche also moves in this direction within his questioning of historiology and its relation to life. This is evident in that when he speaks of the relation of historiology to human life he uses the words *human being, people, culture*, aiming with such determinations toward the essence of the human being (e.g., vol. I, 286f., 294). We will now provisionally sketch the manner in which Nietzsche understands this essence in order to uncover the principal direction and the entire horizon in which his argument develops.

The decisive determination of mankind is, for Nietzsche, the concept of culture. We find a characterization of it in the following two sentences:

"The culture of a people as the antithesis to this barbarism was once, and as I think with a certain justice, defined as unity of artistic style in all the expressions of the life of a people" (vol. I, 314; Nietzsche cites this passage from his *First Untimely Meditation*, p. 183).

"The concept of culture as a new and improved *physis*, without inside and outside, without pretense and convention, of culture as a unanimity between life, thought, appearance and will" (vol. I, 384).

The essence of culture, as Nietzsche develops it, [278] can be determined by means of these two clues. From the first sentence emerges a further concept of essential significance for the concept of culture: the concept of art. In this way we learn that an understanding of the concept of culture is to be gained with regard to the concept of art. But both concepts are essential determinations of the humanity of the human being, and thus of the concept from which the essence of historiology, the proper theme, is to be determined.

Karl Ulmer

Report on the Seminars of December 12 and 14, 1938

In the seminars we attempted to clarify Nietzsche's use of the concepts of *culture* and *people*. We were dealing with the question of culture, to which we had come from the perspective of the guiding theme: *historiology*. Historiology belongs only to the domain of human being, because it has a relation to the past, that is, to being-past, and thus to a determinate being. Because the question of historiology referred us to the domain of *the human being*, we questioned the concept of *culture* as belonging to the essence of man. Nietzsche speaks of this connection in the third paragraph of section I: *"There is a degree of sleeplessness, of rumination, of historical sense, which is harmful and ultimately fatal to the living thing, whether this living thing be a human being or a people or a culture."*

In our reflection on what culture means for Nietzsche we used as a basis the definition from the third paragraph of the fourth section: culture "as unity of artistic style in all the expressions of the life of a people." This means that culture is related to the people. From this the following question arose: *What* is culture in its relation to a people? Is it what makes a people a people, and thus a means? Or is it not rather a goal?

We provisionally left open the question of whether culture is a means or a goal [279] and asked *in what* the goal of culture consists. For if it were only a means it would still have to relate to a goal.

We understood from Nietzsche that culture is essentially codetermined through the concept of art. *"Culture:* the dominance of *art* over *life,"* as Nietzsche says in his notebooks (vol. X, p. 245).

In order to move closer to the question *What is art?* we used Nietzsche's identification of culture and formative education [*Bildung*]. We determined the essence of the latter:

1. in the sense of a forming: as bringing something into its shape [*Gestalt*].
2. in the sense of a preexisting view or image: as a sketch of the manner in which the human being wants to see and possess itself, as imagination [*Einbildung*] in a positive sense.

With this we have Nietzsche's concept of art: he understands it in the wider sense of formation [*Bilden*]. Art in the narrow sense—painting or architecture, for example—belongs to the domain of art in the wider sense. But when he speaks of art Nietzsche *does not mean* it in this more narrow sense.

We determined the *dual signification* of the concept of formative education [*Bildung*] as 1) formation [*Gebilde*], and 2) "images," and maintained that there is no separation of the two. We mean both of these when we say *Bildung*.

In both of these two meanings we find a particular type of *unification*.

1. All bringing into form of images is essentially a simplifying, or negatively expressed, a leaving aside, which means that the unity of the simple plays an essential role.
2. "Images" in the second sense raise and force toward a unity in which everything is gathered. In this sense we speak of transfiguration or illusion.

The *breadth* of Nietzsche's *concept of art*, which we attempted to determine through reflection on the senses of formative education, emerged from a passage in his notebooks: "that the *artistic* also begins with the *organic*" (vol. X, p. 128). That is to say, with the living the artistic is already posited. This clarifies why art is *more extensive* than nature. Nature is an imitation of art, Nietzsche says in his notebooks. [280]

On the basis of this extended sense of Nietzsche's concept of art, we attempted to gain an understanding of his determination of culture in the last section of the text: culture as a new and *improved physis*.

That culture represents an improvement of *physis* is possible only because *physis* has the character of *art* and because *art* is the basis of culture. What is to be improved and what improves both have the character of art.

An improvement of *physis* is possible:
1. in the sense of the putting-into-form: as overcoming of the formless and shapeless;
2. in the sense of a creation of images: as an elevation of what is dull and simply present-at-hand into illusion.

In order to bring out more precisely Nietzsche's concept of art, we questioned the relation of art in the broad sense to art in the narrow sense, and established the limits of art in the narrow sense: that it belongs solely to the domain of human being and that its goal is a *work* of art, posed and created as an existing being. This work-character is decisive for art in the narrow sense.

As understood in a broad sense, art is a particular way of the being of culture. But culture always arises only from the centralizing significance of an art form or of a work of art in the narrow sense.

As a *result* of these reflections that we had carried out, and in order to come closer to Nietzsche's concept of culture, we established the *art-character of culture*.

But culture is also and above all the unity of artistic style. In order to determine this *unity of style*, we first moved on to a clarification of the concept of style.

Stilus means a slate pencil, and the term was used in a transposed sense to denominate word and speech, later also discourse, and then the way of forming something, the rule according to which something is formed. Art is determined as classicism whenever its style can be grasped as a rule. *Classic* style, in contrast, is *authentic style*; it creates in giving the law [281], that is, in an originary manner and according to a new law of its development.

In opposition to uniformity, style is *law giving* and creative of unity. The unity of artistic style means the unity that arises from style; that is, a unity that is formed *in its own expression*.

What, then, is unity of artistic style in all the expressions of life of a people? That these expressions of life—the state, ethical life, the economy, for example—are governed by a unique law of formation.

We took from this definition of culture—as an answer to the question we posed at the outset, namely whether culture is a means or a goal—that the unity of artistic style is that through which a people sees itself, and completes itself as a people.

According to Nietzsche the people is not the *goal* of culture, but rather people *and* culture *and* humanity are there for the sake of great individuals. *Great individuals* (or highest examples, as Nietzsche also names them) do not exist because of humanity, but are rather in themselves peaks and goals. This is one of Nietzsche's essential thoughts, one which permeates his whole philosophy, and is expressed in the 1870 preface to *The Birth of Tragedy* dedicated to Richard Wagner, as well as in the 1886 text *Beyond Good and Evil* (vol. VII, part 4). It is rooted in Western metaphysics and is far from being an arbitrary assertion on Nietzsche's part.

If the individual is the goal of humanity, culture, and thus of the people, then how the *people* is formed is of capital importance. "Create for yourselves the concept of a "people": you could never have a sufficiently high and noble idea of it" (sec. VII, para. 3), as Nietzsche says in our text. The people is a *metaphysical concept*, even in Nietzsche, who takes it from German idealism by the intermediary of Schopenhauer; it cannot be created through offshoots of the sciences such as the study of popular culture or empirical historiology, but rather only through creative thinking. [282]

We closed the reflection on the concepts of culture and people in Nietzsche with this *result*, that people and culture are not their own goal, but rather a condition for the highest goal: great individuals.

December 20, 1938. Ernst Walter Zeeden

Report on the Seminars of December 19 and 21, 1938

In the last seminar we began with the question of the goal of culture and of a people. Nietzsche sees this goal as the bringing forth of the great individual, of the genius. Genius is a concept belonging to modern aesthetics and is used in this sense by Kant and German Idealism. It rests on an essentially modern understanding of human being that is foreign to the ancients. In antiquity the artist was seen as a craftsman. In antiquity the position of the artist, and also of the poet, was essentially different from what it is in modernity. Today the role of the artist is not clearly understood.

Nietzsche takes the concept of genius immediately from Schopenhauer. In the notes to his incomplete *Untimely Meditation* entitled *We Philologists* (1874–1875) he describes the genius as "the only one who is truly able to evaluate and negate life." Negating life must here be understood as a pacification [*zur Ruhe-bringen*] of the will. The genius brings the will in himself to a state of repose in the contemplation of the eternal. Contemplating the eternal only becomes possible once we are diverted from becoming. Nietzsche describes in section X, paragraph 9 the powers that enable the contemplation of the eternal: "I call 'suprahistorical' the powers that lead the eye away from becoming toward that which bestows upon existence the character of the eternal and the self-identical, toward *art* and *religion*."

The idea that the great individual is the goal for culture and a people is maintained by Nietzsche in his later, veritable philosophy, [283] but with one essential modification: Nietzsche characterizes his thinking quite early on as an inversion of Platonism. Platonism means here Western thinking since Plato, which considers what persists and what is constant as beings in the proper sense. Nietzsche's inversion considers becoming as being in the proper sense. The nature of becoming is determined from the perspective of life. Nietzsche says later on: "Genuine being is life" [*das eigentliche Sein ist das Leben*].

In this reversal Nietzsche's determination of the great individual also changes. The great individual becomes the *Overhuman*, a being of the greatest health and accomplishment, in whom the highest possibilities of human-being are realized. In his transfiguration the *Overhuman* incarnates life, becoming as genuine being.

This change in the meaning of the great individual is connected to an essential transformation of metaphysics that is rooted in Nietzsche's doctrine of the *Eternal Return of the Same*. This doctrine appears quite early in Nietzsche's thinking as a possibility, while first being rejected by him.

Nietzsche determined the great individual as the goal of a people. We must conceive the relation of a people to this great individual correctly. It is different from that of community and personality. The differentiation of community and personality is carried out within the people and within human being. It is a political-anthropological distinction. The people and the great individual are distinguished from an essentially different perspective. The great individual stands alongside the people; he is himself something like the people. He is in an exceptional way and on a higher level what the people itself is to a certain degree. The distinction is a metaphysical one.

When the great individual is characterized as the goal of a people, this does not mean that he emerges from an intention of a people to bring him into being. Rather, for the great individual to be able to emerge, the people must believe that it itself is the goal, that everything depends solely on the people.

The distinctions community/personality and [284] people/great individual are established on different levels. Playing off the thought of the great individual against an idea of community confuses these levels.

We moved on to a more precise determination of the idea of historiology in the text at hand. In sections II and III Nietzsche differentiates three modes of historiology: the monumental, the antiquarian, and the critical. This threefold division embraces the multiplicity of what we name historiology. What shows itself here in its continuity is the essence of historiology, its inner possibility.

Each of the three modes is accounted for with respect to its advantages and disadvantages for life. Historiology is something for which a calculative account can be provided and is bound to something that does the accounting, that is, to life. Life is continually engaged in accounting for itself. This reckoning becomes in Nietzsche's true philosophy a calculative account concerning value and nonvalue [*Unwert*]. In this context Nietzsche determines value as condition of the intensification of life, un-value as condition of the diminution of life. The question of values is the most decisive question of Nietzsche's philosophy. This is evident in the subtitle of his planned philosophical masterwork: *Attempt at a Revaluation of all Values.*

The idea that life is always engaged in accounting for itself is also to be found in Schopenhauer, who describes life as a business that does not cover its own costs. The calculative character of life is also included in the traditional determination of human being as *animal rationale* and as ζῷον λόγον ἔχον.

The threefold nature of historiology corresponds to three possible relations to the past, which emerge from three possibilities of life and the living: monumental historiology corresponds to the active and powerful individual, antiquarian historiology corresponds to conservation and veneration, and critical historiology to the being that suffers.

Life needs the service of historiology. Historiology serves the living in three respects, each time according to the way in which the living relates itself to the past. [285]

Monumental historiology serves the active individual by providing archetypes of the past. Antiquarian historiology serves the conservative and venerating individual—as a way of honoring the past and being bound to it. Critical historiology, as a way of judging the past, serves the one suffering from the past.

Next to the differentiation of the three modes of historiology as three possibilities of relating to the past stands our earlier distinction of making present and remembering. Remembering can be understood in a narrow and a broader sense. Remembering in the narrow sense demands a having-been-alongside the remembered [*Dabei-Gewesen-Sein*]. Historiology can be determined as remembering only according to a broader sense of the concept, that is, in grasping remembering as a form of remembrance, as a relation to something past that has an effect on the present, confronting the present and challenging it. Present here means: the presence of life. Life is continually engaged in a reckoning with itself. The present as presence of life is at each time the mastery of the reckoning that life undertakes with itself. In this reckoning the setting of goals for the future is codetermined. In this way, the relation constitutive of historiology reaches above the present into the future.

In each of the three modes of historiology the past suffers in a particular sense, in that it is viewed in a one-sided and incomplete manner. This affirmation presupposes the guiding idea that a relation to the past is at least possible, in which the past can completely and integrally be made present. Behind the question of the possibility of such a complete and integral making present of the past stands the question of historical truth, which will concern us when we examine the individual modes of historiology.

In the division of historiology into the monumental, antiquarian, and critical modes, historiology is not conceived as a science. Historiological science can appear in each of the three modes. These are thought as prescientific relations. [286] Science belongs to all three modes of historiology as a particular way of carrying them out, as a determinate manner of explaining the past. It is in no way a fourth, self-sufficient or higher mode of history.

When historical science governs the three modes of historiology or even wants to replace them, dangers emerge for life and historiology itself. These dangers are the veritable problem in response to which Nietzsche, as untimely, confronts his own time in his text on the *Advantages and Disadvantages of History for Life*.

The treatment of the three modes of historiology is contained in sections II and III of the text. Nietzsche begins the first paragraph of the second section with the division. There then follows the presentation of monumental historiology in paragraphs 2 to 6. Paragraph 7 again contains an overview of all three modes. Antiquarian historiology is examined in section III, paragraphs 1–4, critical historiology in the final paragraph of section V.

It is noticeable, even to a superficial consideration, that Nietzsche treats monumental historiology very thoroughly and critical historiology incomparably briefly.

We moved on to present the three modes of historiology individually:

i. Monumental Historiology

We began with the word *monere*—to exhort. The monumental is past greatness that is urgently exhorted into the memory of the present-day human being as stimulation. The monumental exists in the past as complete, permanent greatness standing out from becoming. As such it is the object of monumental historiology.

Monumental historiology springs from the belief in the eternity of greatness, from the conviction that the great moments in history are bound, as summits of human achievement, [287] to the continuing heights of humanity. This conviction grounds the quest and search for summits in history, and ultimately the demand to find impulses and archetypes for the present and the future in the greatness of the past. Monumental historiology serves life, because it grounds and strengthens the belief that greatness is still and always possible, because it once was, because it always was.

The past necessarily suffers by means of monumental historiology. Past greatness must appear to be eternal, standing out from becoming. This requires ignorance of the fact that it has become, in other words, a neglect of the causes and conditions of its emergence. Greatness is celebrated for itself as effect. What is small in history is forgotten, because it is of no interest. In this way monumental historiology courts the danger of overlooking the historical connections of causes and effects and thus of inventing a fictive historiology.

Disadvantages for life emerge through monumental historiology when it claims exclusive mastery for itself to the effect that it excludes life from the possibility of the other necessary relations to the past and their advantages.

Monumental historiology becomes dangerous for life when it serves talented egoists and enthusiastic villains. Life is urged in the direction of evil. The number of horrifying effects is proliferated.

It becomes dangerous for life in the hands of the weak, powerless, and inactive, when it is used by them in order to judge the greatness of the present in the process of its becoming. They consider themselves exclusively able to see greatness. Only what is monumental, past, and has long been acknowledged counts for them as great. The present can only repeat and is only permitted to repeat what is already there.

In this way monumental historiology can hinder the emergence of greatness when it is misused, when what is proper to greatness is misconceived: that it does not exist in itself or for everyone, but rather only for the powerful and active as a model. [288]

ii. Antiquarian Historiology

Antiquarian historiology looks back to the past as the condition of the emergence of the present and future, and further as the ground from which everything living emerges. The past is not venerated for its greatness, nor is it examined in order to clarify the present. It is venerated in order to bind what is alive today to former times, and conserved so that it can be handed down to future life as an object of veneration and attachment.

Antiquarian historiology settles people down and makes them faithful to what has gone before; it prevents the human being from being wholly delivered over to the latest novelty. In this way it serves life.

But the past suffers also by means of antiquarian historiology. The perspective becomes limited to what is near and native, which is accorded too much importance and seen only in its particularities. Antiquarian historiology does not allow the past to come freely to us and does not do justice to its proportions or differences in value.

The disadvantage of antiquarian historiology for life emerges from its demand that the past as such is to be recognized as worthy of veneration. It derives value merely from the fact that it is old. Everything new and in the course of becoming is immediately suspect and worth nothing, or even harmful, in that, as something new, it necessarily harms traditional pieties. Through antiquarian historiology, in this way, life becomes blind to creativity and hostile to becoming.

iii. Critical Historiology

The critical relation does not concern tradition, but rather turns on the past itself as a judging of it. Judging means: highlighting how accidents, violence, evil, and weakness are at work in history and even in the emergence of greatness. [289]

Critical historiology brings into the light of day that the past as such is worthy of destruction. In this way it serves the living, who from time to time must destroy a past in order to live.

Nietzsche describes the critical mode of historiology as the most dangerous; dangerous in a double sense: life is uprooted by it, for it undermines the right of the historial (the past) in general, and hence also of greatness, to veneration. It endangers the observer herself, in that it leads her, when she judges and condemns the past, to condemn her own origins as well.

Nietzsche's reflection on historiology is essentially determined by the understanding that Western history has been nihilistic for a long time and is coming to its end. From this perspective, critical historiology becomes the most necessary form of historiology; it becomes his way of doing historiology.

We must question, in going beyond Nietzsche himself, the various interactions between the different forms of historiology.

Alfred Franz

Report on the Seminars of January 9 and 11, 1939

The question guiding our work is the question concerning life. Life itself is to be thought, that is to say, conceived philosophically. For the task of philosophy is nothing other than that of determining the fundamental concepts of being.

From the beginning of our reflections we have distinguished two concepts of life: life as beings as such and in general, and life as human life. Although Nietzsche does not explicitly isolate these two senses of life, we have clearly distinguished them.

Our text led us to a reflection on human life since its topic addresses itself exclusively to the human being, given that it treats of the problem of the relation of history to life [290] and that, as we have seen, history can exist only in the realm of human being.

We then posed another question, namely whether we could learn anything essential from the relation of historiology to life that Nietzsche presents in his text for the determination of the concept of life itself. Here we reminded ourselves that we—in opposition to Nietzsche—had distinguished historiology from history, and thus had characterized historiology in the original, etymological sense of the Greek ἱστορεῖν as an inquiry, particularly an inquiry of the past; history, however, we had determined as the happening of the past, and thus as the object of historiology. The examination of the threefold relation of historiology to life as monumental, antiquarian, and critical historiology led us to formulate three essential statements about life:

1. Human life, insofar as it needs and desires historiology, desires a transfiguration of itself beyond itself by using archetypes from the past; this corresponds to monumental historiology.
2. Life implies an attachment to the past, for this presents itself to the human being as the ground of its existence. This is what antiquarian historiology teaches.
3. This relation to the past involves a suffering from which life needs to be freed, and this occurs through the destruction of the past and of what has become by means of critical historiology.

These are three fundamental attitudes of life, which have emerged in reflection on its relation to historiology: it desires transfiguration, it remains attached to the past, it suffers.

Nietzsche himself has not drawn any further consequences for the essential determination of human life from this threefold relation of historiology to life, for he was caught up in the traditional determination of human being as ζῷον λόγον ἔχον. By means of a more originary questioning, though, we come to an essential determination of human being that is fundamentally different from the traditional one. [291]

The three comportments are not developed any further; instead, studying the relation of human being to historiology led us to the correlative relationship of human being to time, which in turn led us to a more essential determination of human being.

Historiology as an inquiry relating to the past is possible and has meaning only in relation to the present and the future. Hence historiology exists only where past, present, and future exist, where time exists. Historiology is possible only insofar as man—inquiring concerning the past—stands in a relation to time. The nature of this relation is revealed by the three modes of historiology: monumental historiology points toward the future; intensification, willing-beyond-oneself means—understood temporally—wanting to go forward. Antiquarian historiology points toward the past, in that it maintains, preserves, and venerates the past. And critical historiology belongs to the present: the destruction of a past happens in the present. In this way the three modes of historiology have a connection to the threefold relation of human being to time, that is, to the past, the present, and the future. This relation is threefold because time is three-dimensional, because past, present, and future belong to it. This threefold nature of time is the ground on which historiology exists. For historiology was determined as "knowledge of the past in the service of the present and the future."

Things and animals also have a relation to time: they came into being once, and thus are related to the past; they exist in the present, and will exist and pass away in the future. Their state changes in the course of time. Insofar as they exist, they are in time, endure in time, are present in time. Their relation to time is a relation according to clock time.

The human being also bears this relation to time—or rather its living-body [*Leibkörper*] bears this relation; but beyond this it has a particular, essential relation to time that constitutes it as human being, [292] and in studying this relation we will push on toward a different way of essentially determining human being than the one that has predominated until today.

The human being thinks and represents to itself time as such: the past appears in the human realm as past, the present as present, and the future as future. For the human being this relation is essential and characteristic, and it is grounded in the temporality of human being. In this way it is distinguished from things and animals.

We have already said earlier that human being is related to beings as beings, that it "comports" itself toward beings and that this constitutes a limit between animal and human being. Consequently this is also where the limit is here to be found. Only the human being has, over and above a simple relation to time, the particular relation according to which it is not in time like the animal, but rather exists, in itself, for its own being, while also continually being bound to time as such. This relation, temporality, is an ex-stasis, a being held out into time, in which it continually finds itself, as past, present, and future. As a being that remembers it is bound to the past as such. As a being that plans and anticipates it is bound to the future, and as an active being within the moment it is bound to the present. The human being cannot exist in any other way. Even when it remains a passive spectator in the face of life it is grounded in temporality; for since this passive condition belongs to the active being of human being, in the same way as death belongs to life, in this situation it also exists in temporality and is bound to time. This particular relation of human being to time is essential and constitutes it as human being. Temporality is the essential ground of the being of the human being, for it makes remembering possible in relation to the past, planning and resolution in relation to the future, and activity in relation to the present.

Since we have just said that it is the threefold nature of time that makes historiology possible, then we must now establish that the ground of historiology is the temporality of the human being, for in the relation between past, present, and future, [293] which was characterized in the definition of history as a standing-in-service, past, present, and future were meant as a relation originating from human affairs. In this way historiology is grounded on temporality.

We will not decide here whether or not the three modes of historiology that Nietzsche establishes result necessarily from temporality, from the particular and threefold relation of human being to time. Let it simply be noted that the three modes, insofar as they involve a relation to time, are grounded in temporality.

On this basis we can also consider the relation between historiology and history, an issue to which we referred briefly at the beginning in characterizing history as the object of the study of historiology. In one passage Nietzsche goes as far as to say that it is first by means of historiology that events become part of history. In order to be able to take up a position in relation to such a claim, it is necessary to go further into the concept of history, which was previously determined as what "really happens." We will delimit the concept more closely by reserving it for the human realm, in the knowledge that beyond this realm the concept is applied indifferently to all kinds of processes, be it a matter of geological periodization or of the evolution of animals.

History exists whenever the human being exists as a remembering, planning, or actively present being, that is, whenever he is in temporality. Given that he can exist, as we have seen, only in temporality, that he can live—that is, be a human being—only in this particular relation to time, we can infer that the human being is always in some sense historial. The human being does not have a history because he grasps himself historically, but rather he has a history because he is historial. Hence history is not originally what it is as an object of historiology, but is rather grounded in the temporality of the human being. We said the same about historiology, and thus we can now say: historiology—the human relation to history—and history—the object of the relation—are both grounded in the temporality of man. [294]

Following this consideration, we turned back to Nietzsche's text with the question of how sections II and III relate to IV and the ones following it, and said that in sections II and III Nietzsche deals with historiology in general by delineating and discussing the three different modes of historiology. It is in section IV that the genuinely untimely meditation begins; here Nietzsche begins his struggle against the present, a struggle fought with the weapons provided by critical historiology. We had seen that in section III this mode of historiology was examined only very briefly. This is explained by the fact that in the *Meditation* and in Nietzsche's work as a whole this mode of historiology is a matter of fundamental importance and represents the principal weapon of his philosophy. In saying this, we should also remember that in section III of the *Meditation* Nietzsche had said that every mode of historiology, when it predominates, falsifies history. Yet Nietzsche is not only a destroyer, but rather also constructs on the ground of antiquarian and monumental historiology. At the end of section IV he says: "Let me say expressly that it is for *German unity* in that highest sense that we strive, and strive more ardently than we do for political reunification, *the unity of German spirit and life after the abolition of the antithesis of form and content, of inwardness and convention.*"

But that is culture, which had been described as the "unity of artistic style in all the expressions of life," as the presupposition of a higher humanity.

Nietzsche's struggle against his own time rests on the idea of life's oversaturation with historiology; a historiology that has become science. The problem is that this science is undertaken for its own sake, for the sake of gaining knowledge, that historians serve science, carrying it out in going beyond what is intrinsically necessary. That leads to oversaturation and consequently to an "inwardness" that no longer corresponds to anything "outer." In this way culture as the "unity of artistic style [295] in all the expressions of life" is destroyed. Hence it is not science that is guilty, but rather the manner in which it is carried out.

If we consider science in general and particularly as historical science, then with the question of how science can take control of historiology, of how historical science becomes possible, we must first of all consider that historiology is a form of knowledge, that is, that it encapsulates knowledge. Nietzsche does not deal with the fact that historiology, as knowledge, can and must, within certain limits, be a science. It is precisely this issue that we must now turn toward.

Knowledge means having something continually present, such as it is. Such a representation is correct or true. The question of knowledge thus presupposes the question of truth, in our case the question of historical truth, which in Nietzsche, in section VI of the text, emerges as a question concerning historical objectivity and also justice: the question of truth that has moved mankind throughout history. We already find the question concerning δίχη in one of Anaximander's fragments.

Otto Rasper

Report on the Seminars of January 16 and 18, 1939

Nietzsche chose the title *Untimely Meditations* to announce a critique of the age. Since then the idea of an "untimely meditation" has become an expression that could serve, in a much wider sense, as a heading for all philosophy, for it belongs to the essence of philosophy to think against its own age.

It reflects on the age critically (critically in a sense that remains to be determined), in order to lead it to confront itself, and consequently to lead it to a knowledge of its own essence, and also to this: to think in advance the possibilities of its future.

The reflection we are undertaking here goes beyond the framework [296] of the text. It determines the manner of our questioning in relation to the text, and is the reason for our critical confrontation with Nietzsche's philosophical thinking in general. Our concern with this must be of a fundamental nature because Nietzsche is the last in the line of philosophers. What has been thought after him is more or less based on his thinking. A confrontation with Nietzsche therefore concerns our own age.

We are all the more entitled to leave to one side what is all too timely in his thinking in order to emphasize the governing, essential questions. The "untimely" in a positive sense will be the theme of our questioning.

Our intention to offer a critical reflection requires an elucidation of the word "critique." We can gain this from the text at hand. Nietzsche himself, who took up critical historiology as a weapon, does not use the concept in the ordinary sense of "criticizing." He uses the term "critique" positively and as synonymous with "judging"; "judging" not understood in the sense of "condemning," but rather as analogous to the Greek sense of the word κρίνειν, meaning "to differentiate." Here one differentiates according to the rank, the value or valuelessness of that which is to be criticized. Here "judging" means: "setting standards."

The guiding idea of "life" in the title already indicated to us at the beginning of our reflection that in the calculative account of historiology and life, life served as the standard of the judging.

We briefly clarified once again the double significance of both the concepts that are brought into the calculative account: on the one hand, life, as human life, in its three relations to time, is the ground of the three possibilities of historiology; on the other hand, precisely because of these relations, historiology is for us a means of learning something about life.

We have therefore seen that on the one hand, life is the measure of judgment, and that on the other hand, it is itself the target of the critical meditation. We learn from critical historiology how life is understood, [297] whether in an elevated or vulgar fashion. Historiology evaluates and sets standards, as all positively carried out "critique" essentially must, and thus itself becomes philosophy.

Within the relation of historiology to life new regions of questions, which Nietzsche only touches upon, present themselves to us: the relation of historiology to science; science as a particular mode of knowledge; knowledge as a kind of truth; and finally truth as a determination of life.

Yet we first of all endeavor further to develop our reading of the text, since it is the foundation and starting point of all our efforts.

We begin with section IV of the text. The first paragraph summarizes what was said about historiology in section II and section III, namely that life needs historiology, and that the latter must serve it in one of the three modes of historiology. This is the "natural relation of an age, a culture, a people to historiology," says Nietzsche; "all of this is simple, as truth is simple."

We wondered why Nietzsche speaks of "natural" relations in this passage. In this passage that examines once again, in a condensed fashion, the relation of historiology to life, the word "nature" gains a particular significance. This holds, too, for what has previously been argued.

The term has two meanings. It can be defined either as a biological concept, or be understood in the sense of an "essential law." Here and previously Nietzsche uses the word "nature" in the first sense. The naturalness of human life is characterized in the same section with the expressions "hunger," "degree of need," "plastic power." This is a consequence of the essential determination of human being as *animal rationale*. Within these limits—that is, within the limits of human being grounded in animality—each of the expressions of life indicate once again a relation to time: hunger wants to appropriate what remains to come in the future, [298] regulated by the past, and carries the plastic power of all becoming life. The need is oriented toward the present.

Historiology had already been considered in the light of natural comparisons, such as in the seventh paragraph of section II, where the three modes of historiology were compared to plants, each of which could flourish only in a particular climate and on a particular soil.

We find the same idea again in the first paragraph of section IV. Here it is said that historiology cannot be chosen arbitrarily, but must be used by each person and each people "according to their particular goals, strengths, and needs."

The second sense of the concept of nature, as what belongs to the essence of a thing, contains for us the sense of universal lawfulness, by which we are not to understand a rule governing a process within beings, but rather *natura*, as an essential law of being.

In relation to human life, nature in this sense is what demands that life be taken up by the human being in an aspiring, conserving, or suffering mode; it is thus the valid, necessary law in which the temporality of the human being is grounded.

Because the human being is temporal, because it takes up what is past as past, what is present as present, what remains to come in the future as futural, it stands in history and makes history. And likewise, because historiology is rooted in temporality, and because its three modes presuppose the three possibilities of the historiality of the human being, historiology depends on the historiality of the human being. Hence it becomes clear at the end of this analysis, which we began with the concept of nature = life, that it falls again to life to have mastery over nature.

The short summary that Nietzsche presents in the first lines of section IV has the character of a recapitulation. But at the same time it serves as a springboard for the subsequent reflection on his own age. We discussed the constellation of life and historiology. Nietzsche begins this new section with [299] the question: "Or has the constellation of historiology and life really changed, because a powerful and hostile star has come between them?" Indeed, a new star has come between them, science, the demand that historiology be a science. Nietzsche characterizes the star as powerful and hostile, but shortly after describes it as luminous and splendid. He was more convinced than anybody of the necessity of knowledge and knew about the fundamental role that science plays in Western history. The star that disturbs the constellation of historiology and science is not, for him, science itself, but rather the demand that historiology be a science.

We asked how such a demand could be grounded, and where its roots were to be found in the spiritual history of the West [*abendländische Geistesgeschichte*].

Such an overinflated evaluation of science is grounded in the conviction that scientific truth is the basic form of truth. Since Descartes coined the phrase *cogito ergo sum*, the Western human being takes to be true what for it is certain, that is, what it knows by virtue of its capacity to know its surrounding world and to draw valid laws from nature. With the aid of rigorous, provable formulae, the greatest scientific systems are constructed on the basis of this article of faith, according to which the human being henceforth determines itself from itself as a thinking being. This self-certainty of thinking has determined our historical existence [*Dasein*] ever since.

Hence scientific historiology also stakes its claim to an absolute truth. It positions itself between the human being and its original relation to the past and seeks to determine this relation in advance. It is only following this determination that the individual is free to take its own perspective concerning this relation.

The sense of the demand for historiology to be a science is not only that it be carried out with the means offered by a scientific technology, but even more so that [300] knowledge of the past should be as secure as possible. The conviction that everything belonging to the past is worthy of being known is decisive in this. "Knowing" [*Wissen*] here has the same meaning as "comprehending" [*Kennen*], and "comprehending" means grasping something as a whole encompassing all that belongs to it. It is in this sense of comprehending that scientific historiology relates to its own subject matter. Nietzsche calls this historiology the "science of universal becoming," for it represents the past in the manner both of what it had become as well as how it had become what it was [*damaliges Gewordensein und vormaliges Werden*]. The "representing to oneself" occurs in the sense of a making present, not in that of a remembering. We saw that remembering was an "if not having been present at the time, then at least being intimately concerned by it." But in scientific historiology any personal relation of the researcher to the past must be excluded. It wants to look at the pure object and thus to be "objective," to use Nietzsche's word.

We come to the third paragraph of the section. Here the consequences of the disturbed relation of historiology and life are addressed. Nietzsche draws an image of the modern human being. Since life no longer limits the knowledge of the past, "historical knowledge floods in ever anew from inexhaustible springs." A question necessarily arises in response to this account of such an excess of knowledge, knowledge that is supposed to be absorbed but that in fact cannot be digested: why does historiology not suffocate itself, or why does the human being not put a stop to it before it gets to the point of oversaturation? The influx of knowledge that Nietzsche describes does not proceed simply by accumulation, but is rather ordered according to a particular point of view, that of comparability. The richer historical knowledge is, the greater the possibility to draw parallels, to make comparisons, and in short to be free to do as one pleases. This gives the human being the idea that it stands above these things, and this makes history so tempting for it. And that is, again, the genuine, innermost foundation of scientific historiology.

Historiology ruling in such an unrestricted fashion results in a [301] bifurcation in the life of the human being. Nietzsche characterizes this as the human being's hopeless disintegration into content and form, according to which the inner corresponds to nothing outer, the outer to nothing inner. To be determined by such a fracture and to live within it is described as the most particular characteristic of the modern human being.

We said "fracture" [*Riß*] and distinguished the term from another word, used erroneously, namely "contradiction" [*Gegensatz*], in order to emphasize that this "fracture" presupposes an original unity. It is the un-form of a unity of inside and outside. The relation is still there, but its correspondence is disturbed.

At this juncture we had to make clear how we were to understand the characterizations "inside" and "outside." A spatial distinction is not intended in the given context. We defined the inside of the human being as the capacity to represent something and to have what is thus made present as existing or being created autonomously. The inside is what is present in and for itself, whereas the outside is the outcome, the deed. This distinction is not quite as clear as it may initially appear.

When, for example, I make something present to myself, I form something that already is, something external; in contrast, in certain realms of action I give form to something inner; for example, in education I form something that still has to come into being.

This clearly shows the reciprocal interplay between the initially separated realms of inside and outside.

Irmgard Hueck

Report on the Seminars of January 23 and 25, 1939

It became clear that we had to elucidate once again the essence of the natural sciences and the concept of truth in the natural sciences.

It is often affirmed that the modern natural sciences are presuppositionless, which seems to mean that [302] they are purely experimental sciences, that they are purely and simply grounded on experiment. But does this affirmation correspond to the facts? Do we not precisely make one presupposition that makes something like experimental science in general possible? A presupposition that dictates that the principles of science, the ones that are to be seen as fundamental and properly scientific, must have the character of mathematical principles.

The breakthrough of the modern concept of truth in Descartes is the foundation of the concept of truth proper to the natural sciences, and consequently the ground of the modern natural sciences in general. It made possible the constitution of modern physics, but it also did violence to several differently organized sectors of the natural sciences such as biology, since the latter's philosophical development, to the same extent as physics', was bound to the Cartesian conception of truth, and thus was unable to adhere to any other ideal than this.

Consequently biology did not attempt to grasp the living being as something living, but rather attempted to capture it in such a way that its results can aspire to the same degree of truth as mathematical physics. And this is why still today in biology the most prized areas are those in which it is possible to work in a physicalist manner. One particular area of biology demonstrates this merely in the way it is named: developmental mechanics.

It is essential for us—and this is the aim of our elucidation of the concept of truth in the mathematical-natural sciences—to recognize that this concept of truth determines the idea of science as such, and that it has become operative to a degree which does not do it justice, as the example of biology as belonging to the natural sciences already indicated.

This point is already grounded in the fact that in the course of the emergence of the particular sciences, the natural sciences, and within these [303] the physical sciences, were primary and hence *oriented* the development of all sciences.

Let us return to our text! The third paragraph of section IV contains the characterization of the fracture between inside and outside, which is the decisive consequence of the scientific predetermination of historiology. But concerning this characterization, it should be noted that the fracture does not occur first of all as a result of historiology becoming a science, but because within this process the fracture is shaped in a particular way.

The fracture has rather existed since the beginning of modernity. It would be easy to pass over this issue, because Nietzsche does not illuminate it in his essay. Nietzsche was not yet able to perceive this situation, because it was still much too close to his own stance.

The fracture emerges with the determination of truth as certainty in and through Descartes. "Certain is what I evidently perceive!" I can (therefore) perceive as evident mathematical principles and consequently the whole of scientific knowledge, which itself is grounded on this determination of truth.

The essential importance that this determination of truth and its transformations have for philosophy and for science, indeed for the whole of life, has now become manifest. And this is why the concept of truth must now also be taken up as a theme. The next question in this connection is that of Nietzsche's determination of truth.

The historical moment in which the *Untimely Meditations* were written is decisive for Nietzsche's concept of truth. A clear indication of this is the essay of 1873: "On Truth and Lies in an Extramoral Sense."

In order to provide a merely preliminary concept of this and in order to clarify in a certain sense the horizon underlying Nietzsche's concept of truth, we note in advance the following propositions offered by Nietzsche:

1. 1883, *Zarathustra*, part 2: "Their madness teaches that [304] truth is proved with blood. But blood is the worst witness of truth."
2. 1885, *Will to Power*, n. 493: "*Truth is that sort of error* without which a particular sort of living being cannot live. The value for *life* is in the end decisive."

This last aphorism is for Nietzsche a basic thesis, and thus it should not be played down by saying that here Nietzsche means: "The true is what is useful." One can therefore not take this aphorism seriously enough, for behind it stand Nietzsche's deepest insights. This suffices for the *preliminary* anticipatory remarks.

Turning back to the text, the fourth paragraph deals with the question of how the fracture between inside and outside is manifest in the life of contemporary Germans. Nietzsche says of the Germans that they have lost form, but form must here be understood in a particular sense. Nietzsche himself characterizes this form, this outside, through the concept of convention. What is convention? It is, for Nietzsche, authentic tradition, tradition brought into form. This concept of convention becomes clearer if we imagine its opposite, namely what is merely learned and lifelessly taken up, for example, the nineteenth-century neo-Gothic.

Nietzsche's view of romance culture is essential for a more developed characterization of this concept of convention. Within this he particularly focuses on seventeenth-century France.

In the fifth paragraph Nietzsche speaks of the particular danger of relying on and abandoning oneself to [*Sich-verlassen*] interiority, namely that it could disappear without our being aware of this.

In the sixth paragraph, in contrast, the value of unscathed inwardness is deliberately emphasized. This sixth paragraph refers back to the third insofar as it clarifies once again the conditions of culture in relation to the particular case of the Germans of his time. And toward the end of the paragraph we find Nietzsche's declaration: "I shall explicitly set down my testimony here that we strive for *German unity* in that highest sense." [305]

The unity in that highest sense is culture, and such culture the Germans need to strive for. According to Nietzsche's statement, the culture of the Germans lacks convention, the concept of which he gained from romance cultures. In order to clarify this so essential concept of convention with particular respect to a possible German culture, let the following be said: the reference to the romance world and specifically to the French world refers to a particular factor that becomes clear in a basic manifestation of the historial human being, that is, in language! Both languages, French and German, although they both are of Indo-Germanic origins, are considerably different from each other:

The French language has been complete for a long time; it is, and will be, continually supervised by the *Académie française*. A Frenchman can say everything that he has to say with his language. In fact, the language is at one and the same time conventional and lively, and thus possesses a particular clarity and suppleness.

The German language, in contrast, has a quite different nature. Both dangers and strengths are to be found in this difference: it allows for the possibility of new creations and for the danger of abuses and decline.

Whereas the French language, with the balance proper to it, has a certain elegance and perfection, the German language often shows an ungraspable uniqueness in expression and often lacks grace.

This difference between the two languages clarifies two things:
1. the nature of French convention
2. that this nature does not conform to what is German.

In order to form a German culture, it would therefore be necessary at least once to think and feel in a purely German way, while the German essence would have to be clarified and elucidated. But to work this out in detail is not *our task* here.

Section IV of the text offered something of an overview of the harms caused by the predetermination of [306] historiology as a science. Section V now presents the properly untimely meditation.

Before we can begin with its elucidation, however, one particular misunderstanding must be eliminated from the outset: the harms Nietzsche points out do not arise from scientificity as such, but rather from the fact that a particular mode of scientific knowledge of the past exclusively attempts to constitute the present's relation to the past. This scientific knowledge of the past claims preeminence over and above the three modes of the prescientific relation. But how, in fact, do matters stand concerning the originality of these relations? It is quite certain that before all science, human beings, whose existence has the character of historial being, have relations to the past by virtue of their essence. These relations are original and essential, and the three that Nietzsche discusses are of that sort.

Within the original region of these relations the following question arises, which is important for an untimely meditation: "How and on what is the specific relation of a particular living present to the past determined and supported?" "Of a living present," that is, of an age in which what is original and essential still governs. This question includes another within it: what the living present thinks of itself and on what basis it values itself, for the interpretation of the past depends on this evaluation. A heroic age, for example, will seek great archetypes, whereas an age like the one to which Nietzsche refers—an age that is no longer fully flourishing, for life itself has been harmed—accords itself so little value that the mere scientific knowledge of the past is more highly prized than the original and essential relations.

Nietzsche has this situation clearly in mind when he says: "What does not serve life is not genuine historiology, and this depends on how high or low you estimate the value of life." [307]

On historiology as science we can now say in summary—for it is not possible here to enter further into the problem of science—that:
1. It is a matter not so much of the scientific character of historiology but rather of its standard defining even the goals of the present.
2. The scientific relation to the past is neither more original than the three modes of historiology, nor is it, next to them, a fourth mode, but it originates after these.

Following the argument of the text, we will now explain the damage to life that emerges from the misrecognition and obscuring of both these points. How does Nietzsche proceed?

Section IV begins with the claim that the damage is fivefold:
1. The weakening of personality (Section IV).
2. The emergence of the illusion [*Sinnbildung*] of a higher justice (Section VI).
3. The destruction, by means of historical justice, of the atmosphere necessary for a culture (Section VII).
4. The setting in of the idea of being latecomers and having arrived at the end of time (Section VIII).
5. Self-irony and cynicism.

The first way in which historiology as science inflicts harm is thus the weakening of personality. To be able to understand this weakening we must first question the idea of personality.

First of all, where does this concept arise from in etymological terms? From the Latin *persona*, or, more precisely, *personalitas*. *Persona* can be derived from *personare*, but the derivation is not that obvious. *Personare* means to "resound through," "to proclaim loudly," and thus *persona* would be what resounds through, reverberates [*Durchtönte*], that is, the mask.

And *persona*, like all concepts in this cultural domain, is also a translation from the Greek. τὸ πρόσωπον is [308] what is before the face—ὤψ meaning the face—and thus, once again, the mask.

In ancient theater the mask is the symbol for the person portrayed, πρόσωπον εἰσιέναι—to portray someone. The contemporary idea of a role therefore corresponds to the concept of *persona* and πρόσωπον. A role is a particular mode and manner of being a human being.

But the word "role" is also used in another sense. One says "he's playing a role" and means: "he is a quite particular individual involved in a decisive manner in the matter at hand." This meaning, which is linked in a particular way to the concept of a theatrical role and thus to the concept of *persona* and πρόσωπον, emerged very early on. The Romans were already familiar with it.

This ancillary sense of the word "role" means for a human being to be preeminent and remarkable. Taken in its broadest sense, it had the same meaning for the Romans, but in a narrower sense it was further characterized by means of the concept of *dignitas*.

The Roman *persona* is someone who possesses to a high degree a quality that veritably and originally constitutes what the human being is as such. The human being was generally determined as *animal rationale*. *Dignitas* is thus grounded on *ratio*. Someone who really is someone, who can really play a role, who possesses *dignitas* in the Roman way of thinking, has this eminent being by virtue of his humanity, that is, *by virtue of his ratio*.

The concepts of *persona* and of the human being are thus closely linked, for the concept of *persona* is grounded on the determination of *human being*. This always needs to be borne in mind.

The first determination of *human being* to follow this ancient one was presented by Christianity. Augustine speaks of the *mixtura anima et corpus*, of the living being that is body *and* soul. This new determination of the human being rests on the former as *animal rationale*.

In this Christian realm *persona* takes on a quite particular meaning, and that in two respects: [309]
1. Human being, the *persona* is determined as an individual soul whose goal and salvation lies in gaining eternal life as an *individual*.
2. God is determined as the essential unity of the three *personae*: God the Father, God the Son, and God the Holy Ghost (Augustine, *De dignitate dei*).

Here we find a clear inflection of the concept of *persona* in the direction of the individual. And within the determination of human being we find here for the first time the idea that he is his own goal and purpose.

In fact, in the Middle Ages Thomas Aquinas goes on to determine *human being* in the following way: *persona est rationalis naturae individua substantia*. *Substantia* here is to be understood as the Latin translation of the Greek ὑπόστασις and not as some idea of substance issuing from a philosophy of nature.

Thomas's determination is particularly important for the emergence of the modern concept of personality. It signifies the undivided self-sufficiency of a rational being; that is to say, the independence of the human being, and consequently that of the *persona*, now appears clearly.

In Thomas's determination of the human being, the extent to which Descartes is influenced by late Scholastic philosophy becomes clear; he takes up its concepts, and hence has to move in the realm of these concepts and their possibilities.

Yet Descartes does add something new and essential, and therefore represents the next decisive stage in the development of the concept of personality.

In the context of the fundamental self-reflection that philosophy carries out, which necessarily also concerns the essence of truth, Descartes forms the basic principle of modern philosophy: *ego cogito, ergo sum*. The *ego cogito* is fundamental here. The being of the human being is now determined through its self-certainty, which corresponds to the determination of truth as certainty. The *ratio* [310] that was involved in all determinations of the human being here receives the particular form of self-certainty, on the basis of which certainty about anything else first becomes possible. This means that the *ego* in Descartes's principle is *the subject lying at the root of everything* (in Greek τὸ ὑποκείμενον).

Therefore the following important event occurs: the human being determines itself now wholly in and from itself, he no longer adds anything of Church doctrine. Since Descartes the essence of the human being appears precisely according to its capacity for self-determination.

The next stage in the determination of the human being, and at the same time in the constitution of the concept of personality, is given with Kant. He determined the concept of personality in two ways:
1. with respect to the difference between persons and things (in the *Groundwork of the Metaphysics of Morals*)
2. with respect to the determination of the human being according to three elements, one of which is the person (*Religion within the Limits of Reason Alone*).

In relation to the first way the following should be remarked: a thing [*Sache*] is certainly a being that can exist in itself, but notwithstanding this independence it is only ever a means.

In contrast, a being that is rational—for Kant, reason is the power of principles—can never be a mere means. It is much rather, precisely because it has reason, its own end.

In relation to the second way, let us note that Kant differentiates the following three elements in the determination of human being:
1. that of animality
2. that of humanity
   (together 1. and 2. form the *animal rationale*)
3. that of personality as a rational and at the same time responsible being.

This third aptitude is in a certain sense an extension of the second, but a quite important one, for here Kant makes a distinction between: [311]
1. Reason as thinking and apprehending
2. Accountability, that is, responsibility.

This distinction is important, for it is possible to think of a being that could think according to the principle of noncontradiction, but which would for all that not be responsible. The human being, however, is responsible, that is, it is free and can act according to principles. These are ethical or, as Kant says, practical principles. The highest of them is the categorical imperative.

What results thus from this self-determination of the human being in Kant is autonomy. *Henceforth it is autonomy that constitutes modern personality.*

It now becomes possible to understand the identification of personality and character that Kant establishes. In order to make this even clearer, however, we will need to question the idea of character:

Character comes from χαράσσω; to carve into—χαρακτήρ, what is carved into something, a distinctive mark.

Character in Kant, however, has another quite particular meaning: character is the mode and manner by means of which a cause is a cause. In relation to human action, Kant distinguishes two types of causes: 1. Intelligible character, 2. Empirical character.

The human being is an intelligible character as a being that is resolute through free and self-determined decision; and it is an empirical character insofar as the latter is the appearance of the intelligible character in *the* willed actions that are subject to causality. Kant therefore needs the two types of character for the sake of his determination of human being as a responsible being. A responsible being must have free will as the cause of his actions. This free will, that is to say, the intelligible character, cannot be found in the human world. In this world, the empirical world, human will is not free; it is conditioned, that is, its character is empirical.

"Personality is equivalent to character." Personality is thus a being that is and [312] acts according to its own responsibility. All other determinations of personality follow from this.

These are the essential outlines of the origin and development of the modern concept of personality, of which we have delineated five stages:
1. The Western determination of the human being as *animal rationale* as the basis for the development.
2. The Roman determination of *persona* by means of *dignitas*.
3. The Christian determination of *persona* as the singular soul, that is, as the individual.
4. The Cartesian determination of *persona* as the self-conscious, self-determining subject.
5. The Kantian determination of personality as *responsible*.

According to this clarification of the concept of personality it becomes clear that Nietzsche does not offer an acute characterization of it. Yet his concept of it, which is based on Kant and Schopenhauer—Schopenhauer only retrieving Kant—, can be adequately characterized through the Kantian conception of personality.

The weakening of personality, for Nietzsche, consists in the fact that it is no longer active, but merely contemplative. It is no longer responsible for anything and becomes timid. Consequently it is no longer able to face up to greatness; it must reduce it so as not to be overwhelmed by it.

Hans-Herrmann Groothoff

Report on the Seminar of February 1, 1939

The report on the previous seminar demonstrated the necessity of determining in more detail the significance and extension of Kant's concept of humanity. We reminded ourselves that the human being is determined as the *animal rationale* in Western philosophy. Here *animal* has the sense of animality, *rationale* that of reason. Reason, [313] in Kant also, is what constitutes the human being as human being. Yet personality is added to this as a third and essential determining moment. In order to avert a common misunderstanding relating to Kant's determination of human being as a rational living being [*Lebewesen*], we looked more closely at this determination. The human being, for Kant, is not only a thinking animal, for at the same time that it is determined as a rational living being it is determined as a being that apprehends principles. The basis of the practical (as a determination), the practical understood in a quite specific sense, is to be found in this faculty of apprehending principles. We distinguished different elements of the practical, as a determination of human being:

Technical praxis as apparent in the production of tools, the construction of a house, and so on. In this the human being is led by thematic principles. These presuppose a particular knowledge of things and of nature for this praxis. We spoke here of the ability to use tools [*Zeugfähigkeit*] and of the knowledge of proportions and relations.

Praxis understood here in a quite specific sense, in the sense of Greek (philosophy); ethical action, which is grounded in practical reason, in the knowledge of the principles of this action. We identified personality in this specific sense with the notion of practical reason and did so on the ground of this determination of the practical. On this basis it becomes clear that, for Kant, knowing belongs to personality and character. To make this claim does not constitute a contradiction, but is rather the fundamental characterization of his determination of the human being. We emphasized that knowledge in the sense of scientific knowledge is in this context of no consequence. Every will as will is already a knowing; a knowing of the law and the realm of decision. Action without such knowing is blind. Knowing without willing is weakness. Knowing belongs to personality and character. The great significance Kant places on knowing provided us with an opportunity to engage with the idea of intellectualism. We characterized intellectualism as a fatality and as a fallacious phenomenon, whose causes lie not so much in the underestimation of the practical and of what relates to character, or even in the [314] disrespect of the will; but which is much rather grounded in the denial of authentic knowing. This misrecognition of authentic knowing is the negative element that gives rise to the undervaluation of the practical and of the will. An overcoming of intellectualism can only be achieved by means of an education in authentic knowing. It was said that contemporary scientists are generally intellectualists, although it was emphasized that this says nothing about the character of scientists. The reason for this intellectualism is that scientists fail to see that a particular knowing, which they have not themselves determined, is presupposed in their science. The attempt to exclude this authentic knowing, or to explain it by mere anthropology and empirical psychology, is what determines contemporary scientists as intellectualist.

Here we turned back to what we had considered in the preceding seminar. The survey of the history of the concept of personality can now provide guidelines for the clarification of the statement that the basic determination of the human being in the whole of Western thought is the *animal rationale*. We recalled that the second paragraph of section V contains the general characterization of weak personality, and repeated that it is due to a lack of autonomy that weak personality is unable both to face up to greatness in history and truly to know itself; it is thus doubly evasive, in the face of history and before itself. In moving on to the third paragraph of section V we remarked that Nietzsche here clarifies his idea of philosophy. Given that the text here presents the first form of the emergence of the fracture, of the weakening of personality, this paragraph gave us cause to question why Nietzsche here suddenly brings in a discussion of philosophy. We reminded ourselves of what we had already said about the *Untimely Meditations* in the context of the treatment of critical historiology. We established that Nietzsche himself [315] does critical historiology and that this critique is philosophical. The question was posed, what sense does philosophy have here? Philosophy is the science that forbids all dissimulation. Hence Nietzsche names it the truest of all sciences and in this sense the honest naked goddess. It is because it falls to philosophy to ground veracity that philosophy must be invoked here.

It is surprising that Nietzsche characterizes philosophy as a science. This is conditioned by the modern conception of philosophy, by the tradition to which Nietzsche belongs. In this paragraph Nietzsche says in relation to his own time: "Philosophy has no rights within historical education if it wants to be more than an inwardly restrained knowing without effect." He means to say that philosophy does not have the same structure as any of the natural sciences, but rather possesses a scientific character that precedes all the ordinary sciences. We clarified the conception of two modes of science that is at stake here:
1. Science: passion for the essential knowledge of being
2. Science = research in a particular region of pregiven being.

Nietzsche continually attempts to bring out the scientific character of philosophy and this often leads to misunderstandings. Viewing Nietzsche as half-philosopher and half-thinker is an erroneous conception that goes against his own most intimate intentions. Nietzsche himself does not give us a clear and definite representation of what at this time he knew about the essence of philosophy and how he considered it. From his writings generally, and from his notebooks in particular, however, it emerges that at this time he was passionately questioning the essence of philosophy. His self-reflection is carried out in two directions:
a) according to historial reflection, [316]
b) according to a basic reflection on the task of philosophy and that of the philosopher in Western culture.

With regard to our coming reflection on truth and higher justice in the present text, and in order to clarify how Nietzsche passionately questioned the essence of truth, significant passages from his notebooks were selected and read. We used the large Kröner edition: *Nachgelassene Werke (Posthumous Works)* by Friedrich Nietzsche, 3rd ed., 1922.

I. Seminar Reports

Volume X of this edition contains, among other things, two studies from autumn and winter 1872: "The Last Philosopher" and "The Philosopher: Reflections on the Struggle of Art and Knowledge." The latter provides the central theme of our coming reflections on Nietzsche's work. The titles alone let it be known that he questions philosophers more than philosophy. A few citations should provide us with a view into the direction of his thinking. Vol. X, p. 109:

> At the right height everything comes together and is unified—the thoughts of the philosopher, the works of the artist, and the good deeds.
> It needs to be shown how the whole life of a people reflects in an impure and muddled fashion the image presented by its highest genii: the latter are not the product of the masses, but the masses are their repercussion.
> Or what is their relation?
> There is an invisible bridge from genius to genius—that is the truly real "history" of a people, all the rest is merely shadowy, countless variations in baser matter, copies from unskilled hands.
> And also the ethical powers of a nation are manifest in its genii.

As an elucidation of this passage, we said that what is expressed here is a conception of the goal of culture, and that Nietzsche is never completely certain about this and seldom expresses an absolute conviction.

The following passage was presented as particularly significant for [317] our purposes, even though it is not worked out precisely and has not been fully thought through.

> The philosopher is a self-manifestation of the workshop of nature—philosophers and artists speak of the secrets of nature's craft.
> The philosopher as *a brake [Hemmschuh] on the wheel of time.*
> The philosophers appear in times of great danger—when the wheel [of time] turns ever more quickly—they and art take the place of declining myth (Vol. X, p. 112).

We remarked here that the philosopher not only eradicates the negative aspects, but also works as a kind of brake on the direction in which the age is moving.

> They will be thrown far ahead of their time, because the attention of their contemporaries only slowly turns toward them.
> A people aware of the dangers that threaten it engenders genius.

From here it emerges that the philosopher has to be untimely.

"Philosophy *not for the people, thus not the basis of a culture*, thus only the instrument of a culture." (Vol. 10, p. 186, "The Philosopher as Physician of Culture")

> It is not possible to ground the culture of a people on philosophy. Hence in relation to a culture philosophy can never have a fundamental, but only an ancillary significance. What is this?
> *Taming of the mythical: strengthening of the sense of truth against free poetizing* [*Dichtung*]. *Vis veritatis* or strengthening of pure knowing. (Ibid. p. 187)

This proposition bears at the same time a reference to the historial reflection on Greek philosophy from which Nietzsche received the decisive impulse for his own conception of philosophy.

"Every philosophy must be able, as I demand, to concentrate a human being—but none at present is capable of this" (vol. X, p. 297, "The Distress of Philosophy"). [318]

"To make *philosophy* purely a science . . . is to throw in the towel" (ibid., p. 299).

Here it becomes clear that the level attained by research does not form the criterion for the determination of the scientific character of philosophy; on the contrary, science is to be determined through philosophy.

As an additional testimony to Nietzsche's historial reflection, we referred to the early spring 1873 fragment "Philosophy in the Tragic Age of the Greeks." This fragment emerged from two lectures that Nietzsche gave on pre-Platonic philosophy in Basel in the winter semester of 1869–1870 and the summer semester of 1872. In this fragment it becomes clear that for Nietzsche, Heraclitus is the exemplary philosopher. We recalled that Heraclitus had already been mentioned in the context of the determination of historiology as inquiry in a critical, judicial sense. At that juncture we had cited the fragment "On the Concept of the Historical." Nietzsche often cites Heraclitus.

It was pointed out that Heraclitus is often superficially understood as counterposing becoming to immobile being. His statements that "everything is in flux" and that "struggle is the father of all things" are well known and often misused. This thinker was, and always remained, the secret role model for Nietzsche. The fragment "Philosophy in the Tragic Age of the Greeks" from spring 1873 provides another instance of the impression that Nietzsche had of Heraclitus (vol. X, p. 44). We did not broach the question of the extent to which Nietzsche is right in his view of Heraclitus.

In conclusion, it was stated once again that philosophy becomes an issue here because the task is to characterize the weakened personality and the avoidance of veracity. This characterization occurs in a critical reflection on the present against the background of Greek philosophy.

The next paragraph involves the repetition of an earlier [319] thought, namely that history can only be borne by strong personality, and that precisely those who call themselves objective, as eternally subjectless, cannot withstand it. All the effects of what happens are discussed ad nauseam, explained and dissolved into psychology. Nietzsche himself had similar experiences within the limits of his own scientific environment. His text *The Birth of Tragedy from the Spirit of Music* suffered the same treatment. As a matter of fact, this paragraph does not have much significance.

We moved on to section VI. This section is not only the most important within the *Untimely Meditations*, but is also the one in which Nietzsche attains for the first time the very kernel of his thinking. The section deals with "true objectivity" and "higher justice." Nietzsche describes his age as that of scientific objectivity. Not because the latter would have accomplished quite particular feats, but rather because scientific objectivity was taken to be the basic form of knowledge supporting everything else.

In the first paragraph Nietzsche poses the question whether objectivity springs from a higher demand for justice as a will to determine and actualize the essence of justice itself as the highest virtue, or whether justice in his age has already been determined and taken for granted as a possession and criterion of objectivity. We now elucidated for ourselves the concept of objectivity in order to see how Nietzsche makes use of it.

Objectivity, from the Latin *obicere*—*obiectum* = what is thrown up against. In the Greek signification of the word, it is more exactly what "stands against" [*Entgegenliegende*]. *Subjectum*—which is as foundation [*Zugrundeliegende*]. These concepts came into medieval Scholasticism in their Greek sense through the appropriation of Aristotelian philosophy.

Subjectum = the object of representation. *Objectum* = that which is represented. Representing is here thought as an activity of the soul. The *objectum* is what belongs to the soul; it is what is [320] represented by the *subjectum*, the object of representation, in the representative activity of the soul. The *subjectum* = what is present at hand, the thing subsisting in itself. It is these meanings that these concepts had in Scholasticism. We saw, by means of examples, that today the meaning of these concepts has been inverted. We find the origin of this in the starting point of Descartes, who put the I, the *subjectum*, that is, the only certain thing for the human being, at the center of his thinking. Everything not belonging to the subject becomes an object, whereas the thing represented, the Scholastic object, becomes subject. Objectivity is now everything that belongs to the thing standing against us [*Gegenstand*], to the object.

In Nietzsche the concept of objectivity takes on a further meaning: objectivity as characteristic and determination of the human being. Only the human being has the ability and capacity to judge and pass sentence, thereby drawing on the state of affairs. In the *Critique of Pure Reason* Kant describes objectivity as the unity of determinations constituting an object as object. But what makes an object such and such an object, or in other words what the objectivity of the object consists of, is, for Kant, the categories. These were named: substance, cause-effect, reciprocal relations [*Wechselverhältnisse*], *qualitas, realitas*. These categories belong in a particular sense to the human subject.

In concluding these reflections it was noted that the subject-object relation as conceived by Descartes underlies these two concepts of objectivity, namely:
1. objectivity as the faculty of judging;
2. objectivity as determined through the categories.

Hans Hübcher

Report on the Seminars of February 6 and 8, 1939

It is in section VI of the text *On the Advantages and Disadvantages of History for Life* that we encounter the central concept of the [321] inquiry, the concept of justice. It appears in relation to the concept of truth and objectivity, with which it seems to be bound in a particular manner, such that understanding it presupposes an understanding of the sense in which Nietzsche uses these concepts of truth and objectivity.

The realm of questions that now opens itself out to us has emerged within the inquiry motivated by our guiding question, that of the relation of historiology to life, which became more precise in the form of the question of the relation of truth to life.

The concepts of objectivity, truth, justice, their mutual relation, and the ground of this particular relation are hence all in question. Truth appears under the heading of objectivity. Justice is presented as the possible ground of the striving for truth.

The ground of the relation in question is to be found in a quite particular interpretation of truth and objectivity, which we should examine first of all. Only on this basis will we be in a position to work through the characteristic ambiguity and indeterminacy that the concepts have in Nietzsche's hands, and to establish what they have in common. This ambiguity goes so far that Nietzsche uses the concept of justice in two different sentences in two directly opposed senses.

The fourth paragraph of section VI states: "Objectivity and justice have nothing to do with one another," whereas the second paragraph states that the "striving for truth" has "its root in justice". To gain some clarity on this it is necessary:
1. to establish the different senses that the concept of objectivity has in everyday language;
2. to recognize the historial transformation through which the concepts have taken on their now apparently self-evident sense;
3. to know that all concepts can be used in their essential and nonessential sense.

It is possible to distinguish three different concepts of objectivity:
[322]
1. Objectivity in the sense of a human capacity to judge on the basis of an understanding of the state of affairs. Hence objectivity is here the title for a human comportment.
2. Objectivity in Kant's sense as the coherence of the determinations that first make an object possible. The question of this making possible appears in Kant under the heading: how are synthetic a priori judgments possible? How are determinations of an object possible that precede empirical cognizance of it? How can I say something about an object before it is given to me? Such a priori determinations are possible according to Kant because they are necessary, because they prefigure the objectivity of objects, originally granting to the object the possibility of being encountered as an object. That is to say, in order to cognize a thing in general as a thing, I must already know what thingness is; in order to see that it stands in relations, I must recognize relation in general and its possible forms. The object must be determined in advance through synthetic judgments a priori; something must be attributed to it for it to be accessible as an object. This pure prefiguration of objectivity occurs in the production of the categories by the understanding. The system of the categories is thus the essential ground by virtue of which an object becomes an object; its objectivity or objectness [*Objektität*].
3. Objectivity can be understood in the sense of scientific objectivity. In this case the concept is used as a determination of the relation of science as a system of true statements to what is expressed in these statements, to the object. This relation is objective insofar as the statements are governed by the object. If this demand is fulfilled, that is, if science is objective, then it gains the character of universal validity and obligation, so that scientific objectivity can also be called: universal validity and necessity. In Kant, all knowledge is universally valid and binding on the basis of its objectivity. [323]

Nietzsche uses the term indeterminately in all three senses without providing any reciprocal clarification of them. The confusion goes back to Schopenhauer's interpretation of Kant. This opacity and lack of clarity in Nietzsche's mode of expression, which has now become more explicit through the presentation of the three different senses of objectivity, signals the necessity of a reflection on Nietzsche's own historial position, and on how the concept of objectivity that he borrows from the language of his time has developed historially. For this it is necessary first of all to examine another concept, which stands in the closest relation to the concept of objectivity, namely, subjectivity. Objectivity can be understood without subjectivity as little as life can be understood without death, or unhistorical being without historical being. (Whether or not it is a matter of the same relations in each instance is a question that here remains open). Each of the two concepts gains its sense only from its relation to the other. It is this relation that takes precedence and it is not, as it might initially appear, a coupling of two independent entities after the fact. There is no more a subject in itself than an object in itself.

This subject-object relation must now be determined in more detail in order to obtain a more explicit concept of both subject and object. Three questions were posed:
1. Where is this relation established?
2. What is its nature?
3. On what is its possibility grounded?

The site wherein it is established is human representation. Here something as something, the object, what can be represented, is contrasted to the being that represents, the subject. If such a representational relation is to exist, what is represented and what represents must be open to one another. The relation presupposes an openness in which it moves, in which it is grounded.

Yet the subject-object relation is not, as it might initially seem, the sole possible way in which this openness becomes real and explicit, but is rather one of the possible forms of the relation of the human being to beings, one which [324] was initially developed within a determinate historical moment, namely in Descartes's philosophy, who also gives a name to this representative relation in designating it as consciousness, which is a translation of *cogitatio* or *perceptio*. Before this moment, neither in antiquity nor in Scholasticism had the subject-object relation and what guarantees it been examined. The human being was determined as *animal rationale*, as a being provided with the faculty of *ratio*, as if with a tool that has the function of cognizing the world, so that he can find his way about.

How do we get from this conception, which is the standpoint of healthy common sense, to the stance according to which the subject-object relation is emphasized and gains predominance over the simply receptive relation? How does the general and undetermined relation of the *animal rationale* to things become the subject-object relationship? In other words, how does the human being become a subject? The ground of this transformation consists in a change of the basic character of the human relation to things. The relation of the simply cognizing human being to things is determined by truth in the sense of *adequatio, rectitudo*, correctness. A judgment is hence true when it accords itself to the thing, when, akin to a piece of malleable wax, it takes on the form of the things, when it conforms itself to them. In this way, what comes from the outside into consciousness and is taken up by the latter is the representation, the object, and what produces the representation, what underlies it, is the subject. If this relation is to be converted into that of the subject-object relationship common in modernity, then the nature of truth itself must change, for truth was the determining ground of the prior relation. The character of truth can only arise as a problem in that very moment that its ground loses its capacity to support, when a need arises to reassure oneself once again of this ground. After the possibility of the simply cognizing relationship has become doubtful, guarantees are sought by means of which the security of the relation can be [325] proved over and against the possibility of illusion. Truth maintains its sense as *adequatio*, as correctness. It is now a matter, however, of finding a notion of truth that allows an unquestionable self-orientation in the sense of a complete insightfulness, perfectly evident to all human beings at any time. Only such a certainly known truth, which can prove itself at any time, can now be truth. Truth becomes certainty.

Where are we to find the knowledge able to satisfy this demand, which can serve as the standard of the truth character of every other form of knowing? Descartes considers this demand to be satisfied in the indubitable certainty of the connection in the human being between representing and being, which he expresses in the well-known statement: *Cogito ergo sum*. In no way does the *ergo* in this statement express a causal connection.

The human being is thus the site where truth is made secure; it is what always must be returned to, the foundation, the subject to which everything knowable is referred. (If the relation is to take the form of the subject-object relation prevalent in modernity).

The ego of the human being thus becomes the preeminent subject in the sense of that which grounds the certainty of truth. Now, however, the concept of subject is equally transformed and takes on another sense. Its literal sense—"what lies at the ground"—was at first only superficially linked to the *ego*, while now it can no longer be separated from it. With the original sense fading more and more, it takes on all the determinations of the human being and almost becomes the human being's sole appellation.

This ego, however, is not the individual I; rather, the concept of *subjectum* comprises all the determinations that constitute egoity as such, that determine every I as I.

In Descartes this determination of egoity is still opaque. The first clear determination of it is to be found in Kant in the sense of the self-determination of the human being in relation to all the standards (determinations) of theoretical and practical [326] comportment. The liberation from the ties of authority, from the church that claims to be in possession of the sole true doctrine of the world, only occurs as an essential consequence of the process through which the human being grasps itself as subject; a process that is grounded, in turn, in a transformation of the essence of truth.

As a further consequence of the determination of truth as certainty, obligation and universal validity come to belong to it as necessary predicates.

What is true is now only what can secure the human being as a being resting exclusively on itself, and that which is of further use for the safeguarding of this autonomy. From here Kant's concept of personality can be understood, the essence of which is autonomy and freedom. The concept of liberalism in its original and genuine sense goes back to this stance of the free and self-assured human being. The negative sense of liberalism, liberalism in the sense of the free capriciousness of the will and the dissolution of all ties, is derived from this.

The historial transformation of the concept of the subject has now become clear to us. In the opposite direction, everything that is knowable, that is given to the subject, to the ego, becomes an object, whereas, as we have already said, in the Middle Ages the *objectum* is what is merely represented, what is therefore, in the modern sense of the word, merely subjective. We can thus see here that the relation of human beings to things is transformed on the basis of a transformation of the essence of truth.

Upon this insight, we now have to clarify anew the idea of subjectivism. Subjectivism is the positioning of human being as the determinant, relational center of all beings, from which everything else can be grasped in its being. In Descartes the human being is understood as consciousness, but this is not the ground of his subjectivism. In this vein Nietzsche's principal attack against Descartes, the accusation that Descartes has conceived the human being only as consciousness while having omitted its real life, the living body, and its animality, is not an attack against his subjectivism, but rather [327] only a struggle against a one-sided form of it. It is not a matter here of overcoming subjectivism, but rather of the human being coming finally into play with all its faculties and powers as a complete subject. Subjectivism does not necessarily have anything to do with intellectualism, and means only that the human being is the relational center, regardless of whether this is conceived as reason, as the living body, as a people, or as society. Nietzsche has come to understand the nature of his own position quite early on. Thus a note from 1873 reads: "It is wholly and simply by virtue of what is *subjective* in us that we are *human*" (vol. X, p. 212).

Everything that the human being brings into play, from itself, is what determines it as human being. We have to hold on to this in order to understand the change in the concept of objectivity.

If the essential element of subjectivism does not consist in the positioning of the human being as consciousness, but rather in the fact that it brings itself into play as determinant and self-determining, then in the question concerning objectivity it is essential to know which faculty of the human being as subject has the decisive role for what is properly binding and objective: knowledge or art.

Is what is binding first grounded through the creative production of form, or is it simply found and taken up as already established? The struggle between knowledge and art, the question of their respective rank, governs Nietzsche's thinking from now on. Because Nietzsche understands the concept of truth first of all in the sense of bindingness, which is grounded by means of science, by means of knowing comportment, he comes to the point where he is able to counterpose art and truth to one another as mutually exclusive. "Art and truth have nothing to do with each other."

We are now in a position to bring the two opposing statements that we mentioned at the outset into harmony, at least if we look beyond the cursoriness of their presentation. Justice in its improper sense, as simply accepting something to be the case, as the passive toleration of reality as it is, has nothing to do with objectivity, if objectivity is [328] taken here in the sense of the bindingness [*Verbindlichkeit*] that is first produced through the unique creativity of genius that does not simply hold to what is already in existence, which is called the actual, but which instead poses anew being and actuality.

In the second statement, "the striving for truth has its root in justice," justice is described in an essential sense as a striving, as a becoming just by means of an active confrontation with beings. The desire for truth, here taken in the sense of scientific truth, is, even though it has become prevalent in the modern age, only a derivative form of a more original striving, which does not have to be actualized in that modern form, and which originally rather comes into its own in art.

The antithesis of subjectivism is objectivism. In subjectivism the human being is the relational center from the perspective of which everything else is determined in its being, whereas for objectivism it is conceived as something incidental and fleeting in the whole of beings. The self-certainty of the first attitude corresponds to the genuine thoughtlessness of the second. What occurs in the equivocal sense of particular concepts, in the concept of life, for example, is only a peculiar coupling of these two approaches. Objectivism is manifest when life is grasped as the whole of beings of which the human being represents only a particular level; but if life is determined as human life, then the latter is conceived as the particular region in which decisions can first of all be made about the character of life in general.

Therese Gisbertz

Report on the Seminars of February 13 and 15, 1939

We began by further developing the reflection on subjectivism. The concept of subjectivism [329] had been presented as, in essence, a point of view that makes the human being—grasped not only as consciousness—the sole *subiectum*, the relational center of all beings. Objectivism can be contrasted to this as its antithesis, as a point of view that puts the object in the place of the subject and conceives of the human being merely as something incidental in the whole of beings, as something accidental among the things of the world. The self-certainty of subjectivism had to be brought into relation with something else, which we characterized as thoughtlessness. The question of the most integral unity of subjectivism and objectivism understood in this way leads us back to our basic reference point, to life in its two senses.

The object of the discussion of the preceding seminar was the concept of justice. The question of justice is decisive for Nietzsche's whole philosophy: justice is the root of truth. Truth is, for Nietzsche, synonymous with objectivity. The latter, in its highest sense, is art. In this way, then, we came from justice to one of the essential determinations of human life. Nietzsche saw in justice the root of the plastic power, that is, of life itself. It is thus of the highest metaphysical significance.

The question concerning justice emerges as the question of *higher* justice, which is not to be understood in the sense of being '"more or less just," but in a more essential sense.

In this sense it is the root of truth. Truth, however, can be determined in two ways. First of all as an inconsequential knowledge, as harmless truth from which nothing arises, as the cognizance of arbitrary states of affairs. But this is not the sense of truth according to which higher justice is named as its root. Here the other conception of truth is intended, truth as judge, judging here not understood as the application of a ready-made [330] law, as guaranteeing right, but rather as the creation of rights, as lawgiving, as the right to shift boundaries.

Justice is more precisely determined as a virtue. This is important because the relationship will later be inverted, with the essence of virtue being derived from higher justice. Here justice is initially the unfathomable sea, in which all virtues congregate; it is the fundamental virtue and as such the rarest of all virtues. Consequently, the just human being is the most worthy of respect, because it is the most human of human beings.

In German, virtue [*Tugend*] is related to being apt and appropriate [*taugen*], and means aptitude, like the Greek ἀρετή. ἀρετή originally means the aptitude of a thing in the sense of being good for something. This sense of the word is then narrowed down to the aptitude of human comportment. In the *Nicomachean Ethics* Aristotle examines ἀρετή in this sense.

We drew two determinations from this:
1. ἀρετή as τελείωσις, completion, consummation, that is, comportment that corresponds to the τέλος.
2. as ἕξις, the holding oneself up and having oneself in one's power.

This was taken up again in the Middle Ages, insofar as *virtus* was determined as *perfectio* and *dispositio*, and *dispositio*, corresponding to ἕξις, as a comportment remaining adequate to the situation. *Virtus* makes any comportment a *bonum*. Something is good if it is directed toward a goal, thus subordinating itself to that goal. And the highest goal is God. The goal is the ideal, in relation to which what is good and what is not good are distinguished.

In the Christian appropriation of all this, obedience, the subordination to God's will, becomes the most fundamental virtue. Concomitantly, rebellion, the failure to adapt to the holy world order, is the proper vice [*Untugend*]. This is the traditional concept of what is good or moral.

Nietzsche sets upon this concept. His higher justice is not a submitting of oneself to an ideal, but rather involves autonomy; it is a supramoral concept, [331] which is not the same as an unmoral one. This finds its expression in the title of the later text *Beyond Good and Evil*. The opposition of good and evil becomes, for Nietzsche, that of good and bad, which is measured according to the intensification of life. *Beyond Good and Evil* does not mean abandoning oneself to the stirring of drives or the arbitrary power of passions, but rather means to stand within a new duty, a duty in a higher sense as a decision to a more essential obligation. Here Nietzsche is often misunderstood and falsely invoked. Merely living out one's life is not yet a justification of that life.

So much for Nietzsche's concept of higher justice. He then characterizes the contemporary and traditional representation of justice, and makes visible the essence of this conception in considering the virtuosity of the historian. This consists of being able to compare everything and anything, a capacity for which nothing is inaccessible. But thereby the human being is only an echoing passivity, avoiding the essential decision.

Nietzsche determines different degrees of the predominant form of justice, and presents them in descending order. The essential determination of justice here is acceptance.

The highest of the four forms that emerge here is generosity, in which the breadth of one's perspective, the security, the superiority with regard to oneself and also to others are present in order to accept what claims to be worthy of acceptance.

The next form is tolerance, the accepting or tolerating without giving in and without weakness, but in which the human being already holds itself apart from what it accepts.

There then follows acceptance out of weakness. A codetermining role is granted to others, which did not yet happen with tolerance. Things are glossed over and one proves to be obliging in order to experience the same in return.

The final level is acceptance out of lethargy and inertia, the avoiding of things, leaving them to themselves. [332]

The opposite of justice as mere acceptance is the higher justice, in such a way that the latter does not stand opposed to what is unjust, for what is unjust belongs to it, in that it is hard and dreadful; rather the opposite to higher justice is cowardice and avoidance.

Higher justice is the root of truth, which for Nietzsche is objectivity. Objectivity appears in two levels. Nietzsche contrasts that of the historian, who describes processes of the past, to that of the poet, of the artist, who reveals inner possibilities independently of isolated facts and their historical correctness. The latter's creating is a poetic elaboration and a continuation in thought of what is historically possible. In this way, artistic presentation is the highest propagation of objectivity.

This insight into two ways of grasping reality is already to be found in Aristotle's *Poetics*: καὶ φιλοσοφώτερον καὶ σπουδαιότερον ποίησις ἱστορίας ἐστιν. Ποίησις is not here a mere reproduction, but rather the self-creation of the possible. As such a creative projection it is at a remove from the arbitrary will and is itself necessary. It is called φιλοσοφώτερον because φιλοσοφία is concerned with the essence of things, and not simply with what is present-at-hand.

If historiology is to do justice to the facts and reveal their inner possibilities, in order to be truly objective, then it requires an element of judgment. This is a dangerous demand—as all essential demands are dangerous—for it seems to leave the door wide open to voluntarism and arbitrariness.

Art and knowledge thus come into conflict, into disaccord, insofar as knowledge shall only depict things that are already present, whereas the task of art is to make essential being visible. In this way the following pronouncement is clarified: "Objectivity and justice have nothing to do with one another." Justice is here understood as knowledge without consequences, and objectivity in an essential sense. But the latter has its root in higher justice and as such it is also a poetic power.

Nietzsche now asks whether an illusion underlies this highest interpretation [333] of objectivity as artistic creating, in that he uses Kant's account of artistic comportment as the suspension of personal interests, as disinterested pleasure. He does this, however, on the basis of a misinterpretation of Kant, which he takes up from Schopenhauer, and which permeates his whole philosophy.

Because Kant intends precisely the opposite of a passive contemplation. He precisely does *not* want to ground artistic contemplation on mere knowing. "Disinterested" is only to be opposed to goals, to pure concepts of knowledge. The relating to art is no crude reception, but rather presupposes an interest of the highest type, a capacity to look beyond what is immediately present-at-hand and to remain open for new ways of being.

Then Nietzsche refers again to what is ambiguous and elusive in the appearance of objectivity and justice. Objectivity is not to be confused with the passive repose of detachment. Justice, that is to say, the right to judge, is not something given merely by the fact of having arrived later [in history], but must rather be properly grounded.

Concerning the one who is just, we have to add that greatness can only be recognized by greatness. And only those who build can be judges, for only they have the sense of measure.

Looking over the whole once again, we have to say that higher justice has not been systematically developed by Nietzsche, but has rather been illuminated in a flash.

[Hermann ter Tell]

Report on the Seminars of February 20 and 22, 1939

In order to gain some clarity about the relationship between higher justice and truth in the Nietzschean sense, both concepts had to be determined again independently of each other. Nietzsche always understands truth and justice in an extramoral sense. Under the heading of morality, he understands first of all Christian morality and [334] its offshoots, while on the other hand morality for him is also any kind of judging according to established, pregiven standards. Consequently, we have to be clear each time which of the two senses is meant.

In order to characterize Nietzsche's concept of justice, we begin with the original sense of the word. Just [*gerecht*], *rectus* in Latin—to be found in words such as *upright, vertical* [*senkrecht*], *forthright, bite-sized* [*mundgerecht*]—means right [*recht*] in the sense of what is suitable and appropriate; thus in *upright*, fitting with respect to the upward direction or in the expression "to fit into all saddles";[1] or taken more generally, right means adapting oneself to a pregiven standard. The human being who judges and acts in such a way is just; and accordingly justice is the concomitant attitude and disposition. The pregiven standards are the claims of human beings or of things, to whom justice is to be done. Justice is thus the equitableness that grants to each their dues; and in relation to the Christian evaluation of life, according to which all human beings are equal before God, it is the capacity to allot the same to all. "Justitiae ratio consistit in hoc quod alteri reddati quod ei debetur secundum aequalitatem," as the Scholastics said. Next to this first account of justice we already find the age-old account of it as a determination of beings themselves, as it is already expressed in Anaximander's *dike*, which, as *rectitudo ordinis*, is here described as the gradation of the particular realms of beings.

Nietzsche's account of truth emerges in the clearest manner in a few significant propositions that he formulates at the high point of his philosophy, in the time of the *Zarathustra*, between 1882 and 1885, mostly outside of any determinate context. In the later years these thoughts fell into the background, and consequently there never emerges in his work a comprehensive interpretation of life, either of human life or of life as beings in general, arising from this basic concept of higher justice. At the time of writing our text, in 1873, Nietzsche had already begun to work out his characteristic concept of justice, which is [335] partially conditioned by his break from Schopenhauer and partially by the idea of a German cultural unity on the basis of Wagner's total artwork. The most important proposition in this context is to be found in volume 13 of the collected works: "*Justice* as a constructive, eliminative, destructive mode of thinking, on the basis of value judgments: *the highest representative of life itself*" (p. 42 [1884]). Hence justice is de-

---

1. The original here is "in der Wendung 'in allen Sätteln gerecht sein'—die eigentlich 'in alle Sättel gerecht sein' heißt"; in other words, the saying is "to be just in all saddles," or to be just in whatever position one finds oneself, while Heidegger points out that it derives from "to be upright in all saddles," which we translate as "to fit into all saddles."—Trans.

termined as a mode of thinking based on value judgments, wherein value means conditions of life and life itself means intensification of life. Justice is consequently the setting up and representation of the conditions for the elevation of life. This way of thinking is first of all constructive, for it neither limits itself to condemning something already existent nor relates itself to a pregiven value system; it is much more a new creation and positing of standards of value, through and in which life first attains its heights. This mode of thinking must also be eliminative and destructive, eliminating everything oppressive and life-denying in life, thus destroying it. This sort of justice is the highest representative of life itself. This means not only human life, the realm into which we were led by the determination of justice as a way of thinking, but rather life as the whole of beings in general presents itself as justice; but not as a kind of outer facade, for life resides essentially in justice, is bound to justice, and justice belongs to beings as such. For life, again considered as the whole of beings, is a continual willing-beyond-itself, a continual self-overtaking; therefore the positing of ever-new standards necessarily belongs to it. This mode of positing standards is characterized more precisely in volume XIV: "*Justice*, as a function of a far-sighted power able to look beyond the narrow perspectives of good and evil, and that therefore has a wider horizon of *advantage*—the intention of preserving something that is more than this [336] or that person" (p. 80 [1885]). The mode of the positing of standards is here determined as the setting up of a horizon and indeed, the broadest possible, in which all perspectives are able to take hold. That is why it is a farsighted power, or, as Nietzsche says in volume XIV: the fundamental condition of justice is the "circumspection proceeding from broad insight" (p. 386), which means: justice arises from an essential knowing. Consequently it is no mere arbitrary will or inconsiderateness, but much more a type of love. In this way Nietzsche says in the first part of *Zarthustra* (1882): "Tell, where is justice, which is love with seeing eyes, to be found." Here love, grasped metaphysically, means the desire that the loved one be what he is, how he is, and how he ought to be; it requires therefore that the lover continually make a gift of himself [*Vorausverschenken*]. In this sense, Nietzsche says in "Judgments and Maxims" (vol. XII, p. 291): "Truly just men are incapable of receiving presents: they give everything back. Thus they are torture for those who love," the latter here understood in an ordinary, inessential sense. Nietzsche's concept of justice gains its most acute expression in the sentence "There is more injustice in revering than in despising" (vol. VII, p. 297). With this, Nietzsche characterizes at one and the same time the opposite of higher justice, which always lies as a danger within it. This consists in giving up the positing of standards, satisfying oneself with a final system of standards, irrevocably closing off the horizon. Corresponding to this is the inertia in human beings that takes the particular form of cowardice, and which, for Nietzsche, accordingly is genuine injustice. For in despising there must be a release from what is despised, and thus an ever new setting of standards even if only in a negative sense, while what is revered offers the possibility of taking shelter from, and thus of giving up on, positing continually developing horizons. In 1878, in the first part of *Human, all too Human*, Nietzsche had already expressed this thought, when he describes justice as a [337] "particular form of geniality" (vol. II, p. 411), whereby at this time for him the genius is already the lawgiver, and this geniality, and thus justice, is characterized as an *"enemy of convictions"*—conviction meaning here the obstinate persistence in the complete lack of questioning in relation to all determinations of beings.

This essential determination of justice is clearly to be differentiated from the un-essence of justice, namely, tolerance, mere acceptance. According to Nietzsche, the latter brings about chaos, the confusion of all orders of beings. The following statement is made in a deliberately ambiguous fashion, supported by the conventional determination of justice, for the essence as much as the un-essence of justice can be understood to be at stake: "Giving to each what he is due: this would be to seek justice while attaining chaos" (vol. XII, p. 291). The *suum cuique* must be replaced with the "I give to each my due," which refers to the one condemned to be just, who thus posits the broadest horizon and within this the narrower perspectives, that is, differentiates each according to his essence. The emergence of chaos is drawn out more clearly by the thought of an immanent justice, when Nietzsche says: "That rewards and punishments already lie in the consequences of actions—this thinking of an immanent justice is completely wrong. . . . All such possible ideas of "immanent justice," "order of salvation," of retributive "transcendental justice" today swim around in *everyone's* head—they contribute to the *chaos* of the modern soul" (1884, vol. XIII, p. 315). Here he wants to characterize the general state of affairs according to which every party sees a punishment in the harmful consequences of the behavior of its enemies, while finding a reward and confirmation of its righteousness in the beneficial consequences of its own behavior. Such a positing of standards on the basis of the particular consequences, such an immanent justice can only lead to chaos. For the consequences of a great action can work against this very action, so much so that it brings about its downfall, in accordance with the basic law that greatness is predetermined to perish while only the small remains in existence. [338]

This determination of higher justice has to be followed by an account of truth in Nietzsche's sense in order to grasp the relation between truth and justice. Let it be clear from the outset that Nietzsche moves completely within the paths of traditional, Western metaphysical thinking, in holding that truth is characterized by cognition, the intellect, judgment, *logos*, and thus the logical. The decisive question that must first of all be answered is, how does the logical stand in relation to life as Nietzsche understands it? Only after this can its relation to justice be determined and the question of the truth of philosophy be answered. In this context, the incomplete and unpublished essay of 1873 that bears the characteristic title "On Truth and Lies in an Extra-Moral Sense" (vol. X, pp. 189–207) is important. A brief account of its contents served to familiarize us with its principal thoughts. Our first question had to be, what does the essay say about the origin of truth? Nietzsche describes the intellect—which means, for him, and as we noted, the same as truth—as an "invention of a clever animal for a short minute of the cosmos." The human being is here apprehended as an individual being. The intellect, the faculty of representation, first of all enables him to know the things around him, and, secondly, grants him the ability to dissimulate his very being. How does this individual, presumed to exist originarily, come to possess a drive to truth, truth that Nietzsche, following Kant, understands as universal validity and obligation for everyone? Nietzsche's answer expresses a thought that found expression in the English philosophy of his time in many ways: first of all from need. The individual needs others precisely in order to be able to exist, and commerce with them is only possible on the basis of a common agreement on what is generally valid. Secondly, from boredom. The individual grows tired of himself and consequently seeks a connection with others, [339] which presupposes the fixed and binding nature of obligation. This signifies for the essence of obligation and for the true itself; it is that to which every member of the community must hold, that on which the existence of the community is secured. We recognized, in a short parenthesis, the importance of the sort of reflection Nietzsche makes use of in describing how binding obligations, for example, concepts, are found. The impression emanated from the object—Nietzsche says—produces a stimulus in the subject, which makes an image arise within the subject. The image is formed into sound, then into the word, and from this the concept is formed, such that the process of knowledge, for Nietzsche, becomes one long concatenation of metaphors. This purely natural-scientific mode of reflection in a philosophical essay shows on the one hand that Nietzsche was still a young man when he wrote it, and on the other hand that despite his stern critique of his time he is tightly enrooted in its opinions. From Nietzsche's conception of the genesis of truth as a constant series of metaphors it emerges, with regard to the essence of truth, that truth is characterized in relation to genuine being as illusion, as appearance. This characterization necessarily presupposes that Nietzsche either knew absolute being or at the very least affirmed the possibility of knowing it. From the fact that Nietzsche does not raise any questions concerning this point, it becomes clear that for him the problem lies elsewhere, and with that insight we turn back to the question that we have already posed, which can now be grasped more precisely: to what extent does truth understood as universal validity serve the conservation and intensification of life? We take as true, binding: A = B. In this something is fixed, constant, which the human being can rely on at any given time. This fixation serves to consolidate life, and this fixedness is necessary for life. If it did not exist, then life would drift away as a continual, ceaseless flow, in such a way that no ties whatsoever between individuals would be possible, ties that are required by them due to need and boredom. [340] In other words, life needs this fixation by means of truth in order to secure its own existence. Hence truth, following the terms of section I of the essay, is identical to the horizon. If we recall that since time immemorial in the Western tradition the essential feature of being is constancy, which for us is synonymous with truth, and that becoming is to be apprehended as the characteristic of life, then it becomes clear that truth harbors a danger for life, namely that of a solidification, a hardening that obstructs life in its essential being, namely as a will driving beyond itself. Thus just as life, on the one hand, needs truth as fixedness, it also needs, on the other hand, a power able to overcome truth in its fixedness and therefore its obstruction. This power is present in art, sustained by plastic power. The latter creates, in continually new forms, illusion, appearance, thus overcoming truth again and again, and allows life, by means of this continually new positing of standards, to be intensified beyond itself, which is its essential characteristic. In this way we move from reflection on the relation of truth and life to an answer to the question concerning the position of truth relative to higher justice. Justice, insofar as it is determined as the power of the ever new positing of standards, is herein comparable to art. Therefore justice is the power that must continuously overcome truth in order to posit new horizons, and it is thus at the same time the root of truth—as is said in section VI of the essay—because it posits all standards, even those that claim truth as obligatory and therefore binding and therefore obstructing life. In order to prove the correctness of these thoughts in Nietzsche, two passages were quoted. In *The Will to Power* he says: "We possess *art* so that we *do not perish at the hands of truth*," and elsewhere in the same text: "But truth does not count as the supreme value, even less as the supreme power. The will to appearance, [341] illusion, to deception, to becoming and change (to objectified deception) here counts as more profound, primeval, 'metaphysical' than the will to truth, to reality, to mere appearance: the last is merely a form of the will to illusion."

It is now possible for us to grasp clearly Nietzsche's position on science, and thus also on historiology as a science. Nietzsche is far from denying the necessity of science. On the contrary, it is necessary, as the creation of something fixed and true, for securing the existence of life. It is solely in this task that its legitimacy consists. It attains its highest goal when it carries out this task exclusive of any other; and that can only happen by means of a science that, as is said, is "closer to life"; and this can only be obtained in the greatest possible elaboration of and concentration of logics, as occurs today to a certain degree in technology.

Now we still have to answer the question posed earlier concerning the truth of philosophy. This will be facilitated by following the last verse of a poem that is the first in a collection of poems called "Songs of Prince Vogelfrei,"[2] which Nietzsche appended to the second edition of his *The Gay Science* in 1887. It was probably written in 1886. Bearing the title "To Goethe," it stands as an antiphon to the end of the second part of *Faust*. The last verse reads:

> World game, the ruling force
> blends false and true
> the eternally fooling force
> blends us in too.

[Annemarie Thuntar?]

Report on the Seminar of February 28, 1939

The last session was concerned with the interpretation of the last verse of the poem "To Goethe," which is to be found in the second [342] edition of *The Gay Science* from 1887, in the appendix that bears the title: "Songs of Prince Vogelfrei":

> World game, the ruling force
> blends false and true
> the eternally fooling force
> blends us in too.

First of all, we once again attempted, by means of two passages on truth from *The Will to Power* and the *Zarathustra*, to gain some clarity concerning the concept of truth and the concept of error.

---

2. Where "Vogelfrei" means "free as a bird."—Trans.

In *The Will to Power*, volume XVI, we read: "*Truth is that kind of error without which a certain living species could not exist. The value for life is ultimately decisive*" (p. 19, n. 493). Truth, according to the predominant conception of it as eternal and universally valid, is something fixed that offers us horizons and secures a standing reserve of things, sustaining continued existence. This truth, as what has been fixed, is determined as error from the perspective of genuine actuality, that is, becoming, to which it, precisely because it has been fixed, can never properly correspond. This "incorrectness" is no deficiency, because Nietzsche does not strive to attain a truth consisting in the correspondence to a thing in itself. This fixedness is the mark and the essence of "truths."

The second passage is to be found in *Zarathustra*, part 2, "On the Priests": "Their folly taught that truth can be proven with blood. But blood is the worst witness to truth."

Here Nietzsche is thinking of the Christian martyrs. Their blood is the worst witness to truth because it renders determinate, one-sidedly established convictions all the more fixed, and in this way obstructs genuine life, which hastens from truth to truth. [343]

The primacy of becoming in relation to being—which comes to the fore, as we have seen, in his thinking about justice—is established very early in Nietzsche's philosophy and emerges from his reflection on pre-Socratic philosophy. His conception of justice is already expressed by Heraclitus, fragment 28:

Δοκέοντα γὰρ ὁ δοκιμώτατος γινώσκει, φυλάσσει· καὶ μέντοι καὶ Δίκη καταλήψεται ψευδῶν τέκτονας καὶ μάρτυρας. (Of the character of appearance is that to which even the most esteemed hold; yet justice, from above, will bring down the artisans of lies, and also those who bear witness to lies.)

Heraclitus sees here a connection between error, appearance and justice, with justice continuously loosening and surmounting fixations, despite the necessity of the latter. This relation was first seen again by Nietzsche. In the meantime it had been forgotten or misunderstood.

Nietzsche here speaks of his own relation to Heraclitus: "Philosophy, in the only way I still allow it to stand, as the most general form of historiology (enquiry into all that which was and which happens), as an attempt somehow to describe Heraclitean becoming and to abbreviate it into signs (so to speak, to *translate* and mummify it into a kind of illusory *being*)" (vol. XIII, p. 23, n. 47 [1885–1886]).

Although every form of truth, according to Nietzsche, is an error, the fixation of what is genuinely actual, that is, of becoming, nevertheless remains the task of philosophy for him. He therefore makes two demands that appear to contradict each other: the demand for fixation, and the demand for the readiness to overcome every particular fixation.

This ambivalence appears the most clearly in Nietzsche's conception of justice; and because the latter constitutes the essence of life, in the sense of both beings as a whole and of the human being, it takes the form, with respect to the first, of a struggle between being and appearance, and with respect to the second, of a confrontation between art and knowledge. [344]

This view of the life of both world and human being is expressed in the verse that we are attempting to interpret; here the essence of the world is more precisely determined as a game. This shows itself to be a perfectly Heraclitean thought when we compare it with fragment 52:

Αἰὼν παῖς ἐστι παίζων, πεττεύων: παιδὸς ἡ βασιληίη. (The world is a child who plays with counters that he pushes one way and another.) This game occurs according to the blending of being and appearance: "World game, the ruling force, blends false and true."

The blending of being and appearance, which does not mean a muddled and arbitrary confusion, but rather the necessary superimposition of the one over the other, and which even after having been interrupted always comes to reconstitute itself, is the basic structure of both world and human being.

Here, on the one hand, and in the sense of the whole of Western metaphysics, being means what is constant, fixed, what is present as what is actual, which as truth is conceived as universal validity, as what is obligatory. But because this truth is an error, being in this sense does not correspond to genuine actuality as a flowing and self-transforming being. Being is appearance. Appearance is used here in the sense of error.

Nietzsche distinguishes this from appearance as art. In this sense appearance is what heightens life and continuously overcomes what has been fixed as truth. Here appearance means intensification and transfiguration. With regard to what it overcomes, namely, truth and being that has been fixed, it is mere appearance. As higher justice, however, it meets genuine actuality. Appearance is being. Hence it emerges that Nietzsche uses the concepts of being and appearance ambiguously, and it is this ambiguity that makes possible the characteristic inversion "being is appearance and appearance is being."

Being means, on the one hand, what is constant and determined, and on the other hand, authentic being, genuine actuality, becoming.

Appearance can mean error, that which does not meet genuine life; as such it is identical with being in the [345] first sense. But appearance also means transfiguration, intensification, and is as such the only way of establishing a relation to becoming. The full sense of the verse can be understood only once this double blending is grasped.

"The eternally fooling force blends *us* in too."

A passage from *The Will to Power* can serve to elucidate what is meant here by the idea of "foolishness": "The animal on earth that suffers most invented for itself—*laughter*" (vol. XVI, p. 356, n. 990).

Being-superior-to-oneself, that to which pain incites the human being, is the ground of foolishness in the sense of a going beyond the habitual and the ordinary. A culture of fools is to be found only where the possibility of self-surmounting is guaranteed in a certain overflowing of life.

This genuinely metaphysical sense of foolishness is to be held apart from another sense, which appears in the expressions "raving madman" and "Zarathustra's ape." Foolishness in the metaphysical sense is merely another name for the fundamental structure of actuality, which renders impossible the possession and safekeeping of a truth, of truth as eternally valid, and condemns the one who wants truth in the sense of actuality, also to want appearance and to renounce truth as a secure possession.

Zarathustra, "The Song of Melancholy" part 4 (vol. VI, p. 431) ends with the lines:

> By a single truth
> All scorched and thirsty:
> —do you remember, do you, burning heart,
> How then thou thirsted?—
> That I should banned be
> From *all* truth!
> Mere fool!
> Mere poet! [346]

"The eternally fooling force / blends *us* in too." The human being is as human being only what it is when it lets itself be blended into this game of being and appearing, when it does not exclude itself from belonging to self-transforming actuality by rigidly sticking with a determinate truth. This transformation occurs within the continual struggle between being and appearance, which is repeated in the human being as the struggle between art and knowledge. In this way, according to Nietzsche, being draws human being into its oppositions and fools him with their contradictions, and this contrary to Goethe's idea that man is raised toward the Ideal.

At the beginning of Nietzsche's essay, as we have seen, life was determined as the domain, measure, and form of enactment of all be-

ings, and of the human being in particular. This starting point, "the interpretation of beings as life," does not come into question and is not justified. This becomes particularly clear in the final, tenth section. According to Nietzsche"s confrontation with his time the question arises, what is to be done? Nietzsche formulates two demands:
1. that we reflect on genuine needs
2. that we organize the chaos in ourselves.

In formulating these demands, Nietzsche appeals to life itself, in the conviction that life is governed by needs that can simply be identified and laid bare.

To the question concerning the criterion of the authenticity of such needs, the answer could be given that a veritable need is one whose satisfaction brings about an intensification of life. What, however, is the criterion for the positing of heights and depths? If this is posited by the great thinkers, then who among them is decisive?

Nietzsche does not respond to these questions. He not only presupposes a concept of life in his early period, but he also fails to ground it in his later work. This interpretation of beings as a whole as life we generally call "biologism." There is no question here of a particular philosophical evaluation [347] of biology, but the basic position that is also merely presupposed by biology is adopted without further ado.

The question of what stands as the genuinely determining moment of this interpretation of the world as life becomes only more acute. For Nietzsche, it is crucial to conceive life not only in opposition to mechanism, to what is dead, but also as a striving beyond oneself, as will to power. Biologism is only a consequence of this dynamism, which is grounded in the essence of power, for power persists only as more power. In this sense, the human being is also not simply determined as something living, but rather as a predator, greedy for prey and victory. Hence the sense of Nietzsche's interpretation is to be grasped not with regard to biologism but rather to the fundamental decision for power itself. Here belongs the definition of justice as "form of enactment of an extensive governing power."

What truth can we find in this interpretation? It cannot be a question here of truth in the scientific sense, for Nietzsche identifies philosophy and art, and in this realm it is not a question of assertions, but rather of projections that can be neither true nor false. The same applies to all interpretations of the world in the sense of worldviews. They rest, as do the sciences, on a presupposed metaphysics; quite determinate decisions about beings as a whole, the essence of truth, and the essence of the human being lie at their roots.

These decisions belong to metaphysics. In order to get to the bottom of a science or of a determinate belief system, we have to take note of these preliminary decisions. Historiology not only as "science," but also as the relation of the three historical perspectives to one another, is grounded on what Nietzsche names plastic art, which we determined more precisely as higher justice. It contains within itself all decisions about the essence of truth and the essence of the human being.

[Therese Gisberts]

II. Postscript by Hermann Heidegger

November 7, 1938

1. Introduction to philosophical concept formation (instruction in learning how to think)
2. On the Advantages and Disadvantages...
3. Nietzsche's philosophy

Thinking in a particular, emphatic sense. To learn thinking in the manner of thinkers (Kant, Leibniz).—There is no such thing as wanting to be a philosopher; one either is a philosopher or one is not.—An introduction to the thinking of thinkers. "Higher" thinking sometimes illuminates simple (technical, calculating, etc.) thinking. The somewhat wrong idea of the philosopher does still belong to the philosopher. Narrower thinking is perhaps only a prolongation of higher, broader thinking, but everyman is unaware of this.—Impositions are the source of abundance. Reflectively following on the path of a thinker, critically, therefore entering into a questioning dialogue.— Reverence toward the thinker must remain, even when we set ourselves against him, or overcome his positions.

Nietzsche, the last thinker of traditional philosophy, brings it to its end. To grasp Western philosophy according to its essential trait; this trait is metaphysics (an editorial term for Aristotle's works; today the "beyond," "over and above" of nature, the suprasensible, nonsensible). We know nothing about the lives of Anaximander, Heraclitus, Parmenides. The greater the thinking and questioning of a thinker, the less remarkable are the details of his life. The work of a thinker can never be understood on the basis of the conditions of his life. What constitutes the core of Nietzsche's thinking?

Born in 1844. Nietzsche's life and thought until *On the Advantages and Disadvantages of History* . . . . Autumn 1873, Basel. Reconstruction of [350] German culture. The college at Schulpforta, two semesters of theology in Bonn 1864–1865. Active in the student association. Goes to Leipzig, classical philology, Schopenhauer (*The World as Will and Representation*).—Friendship with Rohde, and then a falling-out. Meets Wagner (winter 1868), before that a year's service in Naumburg with the horse-drawn artillery. Before gaining a doctorate, recruited as an extraordinary professor in Basel (1868–1869); 1870 ordinary professor.

Jacob Burckhardt lectured on "The Study of History" in Basel 1868–1869. Born in 1818, becomes a *Privatdozent*, in 1844, died in 1897. Burckhardt gave the same lectures in 1870–1871. Other lectures: "On Happiness and Unhappiness in World History" and "Historical Greatness."

In 1870 Nietzsche was an officer in the medical corps, because as a Swiss professor he could not serve as a German reserve officer. Nietzsche's letter to Baron von Gersdorff about Burckhardt's lectures.

November 9, 1938

His best, most profound philosophy is to be found in the writings he did not publish. His letters, which he wrote as an expression of his thinking, are just as important.

On the Advantages and Disadvantages of History for Life. The advantages and disadvantages (the relation) of historiology to life are here calculated. This calculative account presupposes the positing of a goal, which contains the measure, and this is life.—What is the domain within which, the ground on which the relation between historiology and life plays itself out?

What is life? 1. Everything living (collective noun). 2. As a state: a mode and manner in which something is—1. Beings as a whole. 2. Being alive in an emphatic sense.

The measure and the goal is life. Historiology also belongs to life. The relation is established on the basis of life. Only what lives can also be dead. What is lifeless, by its very nature, can neither live nor suffer death. But nevertheless [351] the stone is. There is thus a being proper to what is lifeless and a being proper to what is alive.

Nietzsche identifies life with that which is. Delimitation of the word. ζωεῖν—life in a broad sense, biology. Science works with basic concepts that it cannot explain by its own means. Work is carried out within zoology, botany, et cetera, and what is investigated is called life. Science as science can give no account of what life is.

Nietzsche uses the words history and historiology in the same sense. ἱστορεῖν—inquiring (Herodotus, *Introduction*) in the widest sense, inquiry concerning what is (already) present or past. Becomes historiology as a science. Historiology = inquiring into, understanding the past. History characterizes the thing itself. The historian also presupposes history, but does not elucidate its essence. Not scientifically, but rather in the manner of the thinker. As a historian it is not possible to say what historiology is. In saying what it is, we take a leap into another form of thinking. In the same sense, the mathematician cannot say mathematically what mathematics is.

Section I of Nietzsche's text. It begins with a comparison, a bringing into focus. In a comparison what comes first is the *tertium comparationis*, for without this there can be no comparing (the number three and the "Prince of Homburg"). These two things are different, where is the *tertium comparationis*? We indeed compare them, for otherwise we could not establish their differences. In relation to this something, both are the same; once we have investigated this something, they are dissimilar. For example, a primrose and a motorbike. That they are both something is clear. Physical entities and mathematical entities. One is alive, the other is lifeless, both are self-moving.

1. With respect to what are human being and animal compared?
2. The inner structure of the first section. [352]

November 14, 1938

Historiology—Life / Domain: Life
　　　　　　　　　Measure: Life
　　　　　　　　　The calculative account as itself an enactment and expression of life.

Nietzsche's concept of historiology rests on his concept of life. The delimitation of what historiology is also occurs by considering the relations to the unhistorical and the suprahistorical.

Inner structure: para. 1: the animal is unhistorical; para. 2: the human being is historical; para. 3: and yet the human being must also be unhistorical; para. 4: the historical and the unhistorical belong together in the human being, plastic power as the basic determination of life; para. 5: the unhistorical is primary; para. 6: the suprahistorical (paras. 7–8). Principal themes: historical-unhistorical. Negation of their relation, one sees either *only* historically or unhistorically (Paras. 9–12). Relation of the order of rank to life. "*What* does not serve life is not genuine historiology" (Nietzsche); "this depends, to be sure, on the more or less elevated idea that one has of this life." Thus human life.

The Greeks also understand ἱστορεῖν as inquiry into the future.

Heraclitus (fragment 35): ἱστορεῖν, like an umpire, critical. Passion for the essential knowledge of things, to be listening in to something; this is the old ἱστορεῖν. For Nietzsche, historiology is a being listening in to the past. The animal forgets the moment, the human being cannot forget. Remembering and forgetting are relations to the past. But what is the relation within forgetting? Historiology instigates a relation to the past.

November 23, 1938

No enrichment of knowledge. Seeing more. Human being is characterized by history. Primacy of the unhistorical. [353] Both unified in human being. Consideration of what grounds this unity. Where does the dividing line between human being and animal lie?

ἄνθρωπος	ζῷον λόγον ἔχον	(Roux, a philosophical
homo	*animal rationale*	zoologist in
Mensch	the rational "animal"	Halle, second half of the nineteenth century)

Animality is taken as a genus under which human nature is specified. Nietzsche: the human being is the not-yet-determined animal. The animal in the usual sense is differentiated from the human being as a particular animal; here lies the dividing line. Second case: the human being is not an animal, but an abyss that cannot be covered.

The animal is carried by life itself, for it slips from one moment to the next.

In what does the essence of happiness consist? How is the happiness of a living being to be determined?

The relation to the past, in that something is there, forms a crosscurrent to the constancy of life. The living body is an animated physical body. Every living body can be considered as merely a physical body, but not vice versa. Since an animal can see, it has an eye, and not vice versa. Nietzsche's inner reflection on the animal as that which relates to the milieu in which it moves. The animal always moves within its form of captivation, which is already given. The animal forgets, for it is absorbed in time.

November 28, 1938

What sort of unities are wholes [*die Ganzheit*] and totalities [*die Summe*]? The unity of a totality is a *consequence*. The unity of a whole is its ground, its cause. Aristotle already discovered the whole. The organism conceived as a whole. The animal is an organism. This organism has relations that extend further. The organism does not stop at the external limits of its living body (Uexküll: the inner and outer world [354] of the animal). Relation to the environment (Karl Ernst von Baer). A living body has for its limit an outline that is built into the environment. Forgetting and remembering?

II. Summary by Hermann Heidegger

November 30, 1938

An animal takes up more space than that filled by its living body [*Leib-Körper*]. Nietzsche proposes two extreme, limit cases: the unhistorical animal and the historical human being. The human being is an *imperfectum imperfectibile*, the animal a *praesens perfectum*. (Morgenstern: the pluperfect and future anterior enclose everything). The animal forgets immediately and continually. The human being cannot forget. But everything is interpreted from the perspective of the human being and determined by it. The human being is the world writ small (*microcosmos*) within the cosmos. All modes of being are stored up within him.

Forgetting and remembering: there is an ambiguity in Nietzsche's use of the term unhistorical. Forgetting—absorption in the present, or else the animal sees the present change in a certain way.

Forgetting (Middle High German *gezzen*); to get—hold, thus not-holding, slipping away, *not* retaining, what is forgotten is gone.
Oblivisci, oblino— effacing, rubbing out, also: gone!
ἐπιλανθάνεσθαι—being hidden from itself
"λαθ" in relation to something, also: gone!

Something is no longer present to me. What has been forgotten has disappeared from what is currently present; it has disappeared from the range of what is available. Forgetting is a not/no-longer retaining. (Death as a not/no-longer living). Not-red (yellow, blue, but also angular, proud, etc.). Hence various forms of negation. Forgetting occurs only where there is a retaining. Forgetting—a particular mode (perverted mode [*Unart*]) of retaining. If there are several possible modes of retaining, so are there also different modes of forgetting. If there is no [355] retaining, then there is no forgetting. In Latin and Greek these terms are medial verbs, because there is a reflective relation within them.

What is retaining? The possibility of making something present to oneself (e.g., a number), to represent to oneself, "to make present." In this way the thing itself is made present. I can make present to myself something that is, something that was, something that will be. I can remember that, for example, I have seen Strasbourg cathedral, but I do not remember the cathedral itself. Remembering is always a having-been, a relating to something past as something past. In remembering there must always be a relation to myself. When I remember, I project myself into what has been—I direct myself toward it; when I make something present, I draw that thing in. These are two essentially different forms of retaining, and thus there are also two different forms of forgetting. Memory—the capacity of making oneself present to oneself and remembering-oneself, remembering [*Gedenken*], remembrance [*Andenken*].

December 7, 1938

In making something present to ourselves we are always related to a being as a being, as we are in remembering, but in this case only to something past. This is a comportment. Forgetting is a relation to beings in which the being as such is gone. The comportment of forgetting is really a noncomportment. What is forgotten sinks into forgottenness in becoming forgotten: the vortex character of forgetting. The blackboard is present. We know unconsciously, we understand, what something present as present represents. We think only about the blackboard. This is also a remarkable characteristic of forgetting: we take for granted the "being" of beings as beings.

Does the animal "forget"? In what way does the animal forget?

a) In not-being-able-to-remember and not-remembering. Nietzsche says that the animal does not know what yesterday is; it does not understand the past, and consequently it cannot remember, and thus nor can it forget in the sense of (a). [356]

b) Not being able to make something present to itself. The animal cannot relate itself to something present as present, and thus it cannot forget either. The animal does not have the possibility of retaining anything.

Because the animal stands outside the possibility of being able to retain and forget, it cannot be unhistorical; it is without historiology (lacking history). Only what is historical can be unhistorical (against Nietzsche). The difference between the unhistorical and the historical must be extricated from the context of the opposition of animal and human being. The dividing line cannot be found, the relation is played out only in the human being. Thus we have to investigate further into the human being, both as it is codetermined by historiology and as it codetermines historiology.

Human being: hence the question of the essence of human being. As particular human being it is the real human being (*individuum*). Kant uses the term *Menschheit*, humanity (like *Tierheit*, animality), which is not all human beings taken together, but rather the essence of all and every human being. In order to elucidate the essence of historiology from the essence of humanity, Nietzsche's conception of culture has to be considered. Culture: unity of artistic style. Consideration of art in the human domain.

December 12, 1938

What-being—τί ἐστιν—*quidditas*.

The expression "world" can be used only where beings are understood as beings. The animal's captivation. The opposite of culture: barbarism. For the Greeks: those who do not speak Greek, foreignness. Are the notions of "primitive people" [*Naturvölker*] and "barbaric people" coextensive? Barbarism belongs only to cultured peoples. Culture is something relating to a people. Is culture a means or an end, a goal? And, in the first case, what is the goal of culture? Nietzsche: culture is the mastery of art over life. Nietzsche often identifies culture with *formative education* [*Bildung*]. To be cultured, to know much, a class difference. Nietzsche's [357] concept has nothing to do with this. *Bildung*: 1. formation, shaping, bringing up and into form; 2. that an image is pregiven of how the human being wants to be, an ideal [*Vor-bilden*]. This furnishes us with a determination of art (in the widest sense): a bringing into form.

December 14, 1938

In nineteenth-century thought culture is the highest goal of the human being, a matter of realizing the values of truth (science), of the good, et cetera. If culture is a means for Nietzsche, what then is the goal? (The people?)

Art is a bringing into form, a realization of the actual. ποίησις and τέχνη (without 1. and 2.). The essential element of forming is a simplification, simplicity as a sign of greatness.—Ideals [*Vor-Bilder*] fix the process of forming, constraining it. Nietzsche: "The artistic begins with the organic." (Plastic power, πλάττειν.)—Nature is an imitation of art, a self-constituting bringing into form [*ein sich bildendes Bilden*]. Culture is an improved *physis*. Art is the essence of culture. *Physis* itself is essentially artistic. Art is the higher essence of nature. Forming as bringing-into-shape is an overcoming of the formless. Forming in the sense of creating images is, according to Nietzsche, making them emerge from dull confusion. What stimulates life develops from this, the fact of going beyond oneself. What are the differences between art in the broader and in the narrower sense? What is formed by the human being is created as a being. (Is, for example, Goethe's *Faust* a work in the same manner as the flowering of a flower?). Culture as art in the broad sense plays an important role within art in the narrow sense. In Wagner's art as redemption (Schopenhauer's influence).

It is not only that art should be unified, but also that it should serve to overcome life (*Parsifal*). Music as the highest form of art, because it already sustains the human being. "Culture can only ever arise from the centralizing significance of a form of art or artwork."—How does the unity unify? ("Culture is the unity of artistic [358] style.") What is style? The mode and manner in which one expresses and forms oneself (from *stilus*, a slate pencil, writing, transposed to speech etc.). The rule according to which the forming occurs. Wherever style is graspable as a rule, art has become classic. The essence of style: constituting the law that governs forming. The classical has developed the rule within itself, without the rule appearing explicitly as rule. Style thus as what gives the law. Barbarism has no style. "Unity of artistic style," that is, a unity that corresponds only to self-expression; the law-giving, creative unity is style. Unity as formed through style itself.

A unitary law, first constituting itself in the process of formation, in technology, science, business, et cetera—that is, in expressions of life—holds sway over the whole.

The goal of culture is the singular, great individual (for Nietzsche). The genius, the triad of thinker, artist, and saint. "The goal of nature (i.e., life) is genius"; they do not exist because of humanity, but are rather themselves the goal, they bear within them what is highest in humanity. Later his conception of negation will turn toward the genius as the one who affirms affirmation. Nietzsche says that a people exists in order to engender six or seven great human beings. Riehl's influence on the understanding of the people. Culture as the condition of the goal: great individuals.

December 19, 1938

Nietzsche's concept of genius is influenced by Schopenhauer, for whom the genius comes to rest in the contemplation of the ideas. Nietzsche describes his own philosophy as an inversion of Platonism. Nietzsche views what is actual not as something that persists, but rather as something that becomes (hence the pervasiveness of the concept of life). The goal is not humanity, but rather the Overhuman, and thus his concept of genius turns out to be quite different. The genius brings to expression what becomes in a people, and not what eternally persists. The goal is the great individual, the communal goal is personality. An anthropological and thus [359] political distinction (worldview). Community and personality both belong to the concept of the people. The people—the great individual—relies on a metaphysical distinction.

Life is a calculative reckoning with regard to itself. Value: the condition of the intensification of life. Nonvalue: condition of the diminution of life. "Life is a business that does not cover its costs" (animal *rationale*). We learn three things about human life: it is active or striving, protective or venerating, and it suffers.

December 21, 1938

Monumental historiology is treated in the greatest detail, critical historiology in the briefest manner, and there is also antiquarian historiology (all are dealt with in the first paragraph of section II, and the first paragraph of section IV). The monumental: section II, paragraphs 2–6; antiquarian: section IV, paragraphs 1–4; critical: section III, paragraph 5. "Life needs historiology" and "historiology serves life."
1. The selecting of ideals or models (from the past and in the past)
2. Preservation (of the past)
3. Judging

These relations transport us back into the past, and this in such a manner that the past acts on the present. There is, thus, a relation of the past to the present. Present: in each case the mastery of the calculative account with regard to itself. The future is also included. The past suffers harm in each of these modes of historiology. Sometimes it is even falsified, consciously or unconsciously. Thus there ought to be a reflection on the past in itself and in its fullness; but this does not touch on its possibility. Ranke: the recording of history [*Geschichtsschreibung*] such as it actually happened (objectivity). *Adaequatio* (*intellectus ad rem* = *veritas*, correctness). The question of historical truth. In these three modes historiology is not conceived as a science. Science is built onto and [360] grounded in these three modes of historiology. How can science then be objective? Here historiology appears first of all as something prescientific; and only afterward as a science that seeks to rule over the three modes, to stand out from them as an independent fourth mode that wants to be the truth.
1. *Monumental historiology*: Remembering greatness, inciting it, the past is recalled to the human being. Being-past belongs to the monumental. Nietzsche identifies the nonmonumental with the present. The monumental is removed from becoming; it is what is already there. The conviction that there are summits; this is the ground of monumental historiology, the belief in the high peaks of human being. (section II, paragraph 2)

    Section II, paragraph 3 deals with the advantages of monumental historiology. It shows in the present that greatness is possible in

history, and is once again possible. Section II, paragraph 4: how the past suffers (not accidentally, but rather necessarily) at the hands of monumental historiology. The *causae* are neglected while the *effectus* is emphasized. In Stefan George's circle this mode of recording history [*Geschichtsschreibung*] was brought to the fore. *Non facta, sed ficta!* (Nietzsche). Section II, paragraph 5: disadvantage of monumental historiology when it claims sole mastery, also when it falls into the hands of gifted egoists and villains. Section II, paragraph 6: monumental historiology in the hands of the weak and powerless. They do evoke something great in history, but they say that everything else has already been condemned. They hinder the emergence of new greatness; they do not see that greatness exists only for those who are themselves great; it has to emerge again in the present.
2. *Antiquarian historiology*: it looks to the past as that from which the present arises. The present recognizes itself in the past (section III, paragraph 1). Antiquarian historiology establishes ties to antiquity, a fidelity to what has come earlier. Section III, paragraph 2: truth of antiquarian [361] history. How the past obligates. Narrowing of the horizon. Limitation to what is one's own. Section III, paragraph 3: the past as such is in need of veneration; everything, regardless of what it is. Obstructing the view of what is creative and in becoming.
3. *Critical historiology*: securing of sources; in this domain not a critique of the past, but rather of the tradition (e.g., the critical edition of Goethe). Yet *here*: critique of the past. It shows how accidents are, how evil is also at work. It wants to nullify forgetting. This form of historiology is the most dangerous:
    1) Life can become uprooted, the worthiness for veneration can be affected.
    2) It can endanger the historian himself. History of nihilism (Spengler!).
    3) Critical historiology is in a certain manner the flip side of monumental historiology.

January 9, 1939

Life: 1. Beings as a whole, 2. *human life*. What exactly is human life? Introduction by way of a comparison with the animal, which soon disappears. By means of the three modes of historiology we learn three things about human life: the self-intensification, conservation, and liberation of life. None of this is grounded but rather just presupposed. It is not stated whether there are others. Why does human life need historiology? Historiology produces an effect on the past,

II. Summary by Hermann Heidegger

whenever there are also a present and a future. All creating in relation to the future; all conserving for the past; liberation in the present. Human being stands in time, and thus in a relation to time. The change in section IV. [362]

January 11, 1939

In itself time is threefold: the past, present, and future belong to the essence of time. Thus human being depends on time, while time is not a concept of the human being. Historiology is knowledge, desired and utilized by the human being, of the past in the service of the future. If this relation did not exist there would be no historiology. The past as past, the future as futural, the present as such stand open; here we are speaking of temporality. This also belongs to the essence of the human being. The human being is not only—like, for example, the stool—in time, but rather its being is bound to the past, present, and future. A threefold ecstasis of the human being. Temporality is the ground of historiology. Hegel distinguishes immediate, reflective, and philosophical historiology. Temporality is the essence of the human being. The being of the human being is in itself temporal.

What is known by means of historiology is history. Nietzsche even goes so far as to say that only what has been ascertained historically can become history. Temporality is also essential for history and historial happening. There is history only where there are human beings. The human being is itself history to the extent that it intervenes in its events, makes plans, prepares, et cetera. The human being has history, because it is historial. There is historiology only where man is historial. History is the ground of historiology.

Nietzsche now (section IV) carries out a critical historiology in relation to historiology. But within this critical historiology he also thinks in a monumental and antiquarian fashion. The turning against itself of the present. Here begins the "untimely" meditation. He sees the danger in life's oversaturation with historiology. Science arrogates to itself a primary position. Oversaturation within knowledge by means of science. The consequence of this is a lack of action. The unity [363] that constitutes the essence of culture is torn asunder. Historiology is within certain boundaries scientific, for it is a form of knowing [*Wissen*]. Father: "perhaps science is not even the highest form of knowing." The question of the essence of knowing presupposes the question of the essence of truth. And thus also inquiry concerning historical truth (historical objectivity). The idea of justice in opposition to History.

January 16, 1939

Time, according to an old conception, is one-dimensional. Aristotle: only the present is genuine time. That the human being thinks in three directions within time is a consequence of the fact that it temporalizes itself as a being in time. Being is constancy and presence. Discourse still rules over philosophy today. Criticizing Nietzsche is not an expression of pedantry, but rather a thinking one's way into another philosophical understanding. Heidegger: "Every philosophy is untimely, it thinks against its age so that it may permeate the age with its own essence." Judging is at the same time a setting up of standards; separating the higher from the lower. The object of Nietzsche's critique is historiology in its relation to life when it aspires to scientificity. The truth of historiology is meditation, the untimely meditation indeed falls under the category of critical-historical reflection, but the critical aspect is already a philosophical reflection.

January 18, 1939

The word *life* is full of historial content. We understand historiology as a relation to science, and the latter as a concern with knowledge that demands truth. In connection with truth, life as beings in general, and as the being of the human being. Nietzsche speaks of the [364] natural constellations of the relation of historiology to life. This lies in the essence of human life: the threefold nature of historiology.

Beings as a whole—Life—Being of the Human Being
↑Truth
Knowledge
Science
↑
Historiology

In section IV, paragraph 1 Nietzsche explicitly mentions the constellation of historiology and truth. It leads to destruction. The disturbance, the star that interposes itself in this constellation, is science. Scientific knowledge and scientific truth are the basic form of truth. Nature is the coexistence of countless homogenous points. A knowing, which within certain limits can be proven mathematically, quantitatively. Truth: self-certainty of thinking (Descartes). Historiology shall be a science. Science determines from the ground up the relation to the past; it characterizes the modality of the relation. The realm of the past comprises all that has been; a science of universal becoming.

Consequences of the disturbance: oversaturation with knowledge, the fracture between inside and outside. The wealth of historical knowledge allows for comparison. Interiority is representing oneself to oneself, while exteriority is action. But each extends beyond itself to the other. The Greeks (according to Nietzsche) knew the difference but not the fracture. Or is it not rather the case that neither the unitary nor the fractured difference is known to them? My father: the Greeks did not yet have any interiority. Only in modern thinking has the soul become a subject. Nietzsche wants untainted interiority. Personality is a concept of the human being as being independent. For Nietzsche: lack of personality: absence of subjectivity. [365]

January 23, 1939

The fracture between inside and outside is established with the determination of truth as certainty. 1883: "Their folly taught that truth can be proven with blood. But blood is the worst witness to truth" (*Zarathustra*, chapter on the priests). *Will to Power*, n. 493: *"Truth is the kind of error* without which a certain species of living being could not exist. The value for *life* is ultimately decisive" (1885).

January 25, 1939

Recognizing conventions in language. The French language, for example, is already complete. Incomparable possibility of new constructions. Advantages and dangers (decline, disfiguration of language). The disadvantage of scientific historiology derives from the primacy it demands with respect to the relation between living present and the past. In what is the original relation of the present to the past grounded? The endangering establishes the fracture in *five* respects, the second of which is the emergence of the illusion of an actual higher justice (section IV, paragraph 6). Section V, paragraph 1: ironizing himself, cynicism.

Since this *Second Untimely Meditation* tension between Nietzsche and Wagner, at the beginning particularly with regard to Cosima.

1. The modern human being suffers from a weak personality. *Persona—personalitas* (concrete—abstract (essence of the person)). τὸ πρόσωπον (all such Latin fundamental terms are translations from

the Greek) = the mask, role play. (Cicero: essence of the *persona* consists in *dignitas*). By means of such portrayal, of the presentation of oneself, *persona* becomes *dignitas*; here lies the essence of *persona*. *Dignitas* is determined through *ratio*. *Persona hominis = mixtura animae et corporis* (Augustine). The idea of the person plays a role in the concept of God, and in the [366] same way in the determination of the human being (individuality of the soul). Concept of individuality. *Persona est rationalis naturae individua substantia* (Thomas Aquinas).

Independence [*auf-sich-stehen*] by virtue of reason. The independence of a rational being determines personality as such. Descartes's guiding principle: *ego cogito ergo sum*. The being of human being is determined through self-consciousness. Self-certainty is the presupposition of all other certainty; it is the foundation, the subject (ὑποκείμονον). It now enters into the faculty of knowing of self-determination. The concept of personality, its development; "character" can be understood only on the basis of Kant's doctrine. Kant goes along two paths: distinction of person and thing (*Groundwork of the Metaphysics of Morals*, 1785).

Determination 1: Personality as one of the three elements of the determination of the human being (1794). The thing is essentially determined by its character of being a means. A being that possesses the character of rationality can only be taken as its own goal, and never as a means. Reason is the faculty of the representation of principles, and acts according to them (Kant). The first determination of the human being is the structure of animality. 2. The structure of humanity (the essence of the human being determined as rational). 3. Structure of personality as that belonging to a rational and at the same time responsible being (determined through responsibility). Kant is thus also in need of practical principles. Duty, categorical imperative. An unconditioned ought (antithesis: hypothetical). "Act in such a way that the maxim of your action can at the same time be the principle. . ."

Only a being that freely takes up its actions out of this lawfulness can be held responsible. Human being: personality on the basis of the autonomy of its actions. In Kant, the being-with-others of the individual is already posited. (Influence on 1807–1815.) Identification of personality and character later (χαράσσω; to engrave, carve). χαρακτήρ—trait, attribute. The way in which a cause is a cause is what Kant describes as [367] character. Freedom in Kant: to grant it to oneself and to submit to it. There is duty only where there is freedom; wherever there is freedom, there is also duty. Thus in Kant the practical-ethical reconfiguration.

For Nietzsche: the mere spectator who does not submit to his duty, thus avoiding it, no longer has any genuinely individual law-giving power, and also no longer any resistance against the world surging up against him [*das große Andrängende*].

My father: "Authentic knowing is always an action."

February 1, 1939

Humanity as an essential concept: essence of the human being. Rationality is what constitutes the human being as such. Praxis in the sense of the practical and technical is subordinate to theoretical reason. Every will as a will is a knowing. All action without knowing is blind. All knowing without action is weak. Knowledge of the law. Intellectualism holds scientific knowledge to be the most significant; it does not see the essence of the knowledge of the law. This failing is to be avoided: education in true knowledge. Avoidance of the great things in history and avoidance of oneself is a weakness of personality. The weakened personality is no longer capable of a truthful relation to itself. Science as the passion of the knowledge of being and science as research.

Guiding statements from the notebooks: "The Philosopher: Reflections on the Struggle of Art and Knowledge" (1872), vol. X, p. 109: "At the right height, everything comes together and is unified—the thoughts of philosophers." Invisible bridges from genius to genius: "A people aware of its own dangers produces genius" (p. 112). "Philosophy *not for the people, thus not as the basis of a culture*, and thus only as the instrument of a culture" (p. 186). (The philosopher as a brake.) "None of the great Greek philosophers drags the people after him" (p. 187). Concentration of the human being [368] by means of philosophy (cf. p. 297). In *Philosophy in the Tragic Age of the Greeks* (1873)—the influence of Heraclitus.

Objectivity, *ob-iectum*. ἀντικείμενον. Within representation, what is represented is the object. In Scholasticism, the objective is what today we name the subjective, representing within oneself. A book that is for us today objectively there, was for Scholasticism subjective, the ὑποκείμενον. For Descartes, the I is what is present first of all. The I is the *subjectum*. Everything that does not belong to this subject-I is the objective. For Nietzsche, objectivity is a determination of the subject. (We speak of objective people, people who possess the capacity to understand and evaluate). In Kant: unity of those determinations constituting an object as an object. He names these the categories. But these categories belong, for Kant, to what is subjective.

February 6, 1939

Objectivity, *truth*, justice. Life develops according to their interrelation. Truth under the heading of objectivity. Does objectivity derive from justice? Must the human being consequently feel essentially impelled toward justice? Does the human being imagine such an idea of justice for itself, thus regarding objectivity as something self-evident? Kant: not whether, but rather how connections are possible. Synthetic judgments (a priori). A formula, constituting an object as object. In Nietzsche, the three concepts of objectivity are mixed together. There is no subject in itself and no object in itself. The relation between object and subject is always given, and this relation is, in fact, primary. Only within this relation is something determinable as subjective or objective. Nietzsche: objectivity and justice have nothing to do with one another. [369]

February 8, 1939

Three senses of objectivity: 1. the objectivity of the human being; 2. what constitutes an object as an object; 3. relation of the subject to the object (objectivity of science). Universal validity, validity of a particular science is also a type of objectivity. The subject-object relation is a representing of something as something for that which does the representing. There must be an opening [*Geöffnetes*] between the two. The representative relation presupposes such an openness. Consciousness in the sense of being aware of something (*cogitatio*) is the relation of the representing human being as a subject-object relation. Why does the human being consider itself as a subject? Truth belongs already to knowledge. Truth conceived as correctness, as a directing oneself guided by something. How is truth conceived in the sense of correctness? What is known is simply indubitable; it is a matter of insight independent of any particular doctrine. *Cogito ergo sum*—I think, I am. This relation is given indubitably. In this regard, within this truth or certainty, the human being is what lies at the foundation, the *subjectum* (still in the Scholastic sense). All knowing and everything knowable is bound to it. Here a change occurs: the ego is the authentic *subjectum*, but henceforth the *subjectum* is called the ego. The subjective is now everything belonging to the I. This determination applies to every I as an I. Self-determination of the human being through itself in relation to all standards of action and creation in general. The consequence is a liberation from the ideas of the Church. What is true is now what is immediately evident and certain for every I. Submitting oneself to the law is, for Kant, the essence of freedom. This is a comportment in the sense of freedom (autonomy). Subjectivism is the mode that determines the human being as subject. Nietzsche's reproach against Descartes: he apprehended the human being only as a conscious being. The flesh and the animal have been forgotten; passion. The human being, as subject, is the fulcrum of all relations; that is subjectivism. The *subjectum* can be determined as [370] (human) life. Vol. X, p. 212: "It is by means of what is thoroughly *subjective* that we are *human*."

Nietzsche's concept of objectivity: the faculty of knowledge or art? Which is the most necessary for subjectivism? How are art and knowledge to be ranked in relation to each other? Struggle between truth and art in his late period. Truth is what is binding; it is inferior. Objectivity in an essential sense (in the sense of autonomy) and in an unessential sense (in the sense of the sciences).

February 13, 1939

Objectivism. The human being, as the one who determines, is inserted into the totality of beings. The interrelation of objectivism and subjectivism is bound up in the ambiguity of Nietzsche's concept of life.

The modern concept of truth is grounded on the subject-object relation, hence its doubling of this concept on the basis of the subject-object relation. Justice as a basic faculty of the human being and justice as a basic character of beings as a whole (δίχη). The former concept is thus subjective. Section VI, paragraph 2, what justice is as a virtue: ἀρετή, *virtus*, an ethical concept (ἦθος, comportment), something moral.

February 15, 1939

Higher justice is the veritable root of plastic power. For Nietzsche, the relation between justice and truth is decisive. Nietzsche conceives the essence of virtue from the perspective of higher justice. Virtue is an impossibility, and thus the human being consumes itself in its striving for justice, which is the most fundamental virtue of the human being.

Knowledge without consequences is also a form of truth, but it is only [371] the cognition of what is correct. Truth as judge, drawing new boundaries, setting out new domains and standards, as the power of judgment. Virtue (ἀρετή) = suitability (a thing is good for something), but its sense is narrowed to that of human comportment. Every ἀρετή is a τελείωσις, a being-completed, a ἕξις—disposition. The essence of *virtus* is conceived as *perfectio*, ἕξις as *dispositio*. Essence of virtue: *dispositio perfecti ad optimum*. The comportment becomes ἀγαθόν, *bonum*. That is good which is suitable as a goal (*ordo in finem*), as soon as comportment is subordinated to the *summus* (*deus*). In every conception of morality an Ideal is posited, in relation to which good and evil are distinguished. Virtue is whatever serves to maintain it. Christian virtue is submission. Justice in a nonmoral (not immoral) sense (*Beyond Good and Evil*). Life is not yet justified by simply living out one's life. Paragraph 3: historical virtuosos are passive knowers. To magnanimity belongs force and superiority in relation to oneself, and only then to others. Tolerance, beneath which there is simple acceptance, is in itself weakness. The level beneath this: embellishment. Beneath the latter: acceptance in the sense of lethargy, avoidance, leaving things to themselves. These are all types of justice. Injustice belongs to higher justice, for it is hard. Justice in the usual sense moves aside. The opposite of higher justice is cowardice. Paragraphs 4 and 5: artistic creation is the highest expression of objectivity, insofar as here there is an action derived from the innermost essence of what has happened. This is not a mere reception of objects. Aristotle in chapter 9 of the *Poetics*: καὶ φιλοσοφώτερον καὶ σπουδαιότερον ποίησις ἱστορίας ἐστίν. The historian λέγει not τὰ γενόμενα, but rather οἷα ἂν γένοιτο. Art and knowledge are opposed to each other within historical study, and hence the statement: objectivity and justice have nothing to do with one another. Kant determines the aesthetic state as disinterested pleasure. The relation to the beautiful should not be determined as a mere cognition of the thing. The relation to the artwork presupposes [372] an interest in what is in itself essential. Level 6 can either be an emptiness or a controlled creative force. Like is only known by like (a Greek proposition). (7) Only the great can recognize greatness. The small desire only to diminish; while only the great has the power to aggrandize. Only those who build can be judges, for only they possess the requisite standards. (8) They must ensure that a thing can come to maturity and be recognized as having matured. Knowing mastery of beings and things.

February 20, 1939

Justice, truth in a nonmoral sense, beyond good and evil, as Christian morality, not limited to Church doctrine, but any type of socialism, Kantian ethics. This is all morality in the narrow sense of the term. In a wider sense: every normative establishment of an ideal, a value. 1882–1885, the time of the *Zarathustra*: particular emphasis on reflections concerning justice. Justice, right, *rectus*, bringing into line, conforming, according to a pregiven standard. Justice—acting in accordance with a law (moral or juridical). Divine order. Vol. XIII, p. 42 (1884): "*Justice* as a constructive, eliminative, destructive mode of thought, on the basis of value judgments: *the highest representative of life itself."* The establishment of the conditions for the intensification of life. In justice, life is a wanting to go beyond oneself. Vol. XIV, p. 80 (1885): *"Justice,* as a function of a farsighted power, which looks beyond the narrow perspectives of good and evil, and which has a broader horizon of *advantage*—the intention to conserve something that is *more* than this or that person."

Vol. XIV, p. 386: "Prudence proceeding from broad insight." Justice is a sort of love with clairvoyant eyes, a love which does not blind (*Zarathustra*). What is loved is loved according to what it is and what it should be in its essence. Vol. XII, p. 291: "Truly [373] just human beings are incapable of receiving presents: they give everything back. Thus they are abhorrent to those who love." Danger of committing oneself to already established horizons: "There is more injustice in veneration than in despising" (p. 297).

February 22, 1939

Justice as the setting of standards—*rectitudo ordinis. Human, All too Human*, vol. II (1878). Justice as a form of genius. Enemy of conviction. The opposite of justice in the sense of inertia. *Suum cuique*— "Giving to each what he is due: that would be to seek justice while attaining chaos" (vol. XII, p. 291). I give to each what is mine. The thinking moves between these two types of justice. The chaos of the human soul arises from the idea of an immanent justice. What is right and just here is drawn from its consequences.

Interrelation: justice and truth. Nietzsche's conception of truth falls wholly within the lineage of European thinking; a characteristic of knowledge. "On Truth and Lies in an Extramoral Sense," notebooks, summer 1873 (vol. X, pp. 189–207).

Nietzsche begins with the relation of truth to the intellect, with which the human being as an individual is endowed. How does the drive to truth arise? The true is what is valid, obligatory. From external necessity and boredom. Justice as the acceptance of validity is the root of truth (justice in the simple sense). An impression emanates from an object, this impression produces a stimulus, the stimulus an image, the image a sound, the sound a word, the word a concept (explanation of language). The binding together of individuals on the basis of something common, in view of life.

A is B, in this something is fixed and determined, and shall count as truth. This determination is, in relation to life, consolidating. There needs to be a [374] consolidated domain, so that the human being can live within it. This is the true. The danger of reification remains, for the human being is something that becomes. Being = constancy, life = becoming. In order to maintain life as life in its vitality, art is required, the positing of something that truth does not fix, and that rather produces illusion as something necessary to life, so that life can remain free, growing beyond what has become consolidated at any given time. Life needs truth, but it must also always again overcome it. Justice is what overcomes truth and posits new horizons for life; justice in a higher sense. "We possess *art* so that we *do not perish at the hands of truth.*" What transfigures stands higher than what is reified. "Art is worth more than truth" (truth in the sense of fixed being). "But truth does not count as the highest measure of value" (*Will to Power*, no. 853). The will to truth is merely a will to illusion. An inartistic form of art.

Science is necessary for life. The idea of a science closer to life is nonsense. For science must provide constancy to life, and not run along behind it. *Gay Science*, "Songs of Prince Vogelfrei," "To Goethe": "World game, the ruling force / blends false and true / the eternally fooling force / blends us in too."

February 27, 1939

Truth is that particular form of error that belongs to life. *Will to power—Zarathustra*. Blood is the worst witness to truth (Dogma). Primacy of becoming in relation to being. Heraclitus, fragment 28. Δοκέοντα γὰρ ὁ δοκιμώτατος γινώσκει, φυλάσσει· καὶ μέντοι καὶ Δίκη καταλήψεται ψευδῶν τέκτονας καὶ μάρτυρας. Nietzsche: "Philosophy, in the only form that I myself can still accept it, as the most general form of historiology: as the attempt somehow to describe Heraclitean becoming and to abbreviate [375] it in signs" (vol. XIII, p. 23; 1885–1886). The world game in Nietzsche. Heraclitus, fragment 52. "Being," the constant, solid, for Nietzsche also an error, being is thus appearance. Being (as constant)—appearance (as error)—appearance (in the sense of art, transfiguration)—being (as becoming).

Will to Power, n. 990: "The most suffering animal on earth invented for itself—*laughter.*" Even the foolish is, for Nietzsche, equivocal. The raving madman, Zarathustra's monkey. *Zarathustra*, "The Song of Melancholy" (vol. VI, p. 431): "Mere fool! Mere poet!" "Scorched by a truth, and thirsty." Only through being blended into the world game is the human being what it is.

1. To reflect on the genuine needs (in themselves) and 2. to create chaos in oneself. Intensification of life. Through what is the *height* of

human life posited? Through genius. Will to power as force (δύναμις), as willing to go beyond oneself. The animal (predator), greedy for prey and victory (Power!). Thus not the biological. Justice as a function of a farsighted power.

Metaphysics: decision about life, human being, and truth. Only on this basis can a science (historiology) become transparent. [377]

Editorial Postscript

The present volume makes public for the first time Heidegger's notes for a weekly three-hour seminar held in the winter semester 1938–1939 in Freiburg. This dealt with the interpretation of Nietzsche's *Second Untimely Meditation*.

Originally Heidegger had planned a lecture course for this semester. The title would have been "Introduction to Philosophy." Instead he led this seminar, under the title "Exercises as Introduction to Philosophical Concept Formation." And yet these exercises took on the character of a lecture. I know this from Doctor Hermann Heidegger, Heidegger's son, who participated in and wrote a report on these seminars, and who kindly told me about them. As he remembers, the reason for this change lay in the extraordinarily high number of students, which made student participation in the style of a seminar impossible. It was for this reason that in planning the complete edition of his work, Heidegger himself allocated these exercises that took the form of a lecture course to its Division II, *Lecture Courses*, rather than to its Division IV, which comprises the *Seminar Notes*. Another, more substantive reason for this classification may be that the theme of these exercises belongs both temporally and in terms of their content to the Nietzsche lectures Heidegger gave in the years between 1936–1937 and 1940 in Freiburg.

The manuscript used for this volume comprises 315 numbered pages in A5 format. On each of the handwritten pages there is, on the top-left-hand side, the number of the page and, on the top-right-hand side, the numbering, often also with small letters, of the individual parts of the text. The whole text is structured into twenty sections and 138 parts, which Heidegger has consistently [378] given a title. These are reproduced here by the editor with capital letters and with arabic numerals respectively. Most of these parts are fully worked through and formulated texts, while some parts consist of notes, which Heidegger has mostly arranged in larger or smaller structural plans.

Heidegger more or less consistently comments on Nietzsche's essay section by section and paragraph by paragraph. The sections he has named with roman numerals, the paragraphs with arabic numerals. This denotation has been preserved in this edition.

All quotations have been checked and in places corrected and amended. Punctuation has been simplified. Spelling errors and obviously missing words have been tacitly corrected and amended. There are only a few passages in the text that could not be deciphered, which are indicated by footnotes. Abbreviations have generally been spelled out. Orthography has been simplified, while Heidegger's sometimes idiosyncratic way of writing has been left as it was. The various ways of writing the sharp "s"—ß in German, "ss" in Latin handwriting—have all been rendered as "ß," except in quotations from Nietzsche. These are quoted following the *Großoktav* edition which Heidegger himself used.

The beginning of the manuscript has been changed according to Heidegger's own instructions. It does not begin with the *Introductory Remarks*, but with a reflection on the title and the first section of Nietzsche's text. The reason for this might be that Heidegger wanted to clarify for himself the intention of these exercises with reference to the fundamental position of this text. It is only then that the *Introductory Remarks* follow. In these it is a matter—as the original title of the seminar indicated—of an "Introduction to Philosophical Concept Formation." With respect to this Heidegger notes toward the end of the introductory remarks: "Transition—the text here discussed—: *the title*." It was thus planned not to reflect on Nietzsche's text until *after* this introduction, which is indeed what happened, as can be seen in Hermann Heidegger's notes on the first two meetings. [379] This starting point is of essential importance for understanding these seminars in terms of their character as exercises. It is not a matter here simply of interpreting one particular text of Nietzsche, but, according to Heidegger, of the attempt to learn philosophical thinking by means of a "questioning dialogue with an essential thinker."

Along with Heidegger's manuscript the following texts have been used:
1. A typed transcription by Fritz Heidegger,
2. Fifteen seminar reports by participating students,
3. A summary by Hermann Heidegger.

The typed transcription by Fritz Heidegger has been repeatedly collated with Heidegger's manuscript. A few misreadings and omissions have thereby been corrected and amended.

The seminar reports and the summary have been transcribed and published in the Addenda. They present, each in their own way, the course that the lectures took up to the *Concluding Remarks* in §98. From them it is clear that only the essential outline of the interpretation has been discussed in the seminars. In contrast, Heidegger has also verbally added a few points, such as that concerning the difference between the French and the German language in relation to Nietzsche's concept of "convention" (cf. the seminar report from January 23 and 25, 1939). The paragraphs from §99 onward were obviously not covered in the seminars. These concern some further reflections on the fundamental concept of life in the *Second Untimely Meditation*.

* * *

When Nietzsche questions in his text the uses and disadvantages of history for life, his starting point is an ambiguous concept of life. "Life" here means, on the one hand, beings as such and in general as universal life and, on the other hand, it means human life in an emphatic sense. Against this [380] background Nietzsche compares the historical relation of the human being to the past with the relation that the animal entertains with the present. The criterion of this comparison is life in the broader sense, which is used to estimate the importance of historiology for human life.

But—and this is the fundamental question that Heidegger here poses in the "dialogue" [*Wechselgespräch*] with Nietzsche—is it thus possible to clarify the idea of historiology from the perspective of life as such? Who or what is the human being? Is it—as Nietzsche later says—the "not yet fixed animal," which can intensify and transfigure but also weaken its life by means of the various modes of historiology (monumental, antiquarian, critical)? Or is it not rather *that* being that "comports" itself toward life by means of remembering and forgetting, precisely because it is not (only) an *animal rationale*, a "beast of prey" desiring an unlimited increase in power and intensification of life, but a being that steadfastly stands in the truth of being, a being by means of which life is first of all made historically accessible in its multiple senses *as* world, human being, nature, that is to say, as "beings as such and in general." As Heidegger indicates, this question is of the utmost importance, especially in regard to the historico-ontological [*seinsgeschichtliche*] confrontation with the "Will to Power" of the later Nietzsche.

It is well known that Heidegger has already thematized the *Second Untimely Meditation* in *Being and Time* (cf. §76). On account of the publication of this volume it is now possible to compare Heidegger's existential and his historico-ontological interpretation of Nietzsche on the basis of the same text.

* * *

I wish to express my gratitude first of all to Doctor Hermann Heidegger and Professor Doctor Friedrich-Wilhelm von Herrmann. Both have helped greatly with the corrections and with all other issues in the editing of this volume. [381]

I thank Doctor Bernd Heimbüchel for saving the copy of the typed manuscript onto disk and for having provided me with this electronic version of the text for the elaboration and production of the volume.

Editorial Postscript

I thank Mrs. Gertrud Zimmermann for her competent help with the transcription of the handwritten seminar reports and summary. For careful final corrections and consideration of the completed manuscript, thanks are due to Mrs. Jutta Heidegger, Doctor Paola-Ludovika Coriando and Doctor Peter von Ruckteschell.

Würselen, July 2003   Hans-Joachim Friedrich

CPSIA information can be obtained at www.ICGtesting.com
Printed in the USA
LVOW07*2138120916

504271LV00011B/132/P

9 780253 022660